Mexico's
FEASTS
OF ≈ LIFE

Mexico's
FEASTS OF LIFE

PATRICIA QUINTANA

WITH CAROL HARALSON

PHOTOGRAPHED BY IGNACIO URQUIZA

COUNCIL OAK BOOKS / TULSA

FRONTISPIECE: *A Day of the Dead altar in Oaxaca. During The Day of the Dead (El Dia de los Muertos) on November 1 and 2, altars are assembled throughout Mexico in honor of the departed. They are laden with flowers and sugar-candy skulls, skeleton toys, candles, photographs, bread and chocolate and the favorite food and drink of the returning spirits. El Dia de los Muertos is a family feast that commemorates the dead and at the same time profoundly celebrates life.*

COUNCIL OAK BOOKS
TULSA, OK 74120
1-800-247-8850

PAPERBACK EDITION © 1994 PATRICIA QUINTANA. ALL RIGHTS RESERVED
PUBLISHED 1989.

RECIPES AND "THE FOUR GENERATIONS" © 1989 PATRICIA QUINTANA.
"METHODS AND MATERIALS" © 1989 CAROL HARALSON AND PATRICIA QUINTANA
ALL RIGHTS RESERVED.
98 97 96 95 94   5 4 3 2 1

LIBRARY OF CONGRESS CATALOGUE CARD NUMBER 89-61234
ISBN 1-57178-000-9

Visual and conceptual design ≈ CAROL HARALSON.
Editing, marginalia and supplementary text ≈ CAROL HARALSON.

Collaboration on Spanish text ≈ MARIA LOSON DE FABREGAS
AND AGUSTÍN MONSREAL.

Initial translations ≈ LYNDA FINEGOLD AND ASA ZATZ.

Food styling ≈ PATRICIA QUINTANA.
Props and styling assistance ≈ LORENZA CARAZA-CAMPOS.

Production assistance ≈ CARL BRUNE.

PRINTED IN HONG KONG
THROUGH OVERSEAS PRINTING CORPORATION.

TYPESET BY TYPO PHOTO GRAPHICS INC.
IN CENTURY OLD STYLE AND COPPERPLATE.

CONTENTS

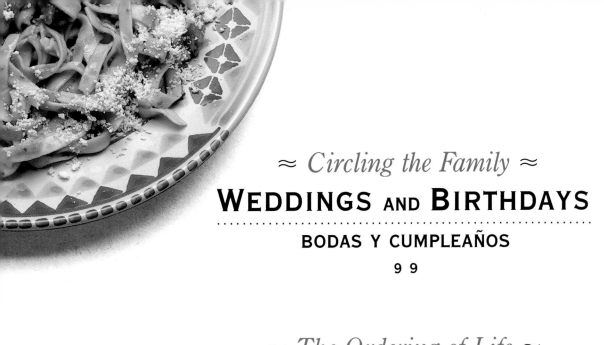

METHODS
AND
MATERIALS

DRY-ROASTING INGREDIENTS.

THE COMAL ≈

In Mexico, the comal is used almost daily for roasting ingredients and cooking tortillas. Metal comals are simple, flat, round surfaces used on conventional stovetops. For cooking over an open fire, a slightly dish-shaped clay comal is used. Any heavy griddle or skillet will serve the same purpose. Cookware used repeatedly for roasting and tortilla-making will cure over time and may blacken; it is a good idea to devote one skillet or griddle to these uses.

Spices, fruits and vegetables are often roasted before being added to a Mexican dish. The most common implement for stove-top roasting is the COMAL, a flat, round griddle made of metal or clay. Any skillet or griddle that conducts heat efficiently will work equally well. The roasting is done without the addition of fats or oils. Once accustomed to this quick technique, you may find it desirable to roast other ingredients to intensify their flavors. Nuts such as almonds or pecans, for example, exude a wonderful essence when quickly roasted before being added to a salad or other dish.

TO ROAST AN ONION: Heat a heavy ungreased skillet or comal to smoking, then lower heat to medium. Place a whole, peeled onion on the heated surface of the skillet or comal and allow to roast approximately 15-20 minutes, turning frequently to avoid burning and to expose all sides of the onion to the heat. Turning with tongs prevents the piercing of the onion and thus preserves all its juice intact. The exterior of the onion will brown but should not char heavily. An alternative method of roasting an onion is to place it directly over the flame of a gas burner. You can allow the onion to rest on the burner, or place a cake-cooling rack or broiling rack over the burner and place the onion on the rack. Roasting intensifies and mellows the flavor of the onion. White onions are generally best for Mexican cooking as the yellow Spanish onions sometimes contribute too much sweetness to the finished flavor of the dish. Roasted onions may be combined in the same dish with raw and/or boiled onions, as each gives a slightly different flavor.

TO ROAST GARLIC: Heat a heavy ungreased skillet or comal to smoking, then lower heat to medium. Add garlic cloves or a whole head of garlic to the skillet. Garlic may be either peeled or unpeeled, according to your preference; flavor will be stronger if you peel the garlic and slightly sweeter if you do not peel it. Roast approximately 10 minutes, turning frequently to avoid burning and sticking, and to expose evenly to the heated surface. Roasting greatly mellows and sweetens the flavor of garlic. Garlic will brown but should not char heavily. If you are roasting unpeeled garlic, cool and peel before using.

TO ROAST A TOMATO: Many sauce recipes call for roasted tomatoes. Start with juicy, ripe red tomatoes with good flavor. (If the only tomatoes available to you are those hybridized for transport and "ripened" with ethylene gas, such as supermarkets sometimes carry in the winter months, it may be better to use whole top-quality canned Italian plum tomatoes, well drained.) Preheat a heavy, ungreased skillet or comal to smoking, then reduce to medium heat. Wash and dry but do not peel the tomato. Add the tomato to the hot skillet and roast, uncovered, approximately 20 minutes, turning frequently with tongs so that all sides of the tomato are exposed to the hot surface of the skillet. You may also roast tomatoes under a preheated broiler: place on aluminum foil and broil approximately 20 minutes directly under the heat source, turning three or four times to roast evenly. Roasted tomatoes will brown but should not char heavily. If the tomato is not fully broiled, it will taste baked and will lack the distinctive roasted flavor. There is no need to peel roasted tomatoes before continuing with most recipes.

PREPARING AND USING FRESH CHILES.

TO ROAST, SWEAT, SEED AND DEVEIN A FRESH CHILE: Fresh cooking chiles such as chiles poblanos are often roasted before use. The procedure is the same for any chile or for sweet bell peppers.

Roast the chile: Wash and dry the chile, then allow it to rest directly on the medium gas flame of a stovetop burner. (Alternatively, you may place the chile directly under the heat source of a broiler.) Turn the chile for even roasting, using tongs to avoid piercing it. Roasting will take 5-15 minutes, depending on the size of the chile and the height of the flame. Skin will become somewhat blackened and blistered. (Extreme charring, however, can produce a bitter taste and may dull the chile's rich color, so stop in time.)

Sweat the chile: When the chile is roasted, remove it from heat, place it in a plastic bag, close the top of the bag, and allow the chile to "sweat" until it is cool enough to handle — approximately 15 minutes — or until you are ready to proceed with it. Chiles continue to cook slightly in the bag, so you can control their degree of softness by the length of time they are sweated as well as the length of time they are roasted. Roasted chiles can be set aside in this way for several hours if you wish.

Peel the chile: Remove the charred skin with your fingers and a small sharp knife. You may need to use some running water but avoid aggressively rinsing the chile or you may rinse away some of the roasted flavor.

Seed and devein the chile: Slice the chile down the side and remove the internal ribs or veins, along with the seeds clinging to

COOKING IMPLEMENTS
≈

Experiment with the many cooking utensils available to North American cooks to find your favorites for Mexican cooking. A wok, used for Chinese stir-frying, works well for sautéeing; a large vegetable steamer is fine for cooking tamales; a stockpot, Dutch oven, or lobster pot is useful for moles and stewed meats. For long-cooking meats or beans, try a crockpot, set to cook slowly overnight, or a pressure cooker to speed the process.

ELEPHANT GARLIC, PINK GARLIC, WHITE GARLIC, AND SHALLOTS ALL ARE USED IN MEXICAN COOKING.

them, and the stem. The heat of a chile is most concentrated in the internal veins and next in the seeds, so be sure to remove these thoroughly if you want a milder chile. Leave the chile whole if you intend to stuff it, or cut it into strips, or RAJAS. When handling hot chiles, you may wish to wear rubber gloves. Be careful not to rub your eyes with hands that have recently handled chiles.

USING A ROASTED CHILE: Rich, roasted chile flavor is an exquisite addition to many dishes. In addition to the uses called for in this book, add roasted chile strips or diced roasted chiles to hot or cold salads, sandwiches, and egg dishes. They are wonderful tossed with a little seasoned oil and vinegar as a side dish or condiment. Chile strips may be mixed with a small amount of olive oil to preserve their moistness and flavor and refrigerated for several days.

TO CHOP A FRESH CHILE: Fresh hot chiles such as jalapeños and serranos are often used as a piquant garnish for Mexican dishes. To prepare them, simply wash and stem, then chop, slice, or mince the fresh chiles. Most of the recipes in this book call for the use of chopped hot chiles with seeds and veins intact, but you can reduce the fire of chiles by removing their seeds and veins if you wish. The greatest heat is concentrated in the internal veins. When handling hot chiles, you may wish to wear rubber gloves. Be careful not to rub your eyes when you have recently handled hot chiles.

PREPARING AND USING DRIED CHILES.

TO PREPARE A DRIED CHILE FOR USE:

Wash and dry the chile: All dried chiles must be scrubbed very thoroughly before using because they are frequently dried in an unprotected outdoor environment. A small, stiff vegetable-scrubbing brush is handy for this purpose. After washing the chile, blot it dry with a cloth or paper towel, particularly if you are going to roast it. Otherwise, the moisture clinging to the chile will cause it to steam rather than roast on the hot cooking surface.

Seed and devein the chile if desired: If you intend to use the chile whole, remove the stem or not, as you prefer. If you will be using the chile without seeds and veins, cut a slit in the side of the chile and remove both seeds and veins, along with the dried chile stem.

Roast or stir-fry the chile: Preheat a comal or a heavy skillet. There is no need to oil it. When the cooking surface has reached medium heat, drop the chile on it and toast lightly, turning with tongs. This process, which takes only a few minutes, releases the perfume of the chile and makes it pliable. Chiles with smooth, brittle skins, such as cascabeles, burn quickly and must be watched closely; larger, wrinkled, more moist chiles, such as anchos, might take a minute or two longer over the heat. The chile should color very lightly, but not char. Chiles to be used in moles are toasted longer, to give a stronger flavor and a deeper color to the sauce.

An alternative to dry-roasting is to stir-fry the chile quickly in a small amount of hot oil in a preheated skillet or wok.

Add the chile to the dish: Add the roasted or fried chile to your dish directly as it comes from the skillet, or take it a step further by:

SOAKING AND PURÉEING: Soak the roasted or fried chile in plain hot water or hot water plus vinegar (2 tablespoons to one cup water) if you wish to reduce its piquancy. You may also soak it in grapefruit juice, bitter orange juice, broth, or other liquids. The chile will soften in 10 to 20 minutes, depending on its type and condition. Then drop it in a blender or food processor and purée, adding a little liquid to facilitate the procedure if required.

CRUMBLING OR FLAKING: Crumble the roasted or fried chile between your fingers or in a mortar, or grind it into powdery flakes using a spice mill.

REMOVING THE PULP: First soak the chile as described above, then lay it out on a flat surface, skin side down, and scrape the inner pulp away from the outer skin, using a spoon or dull knife. Add the roasted pulp to your dish for a delicate chile flavor. This works best for fleshy, thick chiles such as anchos.

An alternative ≈ Using a whole chile: Add whole dried chiles, simply washed and stemmed (or roasted too, if you prefer) to soups, stews, beans, vegetable sautées, or egg dishes. The chile imparts a delicious flavor and you can control the added fire by removing the whole chile at whatever point you wish during the cooking.

SUBSTITUTING CHILES.

Hundreds of chile varieties are grown in Mexico. Differences among them are sometimes unpredictable since they cross-pollinate easily, creating new hybrids, and even the same seed may produce very different results depending on the soil and climate in which it is grown. Many new chiles are being hybridized in the United States now and more are available in supermarkets than ever before, so watch your market for new candidates for Mexican cooking.

Chiles generally fall into two groups: cooking chiles and chiles used for garnish and pickling. Cooking chiles are usually milder and larger and are often roasted before use; the poblano is a good example. Garnish chiles may be smaller and hotter and are often used raw to accent a dish or to make a salsa; the jalapeño is often used this way.

Here is a list of possible chile substitutes that are widely available in U.S. markets. However, you may wish to check with your local grocer, farmer's market, or produce stand for other choices, as they vary widely in different parts of the U.S. and new ones are continually coming on the market. Names of chiles may also vary from region to region.

GARLIC ≈

*Garlic (*ALLIUM SATIVUM*) has been used in cooking and medicine since at least the time of the ancient Egyptians. It is integral to the cooking of the Mediterranean, whence it traveled to Mexico. Medically it has been shown to lower blood pressure and perhaps to lower cholesterol levels. As a flavoring, it enhances many kinds of savory dishes.*

FRESH CHILE SUBSTITUTES:

FOR CHILE POBLANO (MILD)	FRESH ANAHEIM OR MILD FRESH NEW MEXICAN CHILES, MILD BANANA PEPPERS, "LONG GREEN PEPPERS," CANNED MILD GREEN CHILES
FOR CHILE JALAPEÑO (HOT)	FRESH SERRANOS, FRESH CAYENNE CHILES, "LOUISIANA HOTS," CANNED SERRANOS OR JALAPEÑOS
FOR CHILE GÜERO (HOT)	FRESH FRESNO CHILES, HOT HUNGARIAN WAX PEPPERS, HOT BANANA PEPPERS, JALAPEÑOS OR SERRANOS

DRIED CHILE SUBSTITUTES:

FOR CHILE ANCHO OR MULATO (MILD)	DRIED ANCHOS AND MULATOS CAN BE USED INTERCHANGABLY, ALTHOUGH THE MULATO IS SLIGHTLY LARGER AND BLACKER AND HAS A SOMEWHAT RICHER SMOKY FLAVOR. SUBSTITUTE DRIED RED CALIFORNIA CHILES OR DRIED RED MILD NEW MEXICAN CHILES. MAY BE CALLED POD, RISTRA, OR CHIMAYO CHILES.
FOR CHILE DE ÁRBOL (HOT)	DRIED JAPONÉS, DRIED SERRANO, DRIED HOT RED NEW MEXICAN CHILES, CHILES TEPIN OR PEQUIN (OFTEN AVAILABLE IN THE SOUTHWEST), CHINESE OR THAI CHILES (AVAILABLE IN ASIAN MARKETS), CAYENNE PEPPER OR HOT RED PEPPER FLAKES.
FOR CHILE PASILLA (HOT)	HOT DRIED RED NEW MEXICAN CHILES. IF NECESSARY, PURE GROUND CHILE POWDER (NOT THE COMMERICAL TYPE THAT IS PREMIXED WITH OREGANO, CUMIN AND OTHER SPICES).
FOR CHILE CASCABEL (MEDIUM-HOT)	THE NUTTY FLAVOR OF THE CASCABEL HAS NO REAL SUBSTITUTES, BUT IF NOT AVAILABLE, USE CHILE GUAJILLO OR OTHER HOT DRIED RED CHILES.
FOR CHILE CHIPOTLE OR MORITA (SMOKY, HOT)	THERE IS NO REAL SUBSTITUTE FOR CHIPOTLES AND MORITAS, WHICH ARE DRIED, SMOKED JALAPEÑOS, BUT IF YOU CANNOT FIND THEM DRIED, THEY ARE USUALLY AVAILABLE CANNED OR BOTTLED IN HISPANIC AND SPECIALTY MARKETS.

PREPARING A COOKED SAUCE.

Classic Mexican cooked sauces are used with roasted, stewed or baked meats, poultry or fish, in casseroles and stews, with enchiladas, tamales and other dishes. The famous mole (pronounced MO LAY) is a cooked sauce. Cooked sauces are usually made in two distinct steps.

STEP ONE ≈ PREPARE THE INGREDIENTS: Ingredients are roasted, boiled, simply pared and chopped, or a combination of these. Prepared ingredients are then puréed and strained. In a traditional Mexican kitchen, they would be ground to paste or purée in a MOLCAJETE (a rough, black volcanic-stone or clay mortar shaped like an upside-down pyramid on three legs). However, in contemporary North American kitchens they may be puréed in a blender or food processor.

STEP TWO ≈ "FRY" THE SAUCE: In Mexico the strained purée is traditionally cooked in a clay cooking pot called a CAZUELA. A heavy saucepan works well in North American kitchens. It is important to start with a very hot saucepan. Put oil in the saucepan and heat almost to smoking. Then add about one-half cup of purée — it should sizzle loudly when it hits the hot oil — and cook approximately two to three minutes. Adding a small amount of purée at first allows the oil to stay at maximum heat, thus concentrating the roasted flavor of the purée and contributing to the complexity of the finished sauce. After two or three minutes, add remaining purée to the saucepan and reduce to medium heat. Allow the sauce to simmer 40 minutes to an hour, until it develops its full flavor. Tomato-based red sauces cook more quickly than moles, which usually contain a complex combination of chiles, herbs and spices. When the sauce is ready, it will have a thick, homogenous consistency allowing you to see the bottom of the pan when the sauce is stirred back with a spoon. Another cue that the sauce is ready is that the oil you began with will have separated from the mass of the sauce and will be standing separate and visible on the surface of the finished sauce. You may skim it off if you wish. To achieve a velvety texture and the preferred consistency, add broth to the sauce.

PREPARING A SALSA.

The colorful garnishes and condiments called salsas are as common on Mexican tables as are salt and pepper shakers on the tables of North America. Most are fresh, but some are cooked. They usually contain onions, garlic, tomatoes or tomatillos, herbs and chiles. Although the word *salsa* translates literally as "sauce," these zesty condiments are always called "salsas" and the word *sauce* is reserved for cooked sauces used as part of complete dish, such as moles.

The salsa most often seen in North America is a simple fresh one with jalapeños providing the piquant chile flavor. However, there are dozens of other salsas whose varying degrees of heat and subtle flavor differences are supplied by various dried and fresh chiles. This book contains a number of salsa recipes.

The fresh, versatile salsa is a wholesome addition to many menus. It can be prepared without oil, is very low in calories, and may contain little salt yet still retain flavor and interest.

SALSAS AND THE MOLCAJETE ≈

The MOLCAJETE (mol kah HEH TEH) is a three-legged mortar made of black volcanic stone or scored clay in which spices and ingredients for fresh salsas are ground by hand. In modern Mexican kitchens, the pre-Hispanic molcajete may sit side by side with a blender or food processor. To approximate the texture of mortar-ground ingredients, either mince or grate finely or use the food processor carefully in order not to overprocess.

Traditionally, garlic and salt are ground first when a salsa is prepared in a mortar so that their flavors will permeate the other ingredients. Garlic can be roasted before it is ground for a salsa in order to reduce its bite; the garlicky pungence remains but in a mellower form.

TORTILLA PRESS ≈

This inexpensive metal implement has two round surfaces, a hinge and a lever. The masa ball is placed between the two metal plates and pressed flat. Tortilla presses are widely available in kitchen supply stores and Hispanic markets in the U.S.

DRIED CHILES

MORITA
(HOT, SMOKY)

CHILCOSLE OR AMARILLO
(HOT, USED IN YELLOW MOLE)

LARGE MORITA
(HOT, SMOKY)

PASILLA
(HOT, DRIED CHILACA)

ANCHO
(MILD, DRIED POBLANO)

DE ÁRBOL
(VERY HOT)

COSTEÑOS
(VERY HOT)

DRIED CHILES

CHIHUACLE
(MILD)

GUAJILLO
(MILD)

CASCABEL
(MILDLY HOT, NUTTY. DRIED MANZANO)

MULATO
(MILD, MUCH LIKE ANCHO)

CHIPOTLE
(MILDLY HOT, SMOKED AND DRIED JALAPEÑO)

PIQUIN
(VERY HOT)

FRESH CHILES

CHILACA
(MILD, FRESH PASILLA)

POBLANO
(MILD)

GÜERO
(HOT)

POBLANO, RIPE.
(MILD, FRESH ANCHO.)

FRESH CHILES

SERRANO
(FRESH FLAVOR, MILD)

HABANERO
(VERY HOT)

JALAPEÑO LARGO
(MILD)

JALAPEÑOS
(MILD, RED WHEN RIPE. FRESH CHIPOLTE.)

MANZANO
(HOT, FRESH CASCABEL)

HERBS IN MEXICAN COOKING.

Herbs used in Mexican cooking and folk medicine include both Indian plants known since pre-Hispanic times and herbs that have arrived via Spanish, French or other influence. A good number of the hard-to-find plants are extremely adaptable to North American gardens. Page 19 lists sources for seeds and plants.

ALBAHACA.
Basil
ONCIMUM BASILICUM

Sunny annual. Many varieties with flavors ranging from lemony to minty to cinnamon-like. Not often used in Mexican cooking but occasionally in vinaigrette.

CHEPIL.
Chepil, Chipil
CROTALARIA LONGIROSTRATA

A 6-foot flowering shrub, deep-rooted and drought-resistant. Leaves and flowers eaten as a vegetable, sometimes steamed. Flavor like snap beans. Leaves added to tamales.

CILANTRO.
Cilantro, coriander, Chinese parsley
CORIANDRUM SATIVUM

Sunny annual that reseeds easily. Unique tangy flavor used in everything from salsa to mole, with cheese, in broth, rice, beans. Seed has a very different flavor from the fresh leaf. Leaf flavor lost through drying.

CORTEZA DE MAGUY OR MIXIOTE.
Century plant, agave
AGAVE AMERICANA

The leaf membrane of the maguey is peeled and dried to produce a parchment-like material used as a roasting pouch for meats and poultry.

EPAZOTE.
Epazote, Mexican tea, wormseed
CHENOPODIUM AMBROSIOIDEϽ

Tough camphor-smelling perennial that reseeds prolifically. Grows wild in parts of central and southern Mexico. Considered by many to be indispensable to a good pot of beans. Digestive, used for intestinal disorders. Culinary uses are many: chopped fresh and added to sautéed mushrooms or omelets, used in quesadillas, moles, broths. Can be carefully dried for winter use. Very easy to grow.

FLOR DE FRIJOL.
Bean flower
PHASEOLUS VULGARIS

Flowers of the bean group that contains kidney, navy, green, pinto, snap, string and wax beans. Flowers are sautéed fresh, added to cooked beans and fresh salsas.

HIERBA BUENA.
Spearmint
MENTHA SPICATA

A shady perennial, easily propogated from root cuttings. Aromatic flavor added to guacamole, broth, meats, meatballs, cooked sauces. Fresh leaf used in cold drinks.

HIERBA DE CONEJO.
Indian paintbrush
CASTILLEJA LANATA

Zapotec herb used in the cooking of beans and rice. Used fresh or dry.

HIERBA SANTA OR HOJA SANTA.
Hierba santa
PIPER AURITUM

Tender woody-stemmed perennial. Velvety, heart-shaped leaves used in green mole, for wrapping tamales, with chicken, beef, shrimp.

USING DRIED HERBS ≈

Use one-third to one-half as much dried herb as fresh. Potency of dried herbs depends on their age and conditions of storage. Many Mexican cooking herbs work well in their dried state, but some — especially cilantro — lose or change flavor in drying. If possible, obtain dried herbs in leaf form rather than powdered.

HOJA DE AGUACATE.

Avocado leaf

PERSEA AMERICANA

The leaf of the tropical avocado tree is used fresh or dried in broths, chicken dishes, beans, tamales and with fish. Provides delicate, slightly aromatic flavor. It is said that the poorer the fruit of the tree, the tastier its leaves will be. Avocados grown in the U.S. are usually West Indian or Guatemalan races; fragrant, anise-scented leaves and stems are characteristic of the Mexican race only.

HOJA DE MAIZ.

Corn husk

ZEA MAÏS

The husk of any variety of corn is used both fresh and dried, primarily to wrap tamales. Fresh corn is delicious grilled directly in the husk. Remove silk and add butter and salt, wrap husks back around the ear and roast.

HOJA DE PLATANO.

Banana leaf

MUSA PARADISIACA

Banana trees are tropical but can be grown in colder climates if the bulb or root is dug before frost and stored in a cool, dry place. Return to the garden in spring. Will grow annually to 15 feet if handled in this way. Leaves used to wrap tamales.

HUAUZONTLE

Huauzontle

CHENOPODIUM BERLANDIERI

Aztec plant with a flavor like broccoli. Only the tender tip is used, cooked with with onion and garlic, sometimes dipped in batter and deep-fried.

LAUREL.

Bay leaf, bay, bay laurel

LITSEA SSP.

Mexican bay is thinner-leafed, more silvery and more delicate in flavor than Mediterranean bay (LAURIS NOBILIS). It is used for pickling, in cooked sauces, soup, meat dishes.

MANZANILLA.

Chamomile, German chamomile.

MATRICARIA RECUTITA

The Spanish name means "little apple," which describes the aroma of this sun-loving perennial with small yellow, daisy-like blooms. Used in Mexico to make a digestive, mildly diuretic tea, an eyewash, or a hair rinse.

MENTA.

Peppermint

MENTHA PIPERITA

A shady perennial, easily propogated from root cuttings. Used much like spearmint.

PAPALO OR PAPALOQUELITE

Papalo

POROPHYLLUM RUDERALE

Pungent digestive herb eaten raw by the sprig with tacos, guacamole, salad. From PAPALOTL, the Nahuatl for "butterfly."

PEPICHA

Pepicha, Pepicha

POROPHYLLUM TAGETOIDES

Sunny annual with a flavor like cilantro but stronger. Used with squash, corn, cuitlacoche.

PEREJIL.

Parsley

PETROSELINUM CRISPUM

Sun-loving biennial that reseeds easily. Mexican parsley is the flat-leafed variety. Used in rice, stews, casseroles, green mole. Add toward the end of cooking.

QUELITES.

Lamb's quarter

CHENOPODIUM BERLANDIERI

Sunny annual growing to 3 feet. Young growth eaten raw or used as a cooked vegetable, with a spinach-like flavor. Used by Indians of Southwestern U. S. in much the same way as in Mexico. Combined with pumpkin seeds and chile strips in pre-Hispanic cooking.

ROMERITO.

Romerito

SUAEDA TORREYANA

Used fresh or as a cooked green, especially during Lent and The Day of the Dead. Small succulent leaves resemble those of purslane.

TÉ LIMÓN.

Lemon grass

CYMBOPOGON CITRATUS

Tall, sun-loving tender perennial with the appearance of a large clump of decorative grass. Lemon-scented leaves. Traditionally used only for tea but added to chicken broth or soup in contemporary cuisine.

TOMILLO.

Thyme, garden thyme

THYMUS VULGARIS

Sunny aromatic perennial. Used in pickled chiles and marinades, with meats, mushrooms, cooked sauces.

TORONJIL.

Balm-gentle.

AGASTACHE MEXICANA

The citrus-scented toronjil is an annual that grows to 4 feet in good soil and germinates readily from seed. Used to make a diuretic tea which is considered good for weight control and for blood cleansing.

VERDOLAGA.

Purslane

PORTULACA OLERACEA

Low-growing, sun-loving succulent grown as an annual. Archaeological evidence that it was eaten by American natives ca. 1200. Sharp, cooling flavor. Eaten raw in salad or steamed, sautéed with onion and chile, in green mole.

MEXICAN CREAM.

Cream in Mexico is sold in two basic forms: CREMA NATURAL is slightly sour and may be either thick or thin; it thickens as it ages. CREMA DULCE or sweet cream is the equivalent of American whipping cream.

A good substitute for CREMA NATURAL is the French invention crème fraîche, a 30% butterfat cream, fermented by airborne bacteria until it has a thick, rich taste, sometimes slightly sour, and a velvety texture. It is excellent in soups and desserts, or as a topping for spicy chile-flavored dishes in place of sour cream. Yogurt, buttermilk, sour cream and crème fraîche can be made by allowing airborne bacteria to thicken unpasteurized milk, whey or cream. However, pasteurized milk is almost free of bacteria and so will usually spoil before it sours; therefore it is "soured" commercially by the introduction of pure cultures of the desired bacteria.

TO MAKE CRÈME FRAÎCHE

≈

Combine one cup heavy whipping cream (preferably not ultra-pasteurized) with two tablespoons cultured buttermilk, whisking to blend. Cover loosely and let stand in a warm place for 12 to 24 hours. Stir when thickened, then refrigerate. Crème fraîche will keep under refrigeration for a week or more. You may use it immediately after blending, but the flavor will develop more fully upon aging. A quick alternative is to whisk one part heavy whipping cream with one part dairy sour cream. Use immediately, or store in the refrigerator for a week or more.

. . . .

SELECTED SOURCES.

J.H. HUDSON, SEEDSMAN
P.O. BOX 1058
REDWOOD CITY CA 94064
(special collection of Zapotec plants and seeds; catalogue $1.00)

FOX HILL FARM
444 WEST MICHIGAN AVENUE
BOX 7
PARMA MI 49269
(herbs)

HORTICULTURAL ENTERPRISES
P.O. BOX 810082
DALLAS TX 75381
(chiles, tomatillos, epazote)

LOS CHILEROS DE NUEVO MEXICO
BOX 6215
SANTA FE NM 87502
(chiles)

NATIVE SEED SEARCH
3950 WEST NEW YORK DRIVE
TUCSON AZ 85745
(Southwestern and Native American plants)

PEPPER GAL
10536 119TH AVENUE N
LARGO FL 33543
(chiles)

PLANTS OF THE SOUTHWEST
1812 SECOND STREET
SANTA FE NM 87501

REDWOOD CITY SEED COMPANY
P.O. BOX 361
REDWOOD CITY CA 94064
(Mexican vegetable and herb seeds)

TAYLOR'S HERB GARDENS, INC.
1535 LONE OAK ROAD
VISTA CA 92084
(herb plants)

LA PALMA
2884 24TH STREET
SAN FRANCISCO CA 94110
(chiles and achiote)

HAY DAY
2460 DIXWELL AVENUE
HAMDEN CT 06514
(chiles and achiote)

THE MOZZARELLA COMPANY
PAULA LAMBERT, OWNER
2944 ELM ST.
DALLAS TX 75226
214/ 741-4072
(cheeses, Mexican cheeses made to order)

HEART OF TEXAS PRODUCE CO.
MARY MAHAFFEY
PURVEYORS OF UNIQUE SPECIALTY & ORGANIC PRODUCE
777 SHADY LANE /1
PO BOX 6147
AUSTIN TX 78762
(epazote and hoja santa)

OLD SOUTHWEST TRADING CO.
BOX 7545
ALBUQUERQUE NM 87194
(chiles, herbs)

EL AFICIONADO
540 EAST 20TH STREET
NEW YORK NY 10009
(cuitlacoche)

PATTY'S HERBS
ROUTE 1, BOX 31J
PEARSALL TX 78061
(epazote and hierba santa)

SANDY MUSH HERB NURSERY
ROUTE 2, SURRETT COVE ROAD
LEICESTER NC 28748
(herb plants and seeds; catalogue $3.95)

SHEPHERD'S GARDEN SEEDS
7389 WEST ZAYANTE ROAD, DEPT. HH
FELTON, CA 95018
(chile seed collection, herb seeds)

BALDUCCI
424 SIXTH AVENUE
NEW YORK, NEW YORK 10011
(frozen cuitlacoche)

MEXICAN CHEESE ≈

Most of the recipes in this book suggest North American equivalents for Mexican cheeses. Here are some of the basic characteristics of Mexican cheeses.

MANCHEGO. *Mild to slightly sharp, sometimes flavored with herbs or chiles. Used in casseroles, crepes, melted cheese hors d'oeuvres. Melts well.*

CHIHUAHUA. *Nutty and mild. Used to stuff chiles as it melts well.*

OAXACA. *Slightly sour. Shreds easily. Used in stuffed chiles, casseroles, and enchiladas. If well grated, it will melt, but it has a low fat content.*

AÑEJO AND COTIJA. *Salty. Similar to ricotta. Grated finely over quesadillas and enchiladas as a garnish, often with shredded lettuce.*

ADOBERA. *Mild. Melts very well.*

QUESO FRESCO. *Fresh, flavorful, somewhat salty, sometimes tangy. Similar to salted farmer's cheese, or not-so-salty feta cheese. Served sliced with salsa, on tacos with avocado, with fruit pastes, sandwiches, tostadas.*

PANELA. *Similar to fresh mozarella but with a more pronounced flavor. A fresh cheese but not crumbly.*

HERBS

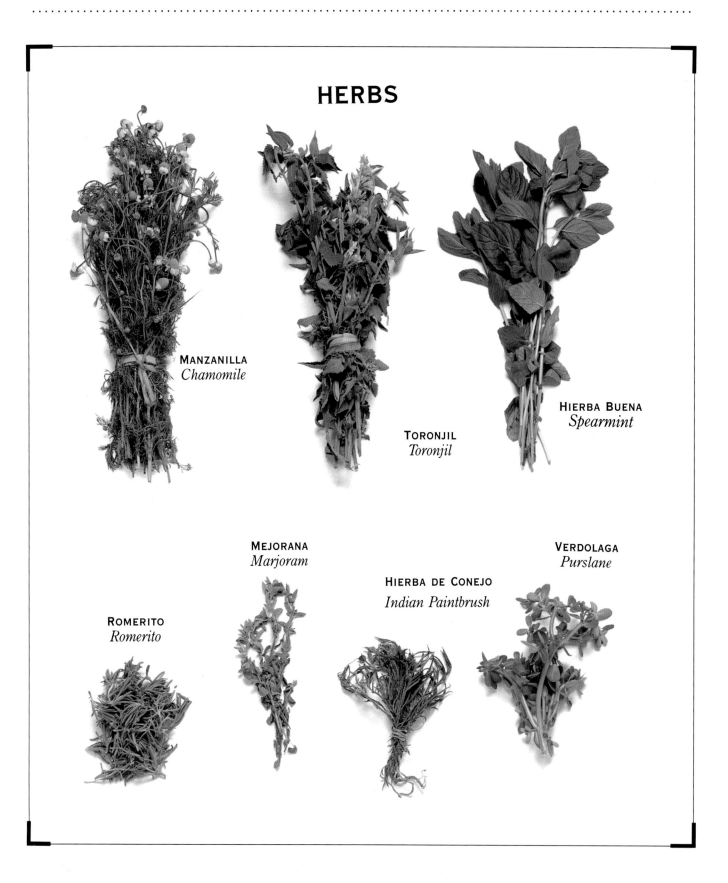

MANZANILLA
Chamomile

TORONJIL
Toronjil

HIERBA BUENA
Spearmint

MEJORANA
Marjoram

VERDOLAGA
Purslane

HIERBA DE CONEJO
Indian Paintbrush

ROMERITO
Romerito

HERBS

TÉ LIMON
Lemon grass

EPAZOTE
Epazote

MENTA
Peppermint

LAUREL
Bay leaf

FLOR DE FRIJOL
Bean flower

CHEPIL
Chepil

TOMILLO
Thyme

THE
FOUR
GENERATIONS

LAS CUATRO GENERACIONES

I would not be guilty of an untruth if I were to say that my love of cooking goes back nearly a hundred years, to when my great-grandmother, Emilia Vasseur, of French descent, discovered that her life's work was to be a cook. Now, as I browse through the family album, I relive in my imagination moments of my great-grandmother's intense, unusual life. As my eyes linger on the sepia photograph of her wedding to Charles East, an English engineer, I also see her on the train that brought the two of them to Oaxaca, the city where she was born. Emilia was back once more in the city of her childhood, in the land of the seven moles, the black clay, and ancient Monte Albán. Now an adult, she would leave her house early in the morning, dressed in a full skirt, a lace parasol on her arm, and stroll through the narrow cobblestone streets on her way to the market. I still remember, not without a slight shiver, her account of the excitement of strolling through the many-colored stands of the market, where one's senses were delighted by the fruits, the tortillas of blue, yellow, and white corn, the red, black, and green squash seed moles, the fresh cheeses, the vast array of chiles, the fragrant herbs, the meats, the fresh fish, the dried shrimp, the vegetables, the sweets, the chocolate — all waiting to be transmuted into an endless variety of delights. She recorded her recipes with exactitude in a great notebook which is a model cookbook to this day. It contains descriptions of ingredients and directions for preparing unforgettable dishes: eggs in *faltriquera; capirotada,* or Mexican bread

---

FISH IN PUFF PASTRY (RECIPE ON PAGE 109). IN THE
PHOTOGRAPH ARE MAGO, PATRICIA AS A CHILD,
MARGARITA, AND GREAT-GRANDMOTHER EMILIA.

CARLOS EAST

pudding; chunks of seasoned cactus cooked in cactus paddles; fresh fish baked in pastry with cream sauce; *buñuelos,* the classic Mexican fritters; and countless others. Lingering over the photographs with nostalgia for that long-ago time, I see one in which, bubbling with good spirits, a brimming market basket over her arm, Emilia returns home on a streetcar drawn by mules. She is in a hurry to prepare breakfast, a daily ritual at the Mexican table.

In this setting of domestic intimacy, the day's first meal begins with freshly squeezed fruit juice, seasonal fruit, eggs in a great variety of guises (a la Mexicana with tomato, onion, and green chile; ranchero style with fried tortillas and green or red salsa; "bricklayer's" style with chile de árbol salsa; scrambled with ham, bacon or chiles serranos), meat stews, or spicy meat with vegetables, all accompanied by the never-failing beans, cooked in the big clay pot or refried, hot chocolate, coffee, fresh tortillas and egg bread.

I appreciate, then, that one of Emilia's deepest satisfactions (with which I sympathize down to its most insignificant detail) was to prepare breakfast in her big, old-fashioned kitchen. The photograph of her kitchen shows white-washed walls adorned with copper, clay, and wooden utensils and vessels and, in the center of the main wall, as a rare and beautiful showpiece, the enormous brick stove with the wide mouths through which it devoured the coal or wood that heated it. Flanking it on either side were the massive wooden dish cabinets and on the side walls, the shelves for storing the food and implements of daily use. Margarita, young Emilia, and Carlos, my great-grandmother's children, were born in this home that radiated warmth and energy. However, misfortune struck. Emilia's husband suffered embolisms in both legs and the family was obliged to move to the city of Veracruz, whose warmth and sea air were prescribed for the patient's recovery. They took over the administration of a farm there and, as I can see in the album, Emilia divided her time between managing the workers, riding on horseback through the banana plantations, and seeing to the care of her husband and children.

In the early 1900s the tranquility of the East family was again disturbed by fate. The outbreak of the revolution of 1910 and the fury of the struggle that ensued compelled my great-grandparents to move to the relative stability of Mexico City. They left the port of Veracruz on the train but, perhaps due to the unrest of the time, or to the trip itself, great-grandfather was weakened and he succumbed to another embolism before reaching their destination.

Emilia, then, had to find the strength to continue alone. She established a boarding house in which she again found surcease in the pleasures of the kitchen, devoting herself to providing succulent meals for her guests. In light of her recent widowhood, Emilia well understood the meaning, both real and magical, of the Day of the Dead. Year after year in the last days of October, she decorated her house with the traditional altar, heaped with flowers and food and aglow with candlelight to keep alive the image of her departed. Likewise, she specialized in the preparation of the most traditional dishes and sweets during these profoundly Mexican holidays: green mole of Oaxaca, corn tamales, Naolinco bread, Oaxacan tamales, lentils cooked in the old way with plantains, yellow mole, caramel custard, guavas filled with coconut cream, egg bread.

Besides the dishes, there appeared on the altar Jamaica water, chia, horchata, and tamarind water, served in small clay mugs; jugs of hot chocolate frothed with a chocolate beater; sweet rolls; sugar skulls; photographs; keepsakes; and all that honored those who had departed this world.

As was the custom in the city at the beginning of the century, Emilia's boarders were usually businessmen, tradespeople, traveling salesmen, or employees of foreign embassies in Mexico. One of these last, a Señor Kant, the cultural attaché of the Swedish embassy, became the second husband of Emilia, who still preserved her youthful grace and beauty.

The young couple decided to settle in Oaxaca, where they bought a farm. For a time, Emilia devoted herself to acquiring a repertoire of the practically inexhaustible gustatory riches of the region. She resurrected for herself and her family such dishes as folded tortillas in chile-tomato sauce; tortillas in bean sauce with avocado leaves, Oaxacan cheese, cream and cured beef; soup made with the tendrils and young leaves of the squash vine; yellow corn empanadas with golden chile sauce; and the fruit drinks of that so very prodigious land.

On the Oaxaca ranch, Emilia experienced the joy of being a mother for the fourth time and the unhappiness of losing her second husband. Again, circumstances forced her to return to Mexico City, this time for good. Again, she established a boarding house where she was to meet her third husband, Roberto Carmen, her companion for the rest of her life.

In her mature years, she was able to devote herself fully to the great passion of her life: cooking. She resurrected traditional dishes and created new ones, drawing from experience and her fruitful imagination. A woman of inexhaustible culinary ingenuity, she left to her descendants the broadest and most invaluable of legacies, the example of strength of will and love of life, and the secrets of the cookery of her beloved country.

Early memories of my grandmother Margarita — daughter of Emilia — are the most treasured of my childhood. One day, when I was very little, I went into the kitchen where she was busily at work. I was so dazzled by the love she lavished on everything she did that from that moment on, and for many years after, I was her inseparable companion. At her side, I acquired not only the skills of cooking but also an appreciation for the immense delight to be derived in the kitchen.

Married at seventeen in Mexico City, where she had lived since she was a small child, Mamanena (as I always called her) was already endowed with the experience that her mother Emilia passed on to her and which she was to transmit with endless patience to me. Her husband, Arturo Fernández, was a hard-working, even-tempered man enamored of his wife's beauty and ingenuity, as well as her tenderness and capacity to enjoy life.

My attachment to Mamanena began when I was a small girl. When my parents announced that we would be going to pay her a visit, I was elated, instantly filled with anticipation of my favorite amusement: cooking. At Mamanena's side, I would concentrate my attention on her white hands and, as she chopped the onions and garlic for the sauces, she would tell me about the two-hour trip on horseback she and her mother Emilia used to make to the market when the family was living on the farm in Veracruz. At other times she would tell me how, basket in hand, she would go daily to the Juárez market in Mexico City to buy vegetables, meat, and fruit. Acquiring a refrigerator was a major event in Mamanena's domestic life because thereafter she would go to the market only twice a week.

MARGARITA, AT LEFT, WITH A COUSIN AND A FRIEND, IN OAXACA.

My grandmother's kitchen utensils were precious treasures to me. The metate, or grinding stone, the molcajete, a volcanic stone mortar, and the molinillo, a wooden implement used for beating chocolate, were the ones I prized most highly. I was also fascinated by the precious wooden basin that Mamanena occasionally allowed me to use, though not without some trepidation. Her caution was justified by memories that this vessel held for her. In her most gentle voice, she explained how Emilia, her mother, had used it to knead the white or yellow dough for delicious handmade tortillas. I was insistent in my curiosity, having eagerly watched everything done by the women who worked on Rancho Chapopote, the family ranch bought by my father Raúl Quintana in the Huasteca region of the state of Veracruz. Sometimes the women would let me help them, and sometimes I was allowed to observe the culinary magic that they performed in the kitchens of their own homes. And so Mamanena, who no longer kneaded her dough but bought it at the market, promised me that one day she and I would prepare the nixtamal, or limed corn for tortilla dough, when we left Mexico City for a visit to the family ranch. She kept her promise, even to the point of taking along her clay comal to show me the difference between a city tortilla and a country one, a point upon which she frequently commented.

On that memorable occasion, Mamanena took a heavy enamel pot filled with water, added the kernels of corn, sprinkled in a little powdered limestone dissolved in water, and set the pot over the fire. After it had boiled for about twenty minutes, she took out one kernel to see if the hull had loosened. Then she took the pot off the fire and let it stand for some hours, an eternity to me, before rinsing the corn until its "teeth" were sparkling white. Next we hulled the kernels in the Indian way, that is, rubbing them together between our hands. What an unforgettable sound it made, the ancient music of the pre-Hispanic hearthside. And she said to me, "Now, we will grind them." Then she placed the wet kernels upon the metate, picked up the mano, or grinding stone, and began to rub the kernels against the curved stone surface they rested upon, as though she were stretching out a sheet of dough with a rolling pin, using a rhythmic and constant backwards and forwards movement. When the kernels were ground to paste, she sprinkled water on them and invited me, finally, to work the corn dough, whose consistency was a brand new experience for me.

It was on the farm, also, that she taught me to prepare exquisite fruit preserves (guava, strawberry, plum, orange) simmered in great enamel pots. She would reiterate the importance of thorough washing of fruits and vegetables and would remind me, as a precaution against accident, never to allow the handles of pots and pans to project over the edge of the stove. She taught me how to control the temperature of the fire in accordance with the

ARTURO FERNÁNDEZ

kind of dish to be prepared. All of this was a pleasurable ceremony for me, filled with surprises and secrets, of which I was the keeper.

Mamanena celebrated family fiestas with great enthusiasm and delighted her dear ones with exquisite dishes that gave her the well-deserved fame she still enjoys. Although she prepared menus that ranged from the simplest to the most complex, she devoted the same pains to whatever she prepared, recording her discoveries in a notebook similar to Emilia's, which covered everything from the measures of beans and liters of milk to the pesos and centavos of her weekly purchases.

As the years went by, my relationship with Mamanena became closer and closer, since, as I grew up, she continued to bestow upon me her culinary skills, but also gradually took me into the loving territory of her confidence. She would relate passages of her life in which happiness was always the dominant note, such as those involving the births of her children and grandchildren. This happiness was expressed through her culinary sensitivity in the baptismal fiesta, which gave her the opportunity to enjoin her imagination and good taste, preparing the dishes most appropriate for such events. She prepared dishes as varied as Tabasco-style enchiladas with chiles anchos, bean soup with garlic, shrimp and avocado leaves; corn torte; chicken breasts stuffed with young squash and corn; figs in mango sauce; and other delights.

Likewise, I remember how Mamanena taught me about the *itacate,* the bundle of succulent foods to be carried away and eaten in another place. Many times, secretly, she put aside for me a few little Monterrey tamales (my weakness) and a slice of cake with meringue. If others asked for seconds, she would say there were none. But when it came time to leave, Mamanena would wink at me and lead me by the hand to the kitchen, where she would present me with the *itacate,* all wrapped in its little bundle, whispering in my ear that there was nothing as delicious as a warmed-over tidbit. Of course, this generosity was not reserved just for me. She often prepared bundles with ample portions for those who came to her house, not only to parties but even to her simplest meals, thus continuing the tradition of the *itacate,* a gesture of trust, affection and goodwill. To this day, when Mamanena tells me incidents of her life unfamiliar to me, I am suddenly ten years old again, and everything this wonderful woman does and says seems to be out of a storybook. The grandmother who taught me to love the world and its beauty and who initiated me into this universe of surprises and magic called gastronomy also brought me to the calling that makes me sure I am alive.

My culinary calling, so rooted in Mexican traditions and customs, was enriched by my mother Mago's inclination towards learning the thousand-and-one secrets of international cuisine.

Mago, Mamanena's daughter, was born and raised principally in Mexico City. She had the good luck to make frequent trips abroad from the time of her early youth, sometimes solely for pleasure, sometimes to study languages, and later on, as I grew up, she passed along to me the fruits of her experiences. Although she managed a household and the rearing of five children, she was able to find a way to cultivate her passion for archaeology and her enjoyment of a highly active social life. It was a source of great pride for her to receive guests in her home and to lavish upon them the most representative examples of Mexican and international cuisine.

It was Mamanena who originated in me a passion for the Mexican markets. But in the company of Mago, marketing took on the intensity of an obsession.

Together we have strolled countless times up and down the aisles of the markets of Mexico, the source of indelible memories for me. Among my favorite markets is the San Juan market in Mexico City, whose gaiety and brilliance gives the impression of a vast, sublime jewel shop of nature. When the visitor recovers from initial bedazzlement, her ear is delighted by that most Mexican symphony of shopkeepers' calls: *"Hay limooooones, hay limooooones, güerita, cuantos le pongo para sus aguas frescas? Andele, Señorita, hay torteeeyas . . ."* (Here are lemons, here are lemons, how many for your lemonade? This way, lady, for tortillas. . .). Over and over, the chanted calls of the vendors fill the air like an ancient chorus, an almost wordless music, all sound, all strange harmony. And before you cascades, stall after stall, the extraordinary wealth of native chiles, dry and freshly picked, red and green and yellow, mild to scorching, pequin tiny as a pumpkin seed to great, fleshy poblanos. Boxes brim over with chromatic riches that stir the appetite at any time of day.

Next, one is struck by an irresistible conjunction of the most varied aromas: handfuls of parsley, coriander, mint, epazote, hierba santa, bay leaves, cilantro, papalo, pepicha, all firing the imagination of the buyer who will combine the fresh herbs with white, yellow or purple onions and the several kinds of beautiful braided garlic.

Once initiated into this world of sensual abundance, the touch awakens, and one strokes the custard apples, blackberries, pineapples, juicy mangoes and sliced melons, the freshly-washed vegetables arranged in pyramids with geometrical exactness, the ruffled, ornamental spinach, the romaine, French and orejona lettuces, the nopal cactuses shorn of their spines, the carrots and scallions; the many mushrooms — *clavito, yema,* bird's foot, champignons, and others of exotic texture and form — all as toothsome as if at that very moment they had risen marveously out of the earth, that exuberant earth that bears so many and such greatly varied prodigies. Finally comes the moment of the "probadita," the tasty little sampling, offered by the shopkeeper as generously as if by nature herself.

As I think of the market, I recall a piece of Mago's advice: "If you want to know a people, go to their market." In the Mexican market is a clear vision of the Mexican essence.

. . . .

Although I acquired my love of cooking from my great-grandmother, grandmother, and mother, it must be said that this love would never have come to fruition without the definitive influence of the magical and marvelous country where I was born, Mexico.

To recognize this influence is to recognize the multiplicity of Mexico, and the distinctive character of each region. Each region is a faithful expression of its aboriginal culture, ancestral habits, customs, and geography, and a record of the interplay between the many different ethnic groups whose language, music, art, and architecture have contributed to its unique and perfect coherence. This coherence can be known through that ritual which is — why not say it? — the most basic way of learning the nature of a people, the partaking of their food. This richness of cultural manifestation is evident throughout the year in the countless fiestas of a pre-Hispanic, religious, popular nature with which the Mexican people celebrate their deepest beliefs and with which they mark the important moments of their private lives.

Since I was a little girl I have been very restless, a kind of industrious little ant, never quiet for a moment. My eagerness to know and to try things in life has brought me some troubles, but, more importantly, it has yielded enormous satisfactions. My interests are very diversified, yet all of them come together in cookery. I have been able to explore the popular traditions of my country, the feasts and celebrations that are a profound expression of Mexico's cultural origins, and the different styles of architecture from one city to another, or one village or another. Each has led me to understand more fully the essence of Mexican cookery, which is as rich and prodigious as the people who created it, expressing their love of ritual, their involvement with nature and their joy of life. That is why, when I speak of cookery, I am speaking of Mexican cookery, and of everything I have learned of Mexico's history, its myths, its heroes, its songs. In each of my dishes is present, in one form or another, the Mexican essence, which is basically my essence.

Further, I am fortunate to come from a family of women who understand the special pleasures and wisdom that spring from and bear their finest fruits in that endeavor that is so intimate and at the same time universal, which is cookery. Because of these influences, and my early awakening to love of the culinary art, I was already giving private cooking classes at eighteen. One day in my twenties I decided to go to Europe to become acquainted with the excellences and varieties of its cuisine, and to avail myself of the tutelage of the best known and most respected international chefs. While studying, in part because of nostalgia and perhaps also because it is in my blood, I began to experiment with the marriage between the materials of the New World and the methods of the Old World, particularly the classical techniques of French, Spanish, German, and Italian cuisine.

I worked unceasingly for a year, with people as wonderful as Michel Guerard and Gaston Lenôtre, and I studied the cuisine of Paul Bocuse, Roger Verge and Pierre Troisgros. The most important adaptations I pursued concern techniques to lighten and color the mixture of elements, and likewise to combine ingredients of foreign origin (Arabic, Chinese, Spanish, French, English, and Italian) with those purely Mexican.

On the basis of the knowledge I obtained both outside and inside the country, I have developed concepts of design of both presentation and aroma, since, as we say in Mexico, "Love is born from sight," and since the aroma of any dish is the most representative aspect of its seasoning. In this way, it is possible to make the values of a dish touch and delight not only the sense of taste but all the other senses. I returned to my native soil with the dream of founding a cooking school. I knew that to achieve it would take much time, work, devotion, effort, resources of many kinds, but my project seemed feasible so I threw myself into putting my ideas into practice. I was helped in very great measure by the activity of teaching. Giving classes was a way of perfecting ideas, strengthening knowledge, and appreciating the true results of experiment. For me, a kitchen that does not experiment, that does not combine styles, that does not develop cuisine with a high degree of imagination, is a kitchen that never will reach its own potential. When, finally, after many years, I was able to establish my own school, experimentation became the core of my philosophy as a cook.

One of the most interesting tasks in my culinary work has been the return to original sources (sometimes the ceremonies of ancient cultures as they are preserved by the early writers, sometimes the accounts of the living native storytellers who inhabit the streets and markets of Mexico) in a search for the essence of Mexico's gastronomic nobility. The purpose, of course, was through them to obtain the necessary elements upon which to base a creative contemporary cuisine. Many of the dishes that follow are the direct result of this continuing work.

Thus, from the amalgamation of two concepts of life, the European and the Mexican, arose my own culinary concepts, which I have sought to place on record, although only in part, in the book, *The Taste of Mexico.* Now a new dream is coming true, that of the publication of *Mexico's Feasts of Life,* which is the culmination of the long process of disseminating the culinary values of my country and is, together with all the love that I put into it, my grain of sand that contributes to an understanding of the breadth and nobility of Mexican cuisine.

· ·

Many people have been involved in the making of this book and I would like to thank some of them. To begin, the book would never have come to be without Ken Tracy, owner of Yorktown Bookstore, a good friend to both books and authors and the people at Council Oak Publishing, Inc., Michael Hightower, Sally Dennison, and especially Paulette Millichap, who believed in the project from its very beginning. I would also like to thank others at Council Oak who provided assistance, especially Ellie Dennison, Judy Carr, Pat Dock and Karen Slankard. Carol Haralson and I would also like to thank those who helped in the research into herbs and chiles and their sources, especially Robert A. Bye, Jr., Ph.D., Investigador Titular, Coordinador de Investigacion, Universidad Nacional Autónoma de Mexico, Tom Gilliland of Austin Texas, and Carl Brune of Tulsa, Oklahoma. People who, in various ways, helped to make the photo sessions in Mexico City go smoothly were the Canales Zapico family, the Caraza-Campos Barrenechoa family, Lopez Montolongo Rene, Ana Seoane de Urquiza and Urquiza Seoane Ignacio. The assistance of Lorenza Caraza-Campos, stylist and prop manager, and Rene Lopez Zarate, photography assistance, was invaluable. I would also like to thank Caroline Brune from The Bakery of Cherry Street in Tulsa for testing some bread and pastry recipes using North American flours. I would especially like to thank Tom Gilliland and Miguel Ravago from the Fonda San Miguel restaurant in Austin. With a great deal of love and skill they took on the task of presenting recipes from my book to almost a thousand guests at a pre-publication party at the Mexican Embassy in Washington, D.C. Also helping to make this party a success were Ed and Susan Auler who provided wines from their Fall Creek Vineyard in Tow, Texas and Davis Tucker who provided Pecan Lager Beer from his Austin brewery.

As you explore the recipes in the book, you will see names accompanying some of the introductory notes. Sometimes my name will appear, but other times you will see the name of one of the other women in my family, from whom the basic recipe was handed down. This is a form of tribute not only of the cooks of my family, but also to the genius of generations of Mexican men and women who have celebrated life through food, collecting, refining and transmitting their knowledge of the fruits of our land.

PATRICIA QUINTANA
Mexico City, 1989

LOS DIAS FELICES
DEL BEBE

≈ *Entering the World* ≈

THE
CHRISTENING
FEAST

BAUTISMO

The first feast experienced by a new soul in the world of Mexico is *bautismo,* the joyous feast of christening. Long before the arrival of Spanish Catholicism in the 16th century, Mayans took part in a *zihil,* an initiatory rite performed for groups of children born on the same day. Priests, godmothers and godfathers accompanied the children to the ceremonial site, which had been purified of evil by the beating of drums. The children were dressed in white and brought before the high priest. Each was given a handful of corn and an ingot of incense to fling into a burning brazier, and then they were blessed and sprinkled with perfumed water. After the ceremony, the participants feasted together.

After the coming of the Europeans, when the village church became the stage for the first ceremonial drama in the life of a child, the great care given

---

LOS DIAS FELICES DEL BEBE, THE HAPPY
DAYS OF CHILDHOOD. IN THE PHOTOGRAPH
EMILIA HOLDS BABY MARGARITA.

to the selection of the godparents or *padrinos* continued. Traditionally, the white garment of the new child is also chosen very carefully. Usually it is very long and full and ornately embroidered. It may be handed down from one generation to the next. It is worn at the baptism to signify the purity of the new soul and the light of hope that surrounds it. During the rite of baptism, the infant is freed from original sin through the purifying action of holy water and is welcomed into the family of the community. The child receives the name by which he or she will be known and to which it is hoped this new being will add honor. After the ceremony, a great cry is set up at the entrance to the church, mainly by the children present. According to custom, the godfather then distributes the *bolos* among those attending. He tosses into the air coins of various denominations which fall in a glittering rain, symbolizing the fruits of fortune that it is hoped will accompany the child throughout his or her life.

After the christening, the infant's parents, the godparents, and the guests gather at the celebration proper, where they will break bread together, feasting on antojitos — "little whims," the hors d'oeuvres of Mexico, served with traditional drinks and fruit beverages, or perhaps a feast of many courses.

In Mexico, as in other Hispanic cultures, children are given the surnames of both parents rather than the name of the father only. Both boys and girls are given a first name, followed by first the father's surname and then the mother's surname. When a Mexican girl marries, she may drop her mother's surname for daily use and add her husband's: Maria Aguirre Mendoza marrying Señor Ramirez may be called Maria Aguirre de Ramirez. However, she may choose not to formally adopt her husband's name but instead to retain the maternal and paternal surnames. Both men and women may keep for formal use several ancestral surnames alternating between the maternal and paternal lineages. The name becomes a compact history of the family, and of the sequence of serendipitous relationships that culminated in the existence of this singular, unduplicable human being.

Once christened, the child embarks upon a life that will be entwined with a rich calendar of feasts, some confirming the life of the community and others accompanying the private celebrations that mark his or her passage through the earthly world.

CAKE BREAD

MARQUESOTE

O ne of the essential characteristics of cake bread is its versatility. If wine is added to the batter, it can be used for a wedding cake, or if prepared in its simpler version, it can be served as a coffee cake or a treat for children. ~
EMILIA

8   EGGS

2   CUPS CAKE FLOUR OR WHEAT STARCH, WITHOUT ADDITIVES (OR RICE FLOUR OR POTATO FLOUR)

1   TEASPOON BAKING POWDER

¾   CUP SUGAR

½   CUP BUTTER, MELTED

    CONFECTIONERS' SUGAR

Preheat oven to 350°F. Separate the eggs, reserving whites and yolks separately. Stir the egg yolks gently. Beat the egg whites until they are stiff. Add three tablespoons of the sugar. Carefully fold in the egg yolks. In a separate bowl, sift together the flour, baking powder, and sugar. Sift a second time. Gradually add the dry ingredients to the egg mixture, folding gently to blend. Add butter and continue folding. Butter and flour a baking pan 4-6 inches by 24-26 inches. Spoon batter into the pan and bake in preheated oven 30 minutes, or until a toothpick inserted in the center comes out clean. Let cool, then unmold. Sprinkle with confectioners' sugar. **SERVES 8.**

VARIATION

Sprinkle the marquesote with sesame seeds before baking. Or serve with sherry-flavored syrup (see page 101).

ALMOND PASTE ROLLS

PASTA DE DAMAS

T his candy was originally prepared by grinding ingredients on a metate (meh TAH tay), a flat grinding stone. The version here is prepared in the fashion of the book ARTE CULINARIO MEXICANO.

FOR THE CANDY

3½   CUPS SUGAR

16   EGG YOLKS

2   CUPS ALMONDS, BLANCHED

¾   CUP WALNUTS

⅓   CUP WATER OR ROSE WATER

FOR THE GARNISH

¾   CUP GROUND CINNAMON

2   STRIPS SILVER FOIL, 4 X 10 INCHES

4   RED RIBBONS, 5 INCHES LONG

Prepare the candy: Place the sugar in a blender or food processor and purée until it is very fine. Transfer to a bowl and add egg yolks. Beat until the mixture is pale yellow. Place the nuts and water in a food processor and purée well. Add to sugar-egg mixture and cook, stirring regularly, until thick, then spoon paste onto a marble counter top and work with a spatula until it cools. Shape into two rolls.

Sprinkle powdered cinnamon over the silver foil. Arrange each roll on foil and wrap. Tie ends shut with ribbon. Almond Paste Rolls make welcome gifts. **MAKES 2 ROLLS.**

TO MAKE ROSE WATER ≈

Fill a saucepan with well-washed red rose petals and add water to barely cover. Bring to a boil, then reduce heat, cover and simmer for five minutes. Cool and strain.

Rose water was praised in 17th-century herbals as a cordial to revive faint spirits. It was also doused on hot fire shovels to perfume a winter room.

FLOUR FOR CAKES ≈

Pastry or cake flour is a soft flour, best for cakes, very finely ground from high-starch wheat. Hard flours, best for bread, are ground from high-gluten wheat. All-purpose flour is a blend of the two; it will not produce the lightest cakes.

MERINGUE-FILLED PASTRY SHELLS

GASNATES

Gasnates (gahz NAH tays), part of the legacy of the Oaxacan confectionery tradition, are served at baptisms and other private festivities. The dough is prepared with eggs and flour, rolled out and shaped into a cone or cylinder, fried, then filled with meringue. ~ MAMANENA

FOR THE DOUGH

6   MEDIUM EGG YOLKS

1⅓ TO 1½ CUPS ALL-PURPOSE FLOUR, OR
    NECESSARY AMOUNT, SIFTED

A PINCH OF SALT

1½ TEASPOONS LARD OR VEGETABLE
    SHORTENING

¼ TO ⅓ CUP WHITE WINE, MESCAL OR
    TEQUILA

3   CUPS VEGETABLE OIL

FOR THE MERINGUE

5   EGG WHITES, AT ROOM TEMPERATURE

A PINCH OF SALT

1¾ CUPS SUGAR

⅓   CUP WATER

1   TEASPOON LIME JUICE

FOR THE GARNISH

8   TABLESPOONS BLANCHED ALMONDS OR PINE
    NUTS, CUT ON THE BIAS AND TOASTED

4   TABLESPOONS CANDY SPRINKLES

Prepare the dough: Combine the egg yolks, flour and salt in a bowl. Mix by hand into a soft dough. If necessary, add more flour. Work in the lard and white wine and continue kneading until dough is no longer sticky. Allow to rest for ½ hour. Then roll out on a floured surface and cut into 3-by-8-inch strips, about 1/16 inch thick (gasnates will puff as they are fried). Heat the oil in a medium saucepan. Brush the ends of the strips with egg yolk to seal them into rings or cylinders. Size can vary depending on your taste. To insure that gasnates will not open during frying, use a pair of metal gasnate tins (see photograph at left). If you do not have gasnate tins, you can improvise with 2 metal cups. Do not get egg yolk on metal cups or gasnates will stick. Fry the gasnates in hot oil until crisp, then drain on paper towels.

Prepare the meringue: Beat the egg whites with salt until they are stiff. Place the sugar and water in a small saucepan and cook until the syrup almost reaches the hard ball stage (about 250°F.) Test by dropping a little in a glass of cold water; syrup should be able to be shaped into a hard, though pliable, ball. Add the syrup to the egg whites, and beat until the mixture is shiny and thick. Add lime juice and beat briefly.

Assemble the gasnates: Preheat oven to 350°F. Butter a baking tray. Arrange fried gasnates on the tray and use pastry bag to fill with meringue. Sprinkle with almonds and sprinkles and bake for 5-8 minutes or until the meringue is no longer sticky. Remove from oven and carefully transfer to a serving dish with a spatula. You may also serve on individual plates with orange-tequila sauce. To prepare the sauce, combine 3 cups orange juice with ½ cup sugar. Simmer together to form a light syrup, then remove from heat and whisk in 3 tablespoons butter and tequila, Gran Mariner or Kahlua to taste. Spoon over gasnates. Garnish with orange slices or strawberries dipped in melted chocolate, then chill. **SERVES 12.**

NOTE

You may also serve without baking. Consistency of the filling will be softer.

MERINGUE, GASNATE TINS,
AND MERINGUE-FILLED
PASTRY SHELLS.

≈

"When they baptized him they invited the relatives and friends so they would be present at the baptism, and then they gave food and drink to all those present, and also to the children of the whole neighborhood. They would baptize him at dawn at his father's house; the midwife would baptize him, saying many prayers and making many ceremonial gestures over the infant."

FRIAR BERNARDINO DE
SAHAGÚN, HISTORIA
GENERAL DE LAS COSAS DE
LAS NUEVA ESPAÑA

YEMITAS

YEMITAS

YEMITAS WRAPPED IN FRINGED TISSUE PAPER.

At the christening feast, sweets shine with a special brilliance of their own. My grandmother Emilia often made this one when there was a family baptism. The egg yolks symbolize life itself. They are called *Yemitas (yeh MEE tez), the diminutive of* YEMA, *or egg yolk.* ~ EMILIA

2	QUARTS WHOLE MILK
1	PINCH BAKING SODA
4½	GENEROUS CUPS SUGAR
24	EGG YOLKS
1½	TABLESPOONS POWDERED CINNAMON
	SUGAR
60	5-INCH SQUARES OF TISSUE PAPER

Put the milk in a heavy saucepan and add the baking soda. Bring to a boil. Remove from heat. Boil a second time and then allow to cool. Add the sugar and simmer until the mixture thickens and you can see the bottom of the pan when mixture is separated with a spoon. Allow to cool.

Beat the egg yolks with cinnamon and add to cooled mixture. Return to heat and stir constantly until the mixture reaches the hard ball stage (250°-266°F.) Remove from heat and allow to cool a little. Transfer to a marble surface. Work with a spatula to blend into a thick, fudgelike consistency. Shape into marble-sized balls and roll in sugar. Allow to harden, then wrap in tissue paper and twist ends closed. **MAKES 60.**

GUAVAS FILLED WITH COCONUT CREAM

GUAYABAS RELLENAS DE NATILLA DE COCO

I*n pre-Hispanic times guavas were offered to the gods. You can also follow this recipe replacing the guavas with fresh pears or other flavorful seasonal fruits. ~* PATRICIA

FOR THE SYRUP

3   CUPS WATER

1½   CUPS SUGAR

4   CINNAMON STICKS, 4 INCHES LONG

FOR THE GUAVAS

16   GUAVAS, FIRM BUT RIPE, WITH TOPS CUT OFF AND SEEDS REMOVED WITH A SPOON

FOR THE COCONUT CREAM

3   CUPS MILK

2   CUPS FRESH SHREDDED COCONUT

3   CINNAMON STICKS

6   EGG YOLKS

14   TABLESPOONS SUGAR

3   TABLESPOONS FLOUR

3   TABLESPOONS CORNSTARCH

½   CUP BUTTER, AT ROOM TEMPERATURE

FOR THE GARNISH

16   GUAVA OR GRAPE LEAVES

Prepare the syrup: Place the water, sugar and cinnamon in a medium saucepan. Bring to a boil and cook for 30 minutes or until the mixture forms a thick syrup. Add guavas to the syrup and continue cooking until the fruit is tender. Be careful not to overcook or the guavas will become mushy and lose their shape. Remove fruit from syrup carefully and allow to cool.

Prepare the coconut cream: Stir together the milk, coconut and cinnamon in a medium saucepan. Place over a medium heat. Meanwhile, beat the egg yolks until they are thick and pale. With a whisk, incorporate the sugar, flour and cornstarch. Add the egg mixture to the hot milk and continue to simmer over low heat, stirring constantly with a whisk until the mixture thickens, about 12 minutes. Then remove from heat and allow to cool. When almost cool, stir in butter.

To serve: Place two guavas on each individual dessert dish. Fill each with coconut cream. Garnish on the side with two guava leaves and a sprinkling of cinnamon. Serve cold. **SERVES 8.**

GARNISH ≈

The Mexican notion of "garnish" extends to the festive wrapping of sweets in colored tissue or silver paper. Try it with candies, candied fruits, or small cakes.

MANGO ≈

The great spreading mango tree is native to India but now thrives in tropical Mexico in many varieties. Its splendid fruit, initially green, ripens to a rainbow of mottled yellows, reds and pinks. At its center is a large seed with clinging fibers. The fully ripe flesh is deeply perfumed and superbly delicious, tasting something like peach, apricot, pineapple, and banana all at once. To ripen a greenish mango, put it in a paper sack pierced with holes and leave it at room temperature until it is fully colored, tender and yielding, but not mushy. Score and peel like an avocado, or halve the mango and scoop out its flesh with a spoon. June is the seasonal height for U.S.-grown mangoes. Mangos can be used in preserves, chutney, pies, sorbet, any way you might use a perfect, juicy peach. Try cooking them in brown sugar sryup to serve as a dessert.

ALMOND AND WALNUT COOKIES

TEJAS DE ALMENDRA Y NUEZ

*T*he lacy, crunchy and buttery TEJAS *(TAY hahz) are a festive favorite, prepared to highlight the conviviality of special family occasions.* ~ PATRICIA

ALMOND AND WALNUT COOKIES, WITH GOLD COINS GIVEN TO THE NEWLY-CHRISTENED CHILD BY ITS GODPARENTS, SIGNIFYING LIFELONG GOOD FORTUNE.

8	EGG WHITES, AT ROOM TEMPERATURE
½	TEASPOON SALT
1½	CUPS SUGAR
¾	CUP ALL-PURPOSE FLOUR, SIFTED
1½ TO 1¾	CUPS CLARIFIED BUTTER, COOLED
1	CUP ALMONDS, BLANCHED, LIGHTLY TOASTED AND GROUND
1	CUP WALNUTS, GROUND
2	TEASPOONS VANILLA EXTRACT
½	TEASPOON ALMOND EXTRACT

Preheat oven to 350°F. Generously butter 4 baking sheets. Beat the egg whites and salt with an electric beater until they thicken. Then gradually add sugar and beat until the mixture becomes glossy. Gently fold in flour by hand. Add 1½ cups clarified butter alternately with ground almonds, walnuts and extracts. If dough is too dry, add remaining butter. Place cookie dough on prepared baking tray by rounded tablespoonsful, slightly flattening each with the back of the spoon until cookies extend to about 2, 2½, or 3 inches, depending on desired size. Arrange 3 cookies on each tray. Bake for 6-8 minutes, turning tray once during baking time to assure even cooking. When golden brown, remove from oven. Remove cookies from tray immediately, with the help of a spatula. While the cookies are still hot, wrap each around a buttered rolling pin, glass or mold, and allow to cool. You may also make the *tejas* smaller, and wrap them over a finger, for miniature cookies. It is important not to prepare too many cookies at a time, or you will not be able to follow this procedure while the cookies are still hot and pliable. Clean and re-butter baking sheets after each batch or next batch will stick. Store cookies in an air-tight container or serve in a chocolate bag (page 104). **MAKES 15-20.**

COCONUT CHARLES COOKIES

CARLITOS DE COCO

T*his candy-cookie originated in Oaxaca. When my grandmother Margarita was born, my great-grandmother Emilia prepared these cookies for the guests at the baptism ceremony.* ∼ EMILIA

FOR THE COOKIES

10   EGGS, SEPARATED
½   CUP SUGAR
½   POUND PASTRY OR CAKE FLOUR, SIFTED
      (OR RICE OR POTATO FLOUR),
      APPROXIMATELY 2 CUPS

FOR THE FILLING

¾   CUP SUGAR
½   CUP WATER
1   CINNAMON STICK, 8 INCHES LONG
1   CUP FRESH COCONUT, GRATED

Preheat oven to 350°F. Butter two baking trays and line with buttered waxed paper.

Prepare the cookies: Beat the egg yolks with ⅓ cup sugar until they are thick and pale yellow. Set aside and separately beat the egg whites until they are stiff. Add the remainder of the sugar to the egg whites and continue beating. Gradually fold the whites into the egg yolks, alternating with the flour. Place by teaspoonful onto the prepared trays and bake 25 minutes or until light brown. When done, remove from oven, and take cookies off tray with the help of a spatula.

Prepare the filling: Place the sugar in a saucepan. Add the water and cinnamon and bring to a boil. Add the coconut and cook until the mixture forms a heavy transparent syrup. Frost the bottom of each cookie with the filling and cover with another cookie, forming a sandwich. **SERVES 8-12.**

CREPES

CREPAS

4   EGG YOLKS
3   WHOLE EGGS
1½   CUPS MILK
¾   CUP WATER
½   CUP HEAVY WHIPPING CREAM
2¼   CUPS FLOUR
½   TEASPOON SALT
⅓   CUP MELTED BUTTER
6   TABLESPOONS MELTED BUTTER

Combine the egg yolks, eggs, milk, water, cream, flour, salt and ⅓ cup melted butter in a blender or food processor and blend well. Add remaining melted butter to batter and allow to set for 3 hours at room temperature or in the refrigerator.

THE VERSATILE CREPE
≈

Sweeten crepes by adding 2 tablespoons sugar and 2 tablespoons Kahlua or tequila to the batter. Fill with Chocolate Ganache (page 48) or butter pecan ice cream and drizzle with chocolate sauce. Garnish with sliced oranges or strawberries dipped in bittersweet chocolate.

Crepes show the French influence on Mexican cuisine but they marry happily with pre-Hispanic flavors. Try them filled with sautéed mushrooms, chiles and squash blossoms, with Chile Strips in Cream (page 146), or with other fillings and sauces from this book.

Heat 2 frying pans or 2 crepe pans, 6-8 inches in diameter. Brush each with butter. Pour about 1 tablespoon of batter in a preheated pan and tilt to spread batter evenly. Cook over medium heat about 1-2 minutes or until the edges begin to lift from the pan. Turn over with the help of a spatula and cook for ½ minute, then transfer to a plate and keep warm. Prepare the crepes using two frying pans to streamline procedure. **MAKES APPROXIMATELY 20 CREPES.**

LIME CREPES

CREPAS AL LIMON

My grandmother developed several quick and easy desserts that my mother as a child devoured. Her favorite was lime crepes, since they had a sweet yet tart flavor. The aroma of these crepes will cause your mouth to water before they come out of the oven! ~ MAGO

FOR THE CREPES

10	EGGS
1	TEASPOON SALT
2	CUPS FLOUR
3½ TO 4	CUPS MILK
½	CUP BUTTER, MELTED AND COOLED
½	CUP BUTTER, FOR FRYING

FOR THE LIME TOPPING

½	CUP MELED BUTTER
	THE JUICE OF 6-8 LIMES (DEPENDING ON SIZE)
	SUGAR TO TASTE

Prepare the crepes: Place the eggs, salt, flour and milk in a blender or food processor and blend. Pour batter into a glass bowl and stir in melted butter. Allow batter to stand for about an hour at room temperature. Heat a 12-inch frying pan, coating with a little butter, pour about a tablespoon of batter into pan and tilt to spread evenly. Cook crepes until the edges begin to dry. Then turn over carefully with a spatula. Stack the crepes on the plate. Be sure to reheat frying pan before preparing each crepe. Add butter to the pan so that they do not stick. Preheat oven to 350°F.

Assemble the crepes: Sprinkle each crepe with lime juice and sugar and roll up. Line crepes on a baking tray or ovenproof dish and brush with melted butter. Sprinkle once again with sugar. Bake until crepes are warm, about 15 minutes. Serve warm. **SERVES 8.**

ROYAL EGGS

HUEVOS REALES

This recipe, which comes from early convent cooking, was given to me by María Dolores Torres Izabal. It is prepared with egg yolks, honey, almonds and pine nuts, foods appropriate to the celebration of a new life. The royal eggs are rich squares of buttery baked egg soaked in cinnamon-scented syrup.

FOR THE EGGS

24	LARGE EGG YOLKS
2	TEASPOONS BAKING POWDER
2	TEASPOONS WATER
2	TEASPOONS BUTTER, MELTED

ROYAL EGGS, SPICED SYRUP, AND SLIVERED ALMONDS.

CAJETA ≈

Hispanic markets sell canned caramelized milk, or CAJETA *(kah* HEH *tah) but you can also make your own. To make it, combine 2 quarts milk, 3 cups sugar and ¾ teaspoon baking soda in a large, heavy saucepan over low heat. Stir to dissolve sugar, then bring to a boil. Reduce heat and simmer gently about 5 hours, stirring occasionally. Caramelized milk is thick and golden. It keeps well.*

SWEET CREPES ≈

Lime crepes can be filled with caramelized goat's milk or apricot preserves and sprinkled with butter, sugar and chopped nuts before baking.

FOR THE SYRUP

5   CUPS SUGAR

6   CUPS WATER

8   CINNAMON STICKS, ABOUT 4 INCHES LONG
    THE JUICE OF FOUR LIMES

1   CUP DRY SHERRY

FOR THE GARNISH

½   CUP DRY SHERRY

½   CUP RAISINS

½   CUP ALMONDS OR PINE NUTS, THINLY
    SLICED AND TOASTED

Prepare the eggs: Preheat oven to 375°F.
Place a pan of water in the oven while
heating, and keep in oven during baking
time, to keep humidity high. Grease an 8-
or 10-inch square baking pan with a thick
layer of butter and line with baking
parchment or buttered waxed paper. Beat
the egg yolks and baking powder with an
electric beater until they are thick and pale.
Fold in the water and melted butter. Spoon
into prepared baking pan. Bake for ½ hour
or until done. Test with a toothpick. Unmold
cake immediately on a damp cloth, covering
with another damp cloth. Allow to cool for
½ hour, then cut into squares.

Prepare the syrup: Place the sugar in a
medium saucepan. Add water, cinnamon
stick, lime juice and sherry. Simmer
ingredients until the mixture thickens.
Carefully lower the royal egg squares into
the syrup with a slotted spatula, a few at a
time if necessary, and allow to cook for 5
minutes or until they absorb the syrup. Or
you may choose to pour syrup over the
squares. Drench with dry sherry and serve
immediately, garnished with raisins, almond
slice, and cinnamon sticks from the syrup.
SERVES 8.

CHOCOLATE MERINGUES
WITH MINT SAUCE.

CHOCOLATE MERINGUES WITH MINT SAUCE

MERENGUITOS A LA MENTA

*T*his recipe was inspired by the famous
French pastry chef Lenôtré. It contains
chocolate, a Mexican staple dating to pre-
Hispanic times when it was considered a
gift of the gods. Innumerable cakes are
made with chocolate but it is very
unusual in meringues, and in this case,
served almost exclusively at baptismal
fiestas. ~ PATRICIA

FOR THE MERINGUES

- 5   TABLESPOONS POWDERED COCOA
- 1   CUP CONFECTIONERS' SUGAR
- 6   MEDIUM EGG WHITES
- 1   PINCH SALT
- ¾   CUP SUGAR

FOR THE GANACHE

- 3   EGG YOLKS
- ⅓   CUP SUGAR
- ½   POUND SEMI-SWEET VANILLA-FLAVORED CHOCOLATE, GRATED
- ½   POUND BITTERSWEET CHOCOLATE, GRATED
- 1   CUP BUTTER, CUT IN PIECES
- 4   EGG WHITES
- 3   TABLESPOONS SUGAR

FOR THE MINT SAUCE

- 6   EGG YOLKS
- ½   CUP SUGAR
- 4   TABLESPOONS CORNSTARCH
- 3½ CUPS WARM MILK
- 2   CUPS FRESH MINT LEAVES, OR TO TASTE
- 1   CUP WHIPPING CREAM, OR MORE

FOR THE GARNISH

- 8   MINT LEAVES
      CONFECTIONERS' SUGAR TO TASTE

Prepare the meringues: Preheat oven to 300°F. Butter two baking trays or line them with buttered parchment paper. Sift the cocoa and confectioners' sugar, and set aside. Beat the egg whites with an electric beater. Add salt and continue beating until stiff. Lower speed and gradually add sugar. Continue beating until stiff. Raise speed and beat until meringue is glossy. Then gently fold in the cocoa and confectioners' sugar by hand. Place this mixture in a pastry bag and press out 50 strips measuring 1x2 inches on the baking trays. Bake the meringues in the preheated oven for about 45 minutes or until they are dry.

Prepare the ganache filling: Bring water to a boil in a double boiler. Heat egg yolks, beating until they are pale yellow. Add the sugar and continue beating until the yolks form a thick string. Stir in the grated chocolate and butter until melted. Remove from heat. Beat the egg whites and sugar until they form soft peaks. Then carefully fold them into the chocolate mixture. Transfer to a deep bowl and refrigerate for 4-6 hours minimum. If prepared a day ahead of time, leave at room temperature for 1 hour before using.

Prepare the mint sauce: Place the egg yolks in a saucepan and beat until pale yellow. Add the sugar and continue beating. Add the cornstarch and warm milk and simmer until the mixture coats a spoon (the consistency should be that of very light cream). Remove from heat and refrigerate 3 hours. Just before serving, place half of the sauce in a blender or food processor and purée with the mint. If the sauce is too thick, add cream. Then stir mixture into remaining sauce. Adding mint at the last moment preserves its color.

Assemble the meringues: Fill a pastry bag with ganache filling. Using a ¼ to ½ inch tip, squeeze a thick ribbon of ganache over the bottom part of a meringue. Top with a second meringue (as if it were a sandwich cookie). Repeat this procedure with remaining meringues. Spoon a bed of mint sauce on each individual dessert plate and place two meringue sandwiches on each plate. Sprinkle with confectioners' sugar or cocoa and garnish with a mint leaf. Serve immediately. **MAKES 12 SERVINGS WITH 4 MERINGUES EACH.**

TO CRYSTALLIZE MINT LEAVES ≈

Brush them with a coating of lightly-beaten egg white, then dip them in superfine granulated sugar, mixed with green food coloring if you wish. Dry overnight on waxed paper and store in an airtight container. Use crystallized mint leaves and violet petals to garnish desserts.

MINT GREEN ≈

For the freshest color, assemble Chocolate Meringues with Mint Sauce immediately before serving so that the chocolate will not darken the color of the mint.

CANDIED LIMES AND FRESH COCONUT.

CANDIED LIMES

DULCE DE LIMÓN

Candied limes, a favorite of both children and adults, are often seen glistening like green jewels in the windows of Mexican sweet shops.

24   LIMES, PEELS VERY LIGHTLY GRATED, SCORED TWICE CROSSWISE AT THE STEM END

    ASH WATER (MAKE BY COMBINING 1 CUP ASHES FROM A WOOD FIRE WITH 3 QUARTS WATER)

3   TO 6 CUPS SUGAR, OR TO TASTE

3   CUPS WATER

    GREEN FOOD COLORING (OPTIONAL)

Scoop pulp out of the limes, then place peels in a medium enamel saucepan. Cover with ash water and bring to a boil. Remove from heat and transfer to a bowl of cold fresh water. Change the water daily for 4 days (this procedure is to reduce the bitterness of the limes). On the fifth day, bring the limes to a boil again and cook until tender. Then drain.

Combine the sugar and water in a large saucepan and cook for about 45 minutes or until the mixture forms a thick syrup. Add the limes and cook for 45 minutes to 1 hour, or until they absorb the syrup. If you wish you may add a little green food coloring to the syrup to intensify the color of the limes, which lose some of their color through the cooking process. Allow to cool, then store in a glass jar or serve immediately. **SERVES 8.**

VARIATION

Fill with fresh grated coconut, Coconut Cream (page 43) or almond paste.

CORN TORTE

TORTA DE ELOTE

This is a perfect dish to prepare ahead of time for a baptismal party. Corn, called "Our Mother" and "She Who Sustains Us" in many Indian languages, is so central to the sustenance of life in Mexico and throughout the Americas that a corn dish seems fitting to welcome a new soul. ~ MAGO

¾ CUP BUTTER

1 CUP SUGAR

7 TO 8 CUPS KERNELS FROM RIPE EARS OF CORN

¼ CUP WHIPPING CREAM

¼ CUP MILK

5 EGGS, SEPARATED

2 TABLESPOONS FLOUR

3 TABLESPOONS RICE FLOUR

1 TABLESPOON BAKING POWDER

1 TEASPOON SALT

Preheat oven to 350°F. Butter a round 9-inch cake pan or bundt pan with waxed paper, then butter the waxed paper and sprinkle with flour.

Beat the butter until creamy, about 10 minutes. Add the sugar and beat another 8 minutes. Place the corn kernels, cream and milk in a blender or food processor and purée. Beat egg yolks. Add corn purée to the butter-sugar mixture, alternating with egg yolks. Then sift together the flour, rice flour, baking powder and salt and add to the mixture. Beat the egg whites until they form soft peaks and fold gently into the mixture. Spoon into prepared pan and bake in preheated oven **for** about 35-45 minutes or until golden brown. **SERVES 8-12.**

CORN TORTE ACCOMPANIMENT ≈

Corn Torte marries well with Chile Strips with Cream (page 146).

CORN ≈

Pre-Hispanic Mexican agriculture was based on the sacred triad of corn, beans and squash. When Europeans arrived, they referred to Indian MAÏS *by the word they used for the staple grain of any country, a word that also meant any small, granular object: corn. The magical corn is actually a grass plant with giant seeds, or kernels.*

HOMINY ≈

The main varieties of corn are popcorn, dent corn (used to feed animals), flour corn (which grinds easily), sweet corn ("roasting ears," or "corn-on-the-cob"), and flint corn. Flint corn was the Indian favorite — it dried easily and could be soaked with ash or lime, then ground into masa, to make Mexico's "daily bread," the tortilla. The large-kerneled flint corn called CACAHUAZINCLE *in Mexico is called hominy in the U.S., where it is the basis for grits, a Southern breakfast staple.*

TAMALES

TAMALES

LIGHT TAMALES ≈

Prior to the arrival of the pig in Mexico, pre-Hispanic cooks made lardless tamales seasoned with honey, herbs, beans and moles. You can make a form of light tamale using kernels from young ears of white corn (not yellow sweet corn). Grind the corn kernels in a food processor, add large-kernel cottage cheese or ricotta for body, season with chile strips or salsa, then wrap in fresh corn husks and steam as with traditional masa-and-lard tamales. These delicious fresh corn tamales were developed by Miguel Ravago of Fonda San Miguel, Austin, Texas, based on a recipe prepared by his grandmother in Sonora, Mexico.

STEAMING TAMALES ≈

Steaming reduces saltiness, so season accordingly. A clean coin placed in the bottom of a steamer will rattle to alert you when there is a need for additional water. Adding boiling water will allow the cooking process to continue uninterrupted.

Test tamale dough for lightness by dropping a pinch of dough into a glass of water. If it floats, the dough is light enough. If not, continue to beat.

T amales have been prepared in Mexico since pre-Hispanic times. Native Indians ground corn into masa, which they combined with various fillings and wrapped in corn husks for steaming. Before the Europeans arrived, most Mexican food was steamed or boiled, not fried. The Indians used sesame or avocado-seed oil for flavoring rather than as a cooking medium. When the Spaniards arrived with pigs, the Indians began adding lard to tamales to lighten their consistency. Today tamales are also prepared with vegetable shortening. They are prepared in many sizes and shapes, with a great range of fillings that includes turkey, coloradito mole, mushrooms, chile strips, cheese, shrimp, shark, pork, pineapple, coconut, guava and many more, and they are wrapped in both corn husks and banana leaves. ~ PATRICIA

FOR THE DOUGH

2¼ POUNDS FRESH MASA OR MASA PREPARED WITH MASA HARINA

1½ CUPS WATER (BOILING THE WATER WITH 30 TOMATILLO HUSKS WILL HELP MAKE THE DOUGH FLUFFIER.)

1½ TEASPOONS BAKING POWDER

½ CUP CORNSTARCH OR RICE FLOUR

1½ TO 2 TABLESPOONS SALT, OR TO TASTE

1 POUND LARD (FOR HOMEMADE LARD, GENERALLY OF BETTER QUALITY THAN COMMERCIAL LARD, SEE PAGE 221)

2 TO 3 BUNCHES CORN HUSKS, WASHED AND SOAKED IN HOT WATER OVERNIGHT OR FOR SEVERAL HOURS, DRAINED AND PATTED DRY

FOR A SALTY FILLING

3 CUPS CHILE POBLANO-CREAM SAUCE (FOR STUFFED CHICKEN BREASTS, PAGE 64) PLUS 2 CUPS FETA CHEESE, CUT IN STRIPS

OR 3-4 CUPS PORK LOIN IN CHIPOTLE SAUCE (PAGE 176)

OR 3-4 CUPS SPICY SHREDDED MEAT WITH TOMATO-CHORIZO SAUCE, TINGA (PAGE 241)

OR 3-4 CUPS SAUCE FOR MONTEZUMA'S PIE (PAGE 63) PLUS 3-4 CUPS SHREDDED COOKED CHICKEN

FOR A SWEET FILLING

3 CUPS SUGAR

1½ TO 2 CUPS CANDIED FRUIT, FINELY CHOPPED (OR CANDIED LIMES, PAGE 50)

1½ CUPS RAISINS

1½ CUPS ALMONDS, FINELY CHOPPED

RED FOOD COLORING, TO TASTE

Prepare the dough: Place fresh masa or prepared masa harina in a large bowl. Add water gradually and knead until smooth and no longer sticky. Add baking powder, cornstarch and salt. (Steaming will slightly reduce saltiness of the dough.) In a separate bowl, beat the lard by hand or with an electric mixer or processor until it is fluffy, about 5 minutes or more. Work the lard into the masa gradually, kneading thoroughly until the mixture is smooth and stiff. (You may also do this in a food processor with a kneading attachment.) Test to see if the dough is light enough by dropping a bit into a glass of cold water. If it floats, it is light enough; if not, continue kneading.

Assemble the tamales: If the corn husks have not been trimmed, cut off the bottom part of the stem end of the husk and trim off the pointed tips at the top. Take two corn husks and lay them flat and overlapping. Spread a spoonful of dough lengthwise over the center of the corn husks, leaving bare husk at the top, bottom and sides for wrapping. Spread a spoonful of filling over the dough. Fold both sides of the corn husk inward, lengthwise, so that they overlap. Fold the narrower end of the corn husks down toward the center, and fold the wider end upward so that the two overlap, closing the tamal into a little bag. Tie the tamal shut with a strip of corn husk or string.

Steam the tamales: Fill the bottom of a steamer with water, dropping in a clean coin (it will rattle if the steamer goes dry). Line the bottom of the steamer with corn husks. Place the tamales in the steamer upright, packing them in somewhat firmly but allowing room for the dough to swell as the tamales cook. Cover with a layer of corn husks, then with a clean cloth to absorb condensed moisture from the lid of the steamer. It is important that the tamales are exposed only to steam heat, not to direct moisture. Water will make them soggy, but steam cooking will make them spongy and light. If water boils away during the cooking process, add more boiling water. Keep the steamer lid on tight. Steam the tamales for about an hour. To test for doneness, remove one and check to see if the dough comes away from the husk easily. If so, they are done. **MAKES APPROXIMATELY 30 TAMALES.**

NOTE

Tamales are excellent reheated on a griddle or in an oven. They will keep in the refrigerator for up to a week, and also freeze well.

PINEAPPLE AND COCONUT TAMALES

TAMALES DE PIÑA Y DE COCO

Sweet tamales bring out the utmost of refinement in Mexican cuisine. This unusual tamal recipe is a favorite among children and adults with a sweet tooth. ~ EMILIA

1½	CUPS BUTTER
1¼	CUPS SUGAR
2¼	POUNDS FRESH CORN MASA OR MASA PREPARED WITH MASA HARINA
1	CUP RICE FLOUR
¾	TO 1½ CUPS WATER
3⅓	POUNDS PINEAPPLE, CRUSHED
1½	CUPS FRESH COCONUT, SHREDDED
1½	CUPS ALMONDS, GROUND
2	TABLESPOONS BAKING POWDER
2	BUNCHES CORN HUSKS, WASHED AND SOAKED IN WATER OVERNIGHT

Prepare the tamales: Cream the butter and add sugar. In a separate bowl, combine the masa and rice flour and work with the hands, adding water until the batter is homogenous and well mixed (amount of required water will depend on moistness of masa). Add the pineapple, coconut, almonds, and baking powder, and knead until well mixed. You may also knead with a food processor. When ready the dough will no longer be sticky. Allow to set for 40 minutes. Assemble and steam the tamales following the procedure explained at left.

TO GRATE A FRESH COCONUT ≈

Pierce two of the eyes of coconut with a sharp instrument and pour out the coconut water. Bake the coconut at 400° for 15 minutes. The coconut may crack from baking but if not, break it with a hammer. Slice out the flesh and grate with a hand grater or in a food processor. A medium coconut makes about 4 cups of grated coconut.

PINEAPPLE ≈

17th-century Spanish explorers in tropical northern South America first called the pineapple by its curious name because it appeared to them to be like a pinecone, then called a "pineapple" (apple being a generic term to describe any fruit). Mexico produces quantities of the luscious tropical fruit, which, because it is extremely perishable when ripe, is perhaps only fully appreciated near the site of its harvest.

Tamales with Pumpkin Seed and Sesame Stuffing

Tamales Rellenos de Pipián Rojo y Ajonjoli, Estilo Culpullapan

These are typical of the Tlaxcala region. Thanks to the almost infinite variety of tamales in Mexican cuisine, special festivities are observed with characteristic tamales in every part of the Republic. ~ MAGO

FOR THE PUMPKIN SEED FILLING

1 POUND HULLED PUMPKIN SEEDS, LIGHTLY TOASTED

6 GARLIC CLOVES, PEELED

2½ CUPS SESAME SEEDS, LIGHTLY TOASTED

4 TO 8 CHILES CHIPOTLES MECOS (STRIPED), WASHED, SEEDED AND DEVEINED, AND LIGHTLY TOASTED OR CANNED CHILES CHIPOTLES (EN ESCABECHE OR ADOBO)

SALT TO TASTE

BLACK PEPPER TO TASTE

FOR THE SAUCE

⅓ CUP VEGETABLE OIL

1 MEDIUM WHITE ONION, PEELED AND GRATED

3½ CUPS TOMATO SAUCE

20 FRESH CHILES JALAPEÑOS, SEEDED AND CUT INTO STRIPS

SALT TO TASTE

BLACK PEPPER TO TASTE

FOR THE DOUGH

SEE INGREDIENTS FOR BASIC TAMAL DOUGH, PAGE 52

OR

2 POUNDS TAMAL FLOUR (AVAILABLE IN SOME HISPANIC, SPECIALTY AND HEALTH FOOD STORES)

SALT TO TASTE

1 TEASPOON BAKING POWDER

WATER

1 POUND LARD

2 TO 3 BUNCHES CORN HUSKS, WASHED AND SOAKED IN HOT WATER OVERNIGHT OR FOR SEVERAL HOURS, DRAINED AND PATTED DRY

Prepare the pumpkin seed filling: Combine the pumpkin seeds, garlic, sesame seeds, chiles, salt and pepper in a blender or food processor, and grind well. The mixture should form a heavy paste.

Prepare the sauce: Heat the oil in a medium saucepan. Add the onion and brown. Stir in tomato sauce and chile strips. Rectify seasoning and cook for about 30 minutes or until the sauce thickens and you can see the bottom of the pan when sauce is stirred back with a spoon.

Prepare the dough: If making the dough with tamal flour, place the tamal flour in a large glass bowl. Add salt, baking powder and enough water to form a smooth dough. Knead the dough well. In a separate bowl, beat the lard until it is light and fluffy. Gradually add the lard to the tamal batter and continue beating until the batter is smooth and light. Test to see if it is light enough, by dropping a little batter in a glass of water. If the batter floats it is ready. Or you may follow the recipe for basic tamal dough, page 52.

Assemble the tamales: Follow basic procedure, page 52. MAKES APPROXIMATELY 30 TAMALES.

PUMPKIN SEEDS ≈

In pre-Hispanic Mexico, pumpkin and squash seeds were valued for their oil and were finely ground for use as a thickener. They are delicious raw or toasted, in or out of the shell, fresh or dried. Shelled, toasted pumpkin seeds provide delicate flavor and crunch to many dishes, including salads and breads. Store in a tightly lidded container in the refrigerator.

CHICKEN TAMALES

CHANCHAMITOS ESTILO COATZACOALCOS

This version of tamales is served in Tabasco and in the south of Veracruz.
~ EMILIA

FOR THE FILLING

14	CUPS WATER
1	WHOLE CHICKEN, CUT INTO PIECES (APPROXIMATELY 2½ POUNDS)
2	LEEKS, WITH MOST OF GREEN TOPS
½	HEAD GARLIC, CLOVES PEELED
3	WHOLE CLOVES
3	BLACK PEPPERCORNS
1	SPRIG FRESH EPAZOTE
	SALT TO TASTE

FOR THE SAUCE

6	CUPS WATER
6	RIPE TOMATOES
1½	MEDIUM WHITE ONIONS, PEELED AND QUARTERED
5	GARLIC CLOVES, PEELED
4	FRESH CHILES JALAPEÑOS, WHOLE
½	CUP VEGETABLE OIL OR SOFT LARD
	SALT TO TASTE

FOR THE DOUGH

1	POUND LARD
	RESERVED CHICKEN BROTH
2	GENEROUS POUNDS FRESH MASA (OR MASA PREPARED WITH MASA HARINA)
2	TEASPOONS BAKING SODA
	SALT TO TASTE

FOR THE TAMALES

50 CORNHUSKS, SOAKED IN HOT WATER OVERNIGHT

Prepare the filling: Place water in a stockpot and bring to a boil. Add chicken, leeks, garlic, cloves, peppercorns, epazote and salt to taste. Simmer for about 45 minutes or until the chicken is tender. Remove from heat and allow chicken to cool in the broth. Then remove from broth and shred into large pieces. Reserve broth separately.

Prepare the sauce: Bring the water to a boil in a large saucepan. Add tomatoes, onion, garlic and chiles. Simmer for about 25 minutes. Allow to cool, then purée in a blender or food processor. Heat the oil or lard in a heavy saucepan and add the puréed mixture. Cook until thick. Add salt and pepper to taste. Add the shredded chicken and cook for another 10 minutes.

Prepare the dough: Place the lard in a glass bowl and beat with a little of the reserved chicken broth until light and fluffy. Add the masa, baking soda and salt and work with your hands until mixture has the consistency of a soft dough. To test if batter is light enough, pinch off a piece and drop it into a glass of water. If it floats, it is ready. If not, continue to beat.

Assemble and steam the tamales: Follow procedure described on page 52.
SERVES 16.

VARIATION

Add chile jalapeño strips to tamales. Prepare the tomato sauce without chicken.

TO MAKE CHICKEN STOCK ≈

Save the bones of roasted poultry, cover with cold water, add a carrot, an onion, and a stalk of celery, simmer one or two hours or more, strain, and use immediately or freeze and save. If you aren't ready to make stock on the day you prepare roasted chicken or turkey, freeze the bones and they will wait till you are ready to use them. When making stock, put the stockpot on a back burner and it will simmer happily as long as there is water to cover the bones. Proceed at your convenience. Freeze stock with its top layer of fat, which provides some insulation in the freezer. When you thaw it for use, it is easy to remove the layer of congealed fat that ascended to the surface of the broth as it cooled.

TO SKIM STOCK ≈

Bring the stock to the first boil slowly, without stirring, in a covered pot. This encourages the foam to rise. Skim thoroughly. The foam that rises to top of the broth is mostly albumen, and it is nutritious; however, removing it makes a clearer stock. Always remove the thin layer of fat that rises to the top of a homemade stock or broth. This is quickly and easily done if the liquid is allowed to cool.

SALBUTES

SALBUTES

*S*albutes *(sahl BOO tays) combine the crunch of a fried tortilla with succulent chicken prepared in an achiote sauce. In the Merida marketplace a version of this recipe is prepared in a larger size, and served with pickled purple onion. The smaller version is a worthy choice for the memorable offerings of the baptismal table.* ~ PATRICIA

FOR THE TOPPING

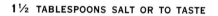

6	SPLIT CHICKEN BREASTS
2	TABLESPOONS ACHIOTE PASTE (AVAILABLE AT SPECIALTY AND HISPANIC MARKETS OR SEE PAGE 107)
6	GARLIC CLOVES, PEELED, ROASTED AND PURÉED
½	TEASPOON BLACK PEPPER, GROUND
½	TEASPOON ALLSPICE, GROUND
1	TABLESPOON DRIED OREGANO LEAVES
½	CUP VINEGAR
½	CUP ORANGE JUICE
⅓	CUP OLIVE OIL
2	BAY LEAVES, CRUSHED
1½	TABLESPOONS SALT OR TO TASTE

FOR THE TORTILLAS

1⅓ POUNDS FRESH MASA OR MASA MADE WITH
    MASA HARINA

2   TABLESPOONS ALL-PURPOSE FLOUR

1½ TEASPOONS BAKING POWDER

1   TEASPOON SALT

⅓   TO ½ CUP WATER

3   CUPS VEGETABLE OIL

    YOU MAY ALSO USE LARGER COMMERCIALLY
    PREPARED TORTILLAS CUT INTO WEDGES
    RATHER THAN MAKING YOUR OWN.

FOR THE ONION GARNISH

2½ CUPS PURPLE ONION, PEELED AND SLICED
    ON THE DIAGONAL

½   CUP VINEGAR

½   CUP ORANGE JUICE

⅓   CUP OLIVE OIL

2   BAY LEAVES, CRUSHED

2   GARLIC CLOVES, PEELED AND PURÉED

1½ TEASPOONS DRIED OREGANO LEAVES

1   TEASPOON FRESHLY GROUND BLACK PEPPER
    SALT TO TASTE

FOR THE GARNISH

4   PLUM TOMATOES, THINLY SLICED

½   BIBB OR BOSTON LETTUCE, WASHED,
    DRIED, FINELY SLICED

Prepare the topping: Place the chicken breasts in a baking tray. In a glass bowl, stir together the achiote paste, puréed garlic, pepper, allspice, oregano, vinegar, orange juice, olive oil, bay leaves and salt to taste. Pour over chicken breasts and marinate for 2 hours. Place chicken breasts in a bowl in a steamer and cook for 30-40 minutes over medium heat. Or you may choose to bake at

350°F. Allow to cool, then shred. Combine with marinade or cooking liquid.

Prepare the tortillas: Place the masa, flour, baking powder, and salt in a glass bowl. Add water and knead for about 4 minutes or until the dough is smooth and no longer sticky.

Heat the oil in a frying pan. Line a tortilla press with two plastic squares. Pinch off enough dough to shape into a 1½ to 2-inch ball. Place on the press and flatten. Carefully peel off plastic squares. Repeat with remaining dough. Fry tortillas in hot oil, basting with the hot oil to cause them to puff. Remove from heat and drain on paper towels. Little tortillas should be puffy and light.

Prepare the onion garnish: Place the onion in a bowl. Add vinegar, orange juice, olive oil, bay leaves, garlic, oregano, and black pepper. Season to taste with salt and allow onion to marinate for about 2 hours.

Assemble the salbutes: For hors d'oeuvres, top each tortilla with chicken mixture, then with pickled onion garnish. To serve as a luncheon dish, top each with pickled onion, tomato and shredded lettuce. **SERVES 16.**

NOTE

If the onion is very strong, soak in salted water for 20 minutes before marinating.

A PLATTER OF SALBUTES GARNISHED WITH A WHOLE CRAYFISH.

PICKLED PURPLE ONION
≈

is a versatile condiment. Try it on toasted open-faced sandwiches or melted cheese hors d'oeuvres.

ALLSPICE ≈

The berry of a tropical evergreen native to Mexico, allspice is picked green and then dried. Spanish explorers exported it to London, where it became a very popular flavoring in the early 1600s. It is called "pimienta grande" or "pimienta gorda" (big pepper, or fat pepper) in Mexico. Its smaller cousin "pimienta pequena" is also spicy but much hotter. Both are commonly available in Mexican markets.

CHICKEN WITH ALMOND MOLE

ALMENDRADO

**CHICKEN WITH ALMOND
MOLE.**

The custom of baptism has numerous
charms: the infant's dress, the invitations,
the church ceremony, and naturally, the
pleasures of the dinner offered in
celebration. Traditional dishes are often
served, among them ALMENDRADO, one
of the seven classic moles of Oaxaca.
Almonds symbolize the essence of life, so
they are perfect in a baptismal dish. ~
PATRICIA

FOR THE CHICKEN

10 CUPS WATER

2 MEDIUM WHITE ONIONS, PEELED AND
QUARTERED

2 GARLIC HEADS, PEELED AND ROASTED

1 CINNAMON STICK, 4 INCHES LONG

8 WHOLE CLOVES

SALT TO TASTE

2 CHICKENS, CUT IN PIECES, OR 4 WHOLE
CHICKEN BREASTS OR 8 SPLIT CHICKEN
BREASTS, APPROXIMATELY 4¼ POUNDS
TOTAL

FOR THE SAUCE

¾   CUP LARD OR VEGETABLE OIL

1½ MEDIUM WHITE ONIONS, PEELED AND QUARTERED

8   GARLIC CLOVES, PEELED

2   CUPS ALMONDS, BLANCHED

1   CUP ROASTED, UNSALTED PEANUTS

1   CINNAMON STICK, 4 INCHES LONG

4   WHOLE CLOVES

16 BLACK PEPPERCORNS

1   CROISSANT, TORN IN PIECES

4   LARGE RIPE TOMATOES, ROASTED

8   DRIED CHILES ANCHOS OR DRIED RED CALIFORNIA CHILES, WASHED, VERY LIGHTLY ROASTED, SEEDED AND DEVEINED AND SOAKED IN HOT WATER

    SALT TO TASTE

½   CUP LARD OR VEGETABLE OIL

2   SLICES WHITE ONION

FOR THE GARNISH

1   CAN CHILES LARGOS OR JALAPEÑOS, PICKLED, ABOUT 8 OUNCES (OPTIONAL)

¾   CUP BLANCHED ALMONDS OR PEANUTS, CHOPPED FINELY

2   TABLESPOONS FRESH PARSLEY, CHOPPED FINELY

Prepare the chicken: Bring the water to a boil in a large saucepan. Add the onion, garlic, cinnamon, cloves, salt, and chicken. Simmer for 25 minutes or until the chicken is partially cooked. Allow it to cool in the broth. Then remove chicken from broth and reserve both chicken and broth. Strain the broth.

Prepare the sauce: Heat the lard in a large saucepan. Add the onions, garlic, almonds, peanuts, cinnamon, cloves, peppercorns, and croissant. Cook for 25 minutes. If the mixture begins to stick, add a little more oil or lard. Place the mixture in a blender or food processor. Add tomatoes and chiles. Purée the mixture. Heat the ½ cup lard in a saucepan. Brown the onion slices. Stir in the puréed mixture and cook until it releases its fat and you can see the bottom of the pan when the mixture is stirred. Rectify seasoning. Add 2-3 cups of reserved chicken broth, or as much as is necessary to slightly thin the sauce. Add the chicken and cook for an additional 25 minutes. Rectify seasoning.

To serve: Serve the almond mole from a large clay pot, garnished with canned chiles, chopped almonds or peanuts and chopped parsley. Accompany with freshly made corn tortillas.

NOTE

For a light alternative presentation use poached chicken, boned and sliced thinly. Measure out 2½ cups mole and thin with 1½ cups chicken broth. Serve a fan of sliced chicken breast over a ladleful of sauce on each individual plate. Garnish with almonds, yellow chiles and baby parsley. Extra mole can be frozen for later use.

KEEPING MOLE ≈

Mole freezes well. Preserve it in pint or quart containers to enhance roast chicken breasts, enrich a stew, or drizzle grilled pork chops.

CINNAMON ≈

Mexican cooks soon adopted cinnamon to blend with their native chocolate after the Spanish Conquest. True cinnamon, CINNAMOMUM ZEYLANICUM, *grows in the Spice Islands and Sri Lanka, but in the west cassia,* CINNAMOMUM CASSIA, *is more common. It is the dried inner bark of an evergreen tree. Cinnamon sticks are used as stirrers in cups of hot chocolate and atole in Mexico.*

BAPTISM ENCHILADAS

ENCHILADAS TABASQUEÑAS

An enchilada is a tortilla dipped in sauce, topped with chicken or other ingredients, rolled up, then drenched with sauce, and sprinkled with cheese and cream. This version is one that my grandmother used to make for baptisms. ~ MARGARITA

FOR THE FILLING

¾	CUP OLIVE OR SAFFLOWER OIL
1	GARLIC HEAD, CLOVES PEELED AND FINELY CHOPPED
½	CUP RAISINS
½	CUP STUFFED OLIVES
2	SWEET GREEN BELL PEPPERS, SEEDED AND FINELY CHOPPED
4	LARGE, RIPE TOMATOES
2	MEDIUM WHITE ONIONS, PEELED AND QUARTERED
1	POUND PORK LOIN, GROUND
1	POUND GROUND BEEF
4	WHOLE CLOVES
2	CINNAMON STICKS, 3 INCHES LONG
1	TEASPOON DRIED OREGANO LEAVES
1	TEASPOON BLACK PEPPER
¼	CUP VINEGAR
	SALT TO TASTE

FOR THE SAUCE

½	CUP VEGETABLE OIL
4	GARLIC CLOVES, PEELED
2	ONION SLICES
4	LARGE, RIPE TOMATOES (2 GENEROUS POUNDS)
2	MEDIUM WHITE ONIONS, PEELED AND QUARTERED
1	VERY RIPE PLANTAIN (ALLOW TO RIPEN FOR A WEEK), PEELED AND FRIED
6	DRIED CHILES ANCHOS, DEVEINED AND SEEDED, WASHED, SOAKED IN WATER WITH SALT (SUBSTITUTE DRIED RED CHILES CALIFORNIA)
⅓	CUP VEGETABLE OIL
2	SLICES WHITE ONION
1	TO 1½ CUPS CHICKEN OR BEEF BROTH
	SALT TO TASTE

FOR THE ENCHILADAS

32	THIN TORTILLAS
½	TO 1 CUP VEGETABLE OIL

FOR THE GARNISH

1½	MEDIUM ONION, PEELED AND SLICED
1½	TO 2 CUPS QUESO FRESCO OR FETA OR FARMER'S CHEESE, CRUMBLED

Prepare the filling: Heat the oil in a medium frying pan. Fry the chopped garlic until brown. Then add the raisins, olives and green pepper. Place the tomatoes and onion in a blender or food processor and purée. Add this mixture to the frying pan and cook until the sauce thickens and releases its fat, about 20 minutes. Then stir in the pork and beef and cook for 45 minutes or until the mixture thickens. Season with cloves, cinnamon, oregano, black pepper, vinegar and salt.

Prepare the sauce: Heat the oil in a medium frying pan. Fry the garlic and onion until brown, then transfer to a blender or food processor. Roast the tomatoes and onions on a comal or in a heavy skillet. Add to the blender along with the fried plantain and chiles, and purée. Place ⅓ cup oil in a frying pan and brown the two onion slices. Add the puréed sauce and simmer for 35 minutes

*"Never will it be lost, never will it be forgotten, that which they came to do, that which they came to record in their paintings: their renown, their history, their memory.
Thus in the future never will it perish, never will it be forgotten, always we will treasure it, we, their children, their grandchildren, brothers, great-grandchildren, great-great-grandchildren, descendants, we who carry their blood and their color, we will tell it, we will pass it on to those who do not yet live, who are to be born, the children of the Mexicans, the children of the Tenochcans. . . ."*

FROM CRÓNICA MEXICÁYOTL, BY THE AZTEC HISTORIAN FERNANDO ALVARADO TEZOZÓMOC

over low heat, or until it has thickened and released its fat. You should be able to see the bottom of the pan when the sauce is stirred back with a spoon. If it thickens too much, add chicken broth. Season to taste with salt.

Prepare the enchiladas: Heat the oil in a separate frying pan. Fry a tortilla briefly until soft. Then dip the tortilla in the sauce, and top with a tablespoon or more of filling. Roll up and arrange on an individual plate or a serving platter. Repeat procedure with remaining tortillas, and then drench the rolled-up enchiladas with sauce. Garnish with onion slices and fresh cheese. **SERVES 8-10.**

LITTLE TACOS

TAQUITOS

Little tacos are perhaps Mexico's favorite snack, hors d'oeuvre or appetizer. They can also be served as a light meal. Paired with one or more fresh salsas, these hot, crunchy and savory bites make wonderful fiesta food. ~ MARGARITA

FOR THE TACOS

48   TORTILLAS, 3 INCHES IN DIAMETER
     SALT TO TASTE
     BLACK PEPPER TO TASTE

6   FRESH CHILES SERRANOS OR 4 FRESH
     JALAPEÑOS, CUT IN STRIPS

2½   CUPS SAFFLOWER OR CORN OIL

2   TABLESPOONS LARD OR VEGETABLE
     SHORTENING

FOR THE FILLING

ANY OF THE FOLLOWING:

2½   CHICKEN BREASTS COOKED WITH GARLIC,
     ONION, BAY LEAVES, THYME, MARJORAM,
     THEN SHREDDED

¾   POUND PORK, COOKED AND SHREDDED

¾   POUND BARBECUED PORK, CHOPPED

¾   POUND BONELESS BEEF, COOKED AND
     SHREDDED

¾   POUND OAXACA OR MANCHEGO CHEESE,
     CUT IN STRIPS, AND EPAZOTE

Prepare the tacos: Heat the tortillas before filling or they may break. Place 1 tablespoon of any of the fillings listed above in the center of each tortilla. Sprinkle with salt and pepper to taste, and place a chile strip in the middle if desired. Roll up tightly and secure with a toothpick. Heat the oil and lard and fry the tacos in the hot oil until crisp. Drain on paper towels. If preparing ahead of time, reheat in the oven for 1 minute.

To serve: Arrange tacos on a serving platter, overlapping. Accompany with any sauces desired (see index for the many throughout this book). You may also serve with rice, or arrange tacos in a baking dish, drench with cream, then bake for 20-30 minutes. Top with shredded lettuce and serve immediately, accompanied with refried beans. **SERVES 12.**

≈

Mexicans are amused by that which is very tiny, including miniature clay vessels, molcajetes and wooden chocolate beaters. This delight in the diminutive extends to the language, in which the diminutive form is often used with children's names and as a term of endearment for adults. Some favorite foods are also called by the diminutive, both in the ancient Nahuatl and in the modern form of the language. For example, onions are "cebollitas," nopal cactus "nopalitos," and little tacos "taquitos."

NEXT-DAY TACOS ≈

Leftover meat, stir-fried till it is crispy and combined with roasted chile strips, makes a wonderful taco filling. Serve with fresh, soft tortillas; salsa and pickled chiles. Leftover shredded chicken is delicious served in this way also. For crunchy tacos, place shredded meat and chopped onion on a tortilla, roll up "cigar-style," close with a toothpick, then fry lightly in a little oil. Serve with salsa, shredded lettuce, and pickled chiles.

CHICKEN TART WITH NUTS, OLIVES AND RAISINS

TARTA DE POLLO ESTILO VILLA JUAREZ

I adopted this memorable tart from my mother, who served it as a culinary delight worthy of the unique moment when a new being joins the family. It is a main course that can be prepared ahead of time, perfect for any gathering. ~ PATRICIA

FOR THE CRUST

2½   CUPS ALL-PURPOSE FLOUR

1   TEASPOON SALT

1   CUP CHILLED BUTTER

3   EGG YOLKS

5   TO 8 TABLESPOONS ICED WATER

FOR THE FILLING

6   CUPS WATER

1   MEDIUM WHITE ONION, PEELED AND SLICED

4   GARLIC CLOVES, PEELED

8   WHOLE ALLSPICE

4   BAY LEAVES

6   SMALL SPLIT CHICKEN BREASTS

    SALT TO TASTE

⅓   CUP BUTTER

⅓   CUP OLIVE OIL

2   MEDIUM WHITE ONIONS, PEELED AND GRATED

4   GARLIC CLOVES, PEELED AND PURÉED

3   LARGE RIPE TOMATOES, PURÉED

2   CUPS CANNED TOMATO PURÉE OR CANNED ITALIAN PLUM TOMATOES

½   CUP CANNED CHILES JALAPEÑOS, CHOPPED

¾   CUP STUFFED OLIVES, FINELY CHOPPED

1   CUP BLANCHED ALMONDS, FINELY CHOPPED

½   CUP YELLOW RAISINS

½   CUP RAISINS

½   CUP PINE NUTS

1   TEASPOON GROUND BLACK PEPPER

    SALT TO TASTE

FOR THE GARNISH

½   CUP MILK

2   EGG YOLKS

Prepare the crust: Butter a 9-inch deep-dish pie pan. Combine the flour and salt in a medium bowl. Cut in butter with two knives until the mixture takes on a sandy consistency. Add the egg yolks and iced water, working with the fingers. Knead dough for 3 minutes, then shape in a large ball and refrigerate for 1½ hours. Remove from refrigerator and divide into 2 equal portions. On a floured surface over waxed paper, roll out one portion of dough evenly until it is about ⅛ inch thick. Cut into a large circle and place inside pie pan to line. Trim excess dough from edges of pan and reserve.

Prepare the filling: Heat the water in a medium saucepan. Add onion, garlic, allspice, bay leaves, chicken and salt to taste and cook for 25 minutes over a medium heat. Remove from heat and allow chicken breasts to cool in the broth. Then bone and shred chicken.

Heat the butter and olive oil in a medium saucepan. Brown the grated onion and puréed garlic. Then add the puréed tomatoes, tomato purée, chiles, olives, almonds, currants, raisins, pine nuts and shredded chicken. Season to taste with salt and pepper and cook for 45 minutes or until the mixture thickens to desired consistency. Remove from heat and allow to cool.

≈

The olive was carried from its home in the Middle East to the Mediterranean and from Spain to Mexico. In Mexican cooking it appears most often in dishes with a Spanish flavor.

STOCK AND BROTH ≈

Broth left over from the cooking of meat or poultry freezes well. Save it for cooking soups, sauces, pasta, dumplings, vegetables or rice. To save freezer space, you can reduce the broth before storing it. Cook it over moderately high heat until its volume is reduced through evaporation to half or one-third.

TO CLARIFY STOCK ≈

Drop in a whole head of roasted garlic or a whole roasted onion and simmer gently. Remove before serving.

Assemble the pie: Preheat oven to 350°F. Fill the prepared pie crust with chicken filling. Roll out remaining portion of dough on floured waxed aper. Cut into a circle larger than the pie pan. Lay dough over top of filled pie. Trim excess from edges and pinch all the way around to seal bottom and top crusts together. Collect dough trimmings and roll out again. Cut into strips ¾ inches wide. Brush strips with milk. Place strips around outer rim of pie and pinch to adhere to the crust. Whisk the egg yolks into the milk and brush over top crust of pie. Bake in preheated oven for 45 minutes or until the crust is golden brown. Serve immediately accompanied with a spinach or green salad. **SERVES 8.**

MONTEZUMA'S PIE

PASTEL DE MOCTEZUMA

This recipe pays homage to the emperor Montezuma, who was said to have been served 300 different dishes at a time, all kept warm on grills, for his choosing. Montezuma's Pie is layer upon layer of delicious ingredients baked in a clay pot. It is easy to prepare ahead of time for special occasions. Simply reheat before serving. ~ MAGO

FOR THE SAUCE

8   CUPS WATER
4½ POUNDS TOMATILLOS, HUSKED
1   MEDIUM WHITE ONION, PEELED AND QUARTERED
4   GARLIC CLOVES, PEELED
10   FRESH CHILES SERRANOS OR 5 JALAPEÑOS
2   CUPS FRESH CILANTRO, CHOPPED

½   CUP VEGETABLE OIL
½   CUP BUTTER
1½ MEDIUM WHITE ONIONS, PEELED AND GRATED
4   GARLIC CLOVES, PEELED AND PURÉED
     SALT TO TASTE

FOR THE FILLING

1½ CUPS VEGETABLE OIL
36   TO 46 MEDIUM TORTILLAS
2   CUPS PLAIN CREAMY YOGURT
1   CUP HEAVY CREAM
     SALT TO TASTE
3   CHICKEN BREASTS, COOKED FOR 20 MINUTES IN WATER WITH GARLIC, ONION, AND SALT, THEN BONED AND SHREDDED
8   CHILES POBLANOS, ROASTED, SWEATED AND PEELED, SEEDED AND DEVEINED, CUT INTO THIN STRIPS
1   POUND CHIHUAHUA, MOZZARELLA, FONTINA OR OTHER MILD CREAMY CHEESE, GRATED

Prepare the sauce: Place the water in a medium saucepan. Add the tomatillos, onion, garlic and chiles and simmer for 25 minutes. Then transfer ingredients plus 1½ cups cooking water to a blender or food processor, add the chopped cilantro and purée.

Heat the vegetable oil and butter in a medium saucepan, and brown the grated onion and puréed garlic. Add the puréed sauce and season to taste with salt. Simmer ingredients for about 40 minutes or until the sauce thickens.

Prepare the filling: Heat the oil in a frying pan. Fry the tortillas one at a time and drain on paper towels. Mix together the yogurt and cream with a little salt. Shred the chicken and prepare the chiles. Grate the cheese.

MONTEZUMA ≈
Montezuma was the ruler of the Aztecs when the Spanish arrived in Central Mexico in 1519. Mexico-Tenochtitlan, the Aztec capital, was a magnificent metropolis built in the center of a lake with 78 ceremonial buildings, palaces, temples, a great market, orchards, gardens, streets, canals and causeways. The Aztecs, arriving in the valley of Mexico in the 1200s A.D., built on the knowledge of earlier civilizations such as the Tecpanecs and Culhuacans. They had written literature, sculpture, painting, music, several kinds of schools, and, of course, a fully developed cuisine.

Assemble the pie: Preheat oven to 350°F. Butter a large, very deep casserole, earthenware pot or ovenproof baking dish. Place a layer of tortillas on the bottom of the dish. Cover with a layer of sauce, shredded chicken, chile poblano, cream mixture and grated cheese. Repeat a second layer of the ingredients, ending with grated cheese. Bake the pie for 1-1½ hours or until the cheese is golden brown and moisture has been absorbed. Serve immediately accompanied with a green salad or refried beans. **SERVES 10-12.**

STUFFED CHICKEN BREASTS WITH CHILE POBLANO-CREAM SAUCE

PECHUGAS RELLENAS DE CALABACITAS CON ELOTES EN SALSA DE CHILE POBLANO Y CREMA

As in all creative activities of life, imagination plays a primary role in the kitchen. It is fundamental to the origination of an unusual dish such as this, a good choice to present along with more traditional offerings in celebration of a new life. ~ PATRICIA

FOR THE CHICKEN

12   WHOLE BONELESS CHICKEN BREASTS, SLIGHTLY FLATTENED

      SALT TO TASTE

      BLACK PEPPER TO TASTE

FOR THE FILLING

½   CUP OLIVE OIL

6   GARLIC CLOVES, PEELED AND MINCED

2   MEDIUM WHITE ONIONS, PEELED AND CHOPPED

4½   CUPS OF KERNELS FROM YOUNG EARS OF CORN

2½   CUPS ZUCCHINI, CHOPPED FINELY

5   CHILES POBLANOS OR ANAHEIM, ROASTED, SWEATED AND PEELED, DEVEINED AND SEEDED, SOAKED FOR 15 MINUTES IN SALTED WATER, FINELY CHOPPED

4   LARGE TOMATOES, PEELED AND CHOPPED

½   CUP FRESH CILANTRO, FINELY CHOPPED

      SALT TO TASTE

      BLACK PEPPER TO TASTE

FOR THE MARINADE

2   CUPS WHITE WINE

1   CUP CHICKEN BROTH

1   CUP BUTTER, IN PIECES

3   BAY LEAVES

4   FRESH SPRIGS THYME

4   FRESH SPRIGS MARJORAM

⅓   CUP SOY SAUCE

1½   TABLESPOONS POWDERED CHICKEN BOUILLON OR SALT TO TASTE

½   TABLESPOON GROUND BLACK PEPPER

FOR THE CHILE POBLANO-CREAM SAUCE

2   MEDIUM WHITE ONIONS, PEELED AND QUARTERED

8   GARLIC CLOVES, PEELED

10   TOMATILLOS, HUSKED

12   CHILES POBLANOS, ROASTED, SWEATED AND PEELED, SEEDED AND DEVEINED SOAKED IN SALTED WATER

2   TO 3 CHILES POBLANOS, RAW, WASHED, SEEDED AND DEVEINED

½   CUP OLIVE OIL

½   CUP BUTTER

      SALT TO TASTE

      BLACK PEPPER TO TASTE

3   CUPS HEAVY CREAM

1½ CUPS PARMESAN CHEESE, GRATED

1½ CUPS CHIHUAHUA, MONTEREY JACK OR
     FONTINA CHEESE, GRATED

Prepare the chicken: Preheat oven to 350°F.
Sprinkle salt and pepper over the chicken
and refrigerate while preparing filling.

Prepare the filling: Heat the oil in a frying
pan. Brown the garlic and onion lightly. Add
corn, zucchini, chile, and tomato and cook
until the mixture thickens, about 45
minutes. Add cilantro and season to taste
with salt and pepper. Spoon filling into the
center of each chicken breast and roll up.
Secure with a toothpick. Arrange in a baking
dish.

Prepare the marinade: Combine the white
wine, broth, butter, bay leaves, thyme,
marjoram, soy sauce, bouillon and pepper in
a medium bowl. Pour over the chicken, and
bake for 10-15 minutes or until slightly
tender. Remove from oven and drain.
Reserve 1 cup of cooking liquid for chile-
cream sauce. Place in a saucepan and
simmer until reduced to ¾ cup.

*Prepare the chile-cream sauce and complete
the dish:* Cook onions, garlic and tomatillos
in water to cover for 15 minutes. Drain,
transfer to a blender or food processor, and
purée. Add roasted and raw chiles and purée
again. Strain mixture. Heat the olive oil and
butter in a saucepan. Add the strained sauce
and cook until the mixture thickens, about
45 minutes. Season to taste with salt and
pepper, then add the reduced cooking liquid
from the chicken and the cream. Continue
cooking until the mixture thickens once
again.

Place the cooked chicken breasts in a baking
dish. Cover with chile-cream sauce. Sprinkle
with cheese. Bake for 20-30 minutes.

Transfer to a broiler to brown the cheese.
Serve direct from the baking dish,
accompanied with rice. **SERVES 12.**

CHILE POBLANO SOUP

SOPA DE CHILE POBLANO

½   STICK BUTTER

¼   CUP OLIVE OIL

1   MEDIUM WHITE ONION, PEELED AND
    GRATED OR PURÉED IN BLENDER

3   GARLIC CLOVES, PEELED AND PURÉED

5   CHILES POBLANOS, ROASTED, SEEDED AND
    DEVEINED, SOAKED IN SALTED WATER TO
    REMOVE PIQUANCY, THEN SLICED INTO
    STRIPS

1   POUND FRESH OR FROZEN GREEN PEAS,
    COOKED IN SALTED WATER UNTIL TENDER

1½ QUARTS CHICKEN BROTH

1½ CUPS HEAVY CREAM

3   POTATOES, COOKED, PEELED AND DICED

3   CHAYOTES COOKED, PEELED AND DICED

1   TABLESPOON POWDERED CHICKEN BOUILLON

1½ CUPS GRUYERE CHEESE OR OTHER MILD
    CHEESE, CUT INTO CHUNKS

In a large saucepan, heat the butter
together with the olive oil. Lightly brown
the onion and garlic, then add the prepared
chile strips. Place in a blender or food
processor, with cooked peas and 1
tablespoon of chicken broth. Process until
the ingredients are well blended. Return
mixture to a saucepan and heat for about 10
minutes. Warm the cream separately. Then
add the cream to the soup base along with
remaining broth, diced potatoes and
chayotes. Cook for about 25 minutes over
medium heat. If necessary, season with
bouillon. Immediately before serving, stir in
cheese, heating soup thoroughly without
bringing to a boil. Serve hot. **SERVES 8.**

CHILE POBLANO ≈

*The versatile chile poblano
can be used as a main
course or to season
everything from salads to
soups. It takes its name
from Puebla, the area
where it originates. When
dried, it is known as chile
ancho. Fresh, it is fleshy
and slightly hot, with a
rich flavor. Chile poblano
is shaped like a pointed
version of the green bell
pepper common in North
America, but its flavor is
not the same. In Mexico,
bell peppers are called*
PIMIENTOS — *not chiles.*

≈

*Other ways to serve Chile
Poblano Soup: Place
chunks of cheese into soup
bowls and ladle hot soup
over them. Place roasted
chile poblano, cooked
potatoes or chayotes in
individual soup bowls,
warm them in the oven,
and ladle in soup at
serving time. Shrimp and
clams may also be added to
the soup.*

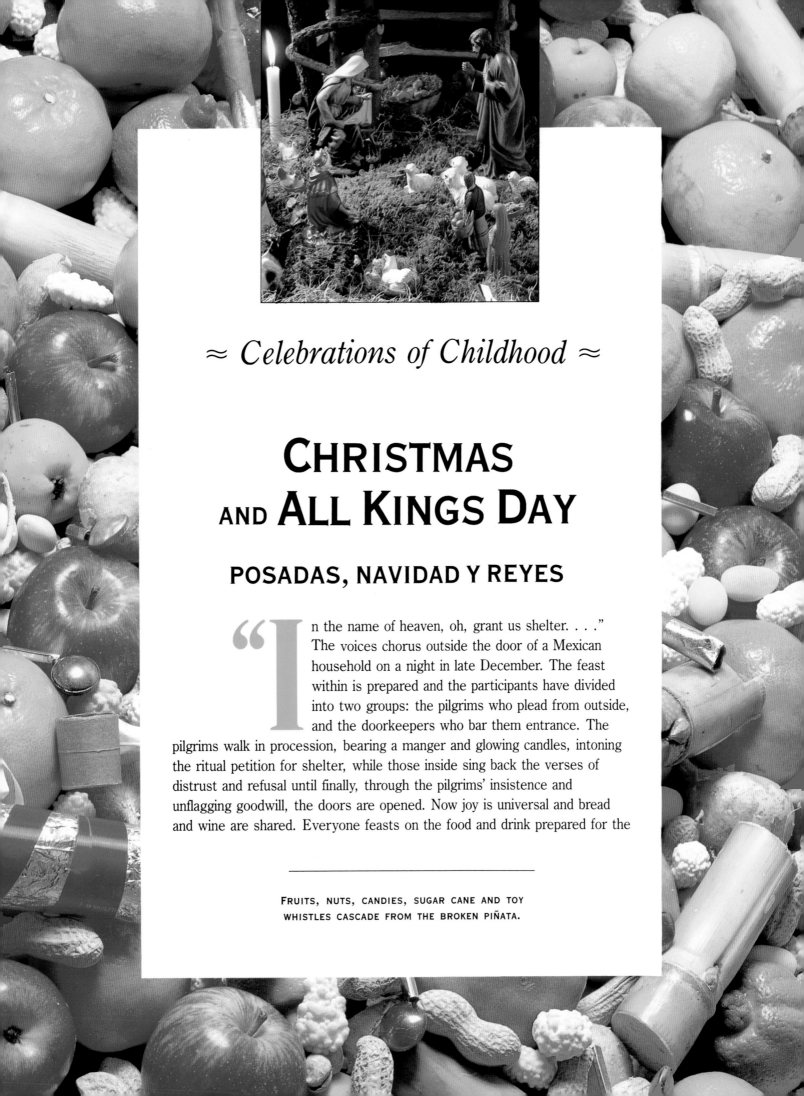

≈ *Celebrations of Childhood* ≈

CHRISTMAS
AND ALL KINGS DAY

POSADAS, NAVIDAD Y REYES

"I n the name of heaven, oh, grant us shelter. . . ."
The voices chorus outside the door of a Mexican
household on a night in late December. The feast
within is prepared and the participants have divided
into two groups: the pilgrims who plead from outside,
and the doorkeepers who bar them entrance. The
pilgrims walk in procession, bearing a manger and glowing candles, intoning
the ritual petition for shelter, while those inside sing back the verses of
distrust and refusal until finally, through the pilgrims' insistence and
unflagging goodwill, the doors are opened. Now joy is universal and bread
and wine are shared. Everyone feasts on the food and drink prepared for the

---

FRUITS, NUTS, CANDIES, SUGAR CANE AND TOY
WHISTLES CASCADE FROM THE BROKEN PIÑATA.

occasion, hot quesadillas filled with mushrooms, squash blossoms, spiced potatoes or cheese, tacos with fresh, vivid salsas, chicken tostadas, tamales, salbutes, carnitas and innumerable other dishes, accompanied by the ever-present punch made of tecojotes, sugar cane, guava, raisins and apples, which for the adults is laced with a shot of liquor.

It is the time of the *posadas,* nine magical days leading up to Christmas Eve, which commemorate the lonely wandering of Joseph and Mary in the city of Bethlehem and the moment when they at last found kindness and shelter. Families and friends gather together nightly to reenact the days preceeding the birth of Christ.

In Mexico the coming of December brings with it a joyousness that starts with the setting up of the family Christmas tree and continues with the first scent of jicama and tecojote that characterizes the posadas. In every home and place of commerce a *nacimiento* or crèche scene appears; the market stalls are bulging with clay and papier mâché figures of angels, shepherds and the holy family. Contributing to the sense of anticipation is the empty manger in which the Christ child figure will finally be placed on *Buenanoche* or Christmas Eve. It is an enchanted time for children, and for that element in all Mexicans that remains childlike in spite of age.

Along with the costumes, candles and chorusing of the posada ritual, and the euphoria of eating and drinking, there is also that exhilarating festivity, the breaking of the piñata. Its origins are uncertain, but the idea may have been brought to Italy from the Orient by Marco Polo. The Spanish, who borrowed the diversion from the Italians, brought it to Mexico. In Mexico, the piñata takes the form of a plain clay cooking pot fancifully embellished with tissue paper, silver paper, fringed streamers or cones resembling the points of a star. It may take the form of a burro, parrot, fish, peacock, elephant or some legendary figure. Inside the pot concealed within the piñata are sweets and toys.

Generally at least two piñatas are broken, one for children and one for adults. The children take turns batting at the suspended piñata according to height. If they are very little they will try to break the piñata unblindfolded; older children and adults are blindfolded and spun to make them lose their sense of direction, which serves to heighten the suspense and excitement. A broomstick is placed in the hands of the player and he bats at the piñata while the crowd chants and claps. Finally a lucky player lands a solid hit in the "belly" of the piñata and it is smashed open. All the guests, regardless of age or sex, rush to gather the pot's contents: limes, tecojotes, sugar cane, tangerines, peanuts, hard candies, lollypops, peppermint sticks, caramels, coated candies and litle toys such as tin whistles and noisemakers.

Thus in the midst of great celebration, Christmas, with its charm and serenity, comes to the Mexican home. The family gathers to wish each other, and the world, peace and happiness. The domestic table is dressed in white, with candlelight and brilliant poinsettias all providing a background for delicious dishes such as cream of walnut soup; codfish stew; turkey stuffed with chiles, spices, pulque and dried fruits; cakes; pine nut balls and many other delectables.

After Christmas Day, the next fiesta, eagerly awaited by children, is only days away. This is the celebration of All Kings Day, or *Reyes,* on January 6. It begins with a symbolic reenactment of the fabled journey of the three astrologers to the birthplace of the Christ child and their offering to him of gold, incense, and myrrh. On the night of January 5, children carefully place their best shoes at the foot of the Christmas tree, in hay representing the manger in which the Christ child lay. Parents play the role of the Magi, bringing gifts to their children. When morning comes, the surprise and happiness of the children is enormous and in the homes, streets, parks and village squares, joy is manifest in headlong races on gleaming bicycles or swift roller skates and in the tender mimicry of the little girls with their unfailing dolls.

At night the tone of the celebration changes since now it is primarily one of sharing amidst the family and friends the inevitable *rosca de Reyes,* or King's Cake, which dates to the time of the Franciscan missionaries. Originally, the feast was celebrated at suppertime with foamy hot chocolate and a *tarta* or sweet cake which in time became transformed into a *rosca* or ring, to symbolize a crown and to pay homage to the three kings who recognized the divinity of the Messiah. From that time on, partly as ritual, partly as fiesta, the rosca is divided and distributed. Inside it, also following the Franciscan tradition, is baked a tiny infant doll or figurine to symbolize the coming of the divine creature. The figurine was originally made of clay, but now is of porcelain or plastic. The *rosca,* or ring, is decorated with powdered sugar and crystallized fruit. Each guest cuts a piece for himself. The one whose slice contains the doll is considered the king of the fiesta and he selects a queen. Between them, they offer the traditional dinner on February 2, Candlemas Day, when the candles are lit for the purification of the Virgin Mary. Throughout Mexico almost every family puts a King's Cake on the table on January 6, accompanying it with coffee, chocolate, atoles flavored with strawberry, pineapple, vanilla or pine nuts and salty or sweet tamales.

"Dale, dale, dale
No pierdas el tino
Porque si lopierdes
Pierdes el camino. . ."

"Hit it, hit it, hit it
Do not lose your aim
For if you should lose it
You will lose the way. . ."

TRADITIONAL PIÑATA SONG

Piloncillo (semi-processed dark brown sugar sold in cones), cinnamon and the seasonal fruit called tecojote add characteristic flavor to Christmas Punch.

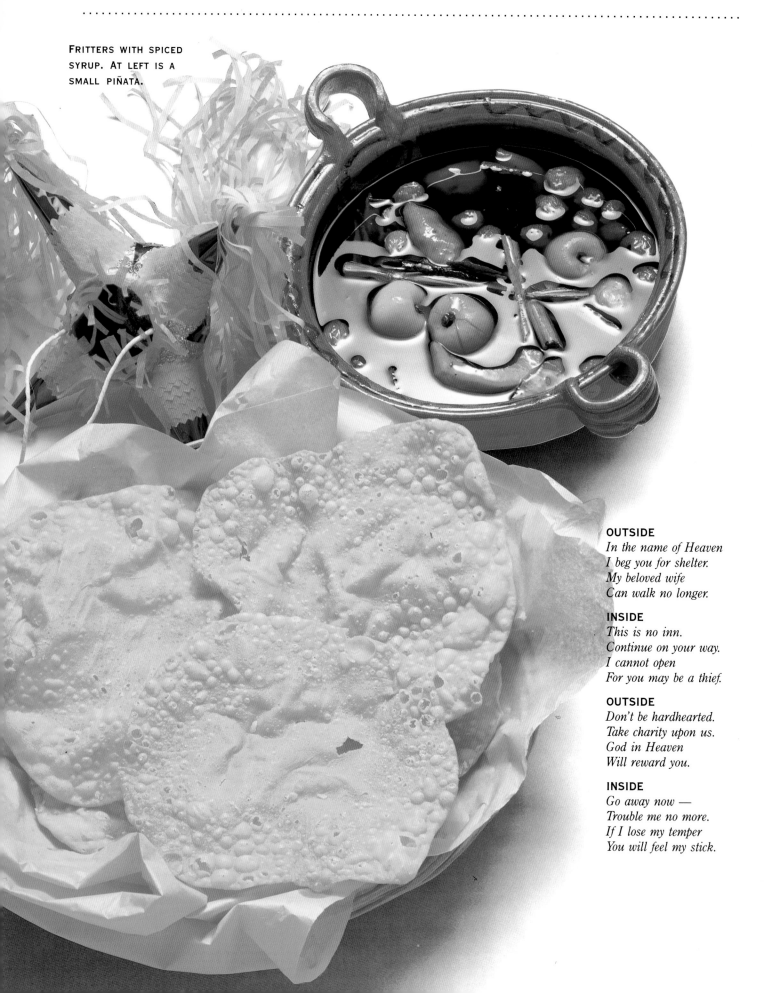

FRITTERS WITH SPICED
SYRUP. AT LEFT IS A
SMALL PIÑATA.

OUTSIDE
In the name of Heaven
I beg you for shelter.
My beloved wife
Can walk no longer.

INSIDE
This is no inn.
Continue on your way.
I cannot open
For you may be a thief.

OUTSIDE
Don't be hardhearted.
Take charity upon us.
God in Heaven
Will reward you.

INSIDE
Go away now —
Trouble me no more.
If I lose my temper
You will feel my stick.

FRITTERS

BUÑUELOS

*F*ritters are reminiscent of Arab sweets brought to Mexico during the Spanish Conquest and adapted by the natives. In this recipe the fritters are rolled out rather than prepared in a mold. Both kinds of fritters are served around Lent and Christmas. ~ EMILIA

FOR THE FRITTERS

1	TABLESPOON DRY YEAST
½	CUP WARM MILK
1	POUND ALL-PURPOSE FLOUR
1	TEASPOON SALT
8	EGG YOLKS, BEATEN UNTIL THICK
4	EGG WHITES, BEATEN UNTIL SOFT PEAKS FORM
2	TABLESPOONS SUGAR
2	TABLESPOONS SOFTENED BUTTER
1	TABLESPOON ANISE SEED
⅓	CUP LARD OR VEGETABLE SHORTENING
½	TO 1 CUP BOILING WATER, CONTAINING 10 TOMATILLO HUSKS (HUSKS IMPART SLIGHT LEAVENING TO THE WATER)
2	CUPS LARD OR VEGETABLE SHORTENING
2	QUARTS VEGETABLE OIL

FOR THE SYRUP

6	CONES PILONCILLO OR 6 CUPS DARK BROWN SUGAR
4	STICKS CINNAMON, EACH 4 INCHES LONG
6	GUAVAS, THINLY SLICED (SUBSTITUTE APRICOTS OR PEACHES IF GUAVAS ARE NOT AVAILABLE)

Prepare the fritters: Dissolve yeast in milk. Place flour, salt, egg yolks, egg whites and yeast mixture in a medium bowl. In a separate bowl, mix together the sugar, butter, anise seed and lard. Add flour mixture and knead dough with hands, adding a little boiling water. Continue kneading dough on a floured pastry board until elastic and not sticky. It may be necessary to add up to 1 cup more of flour to obtain desired consistency. (Process by machine 10-15 minutes if preferred.) Form a ball and coat it with a little oil. Cover and set dough aside until it doubles in volume.

Heat oil and lard or vegetable shortening in a large skillet or deep fryer. Meanwhile, turn a round-bottomed cazuela (clay pot) upside down. Cover the bottom of the cazuela with a dishcloth. Sprinkle cloth with flour. Pinch off about 1½-inch ball of batter and roll out on a floured surface until it extends to about 3-4 inches in diameter. Place on the cazuela and carefully pull on edges, working around until the circle stretches to roughly 9 inches in diameter. The dough should be stretched very thin — almost transparent. Place fritter in oil and fry, basting it constantly with oil. Turn it two or three times until it is evenly light brown. Then remove fritter from oil and drain on paper towels. Repeat the same procedure for remaining batter. Traditional fritters are round and thin, but you may prepare them in rectangles using a pasta machine if you prefer, or roll them out on a floured surface.

Prepare the syrup: Heat the sugar with enough water to cover. Add cinnamon and fruit. Cook over high heat for about 45 minutes or until the syrup is thick.

To serve: Break fritters into quarters. Place in individual bowls. Drench with hot syrup.
MAKES APPROXIMATELY 80 FRITTERS.

QUESADILLAS

ENTREMES MEXICANO

A quesadilla *(kay sah* DEE *yah) is a tortilla filled with any of a wide variety of delicious mixtures, folded over and fried or grilled. They are a perfect example of the Mexican* ANTOJO *(an* TOE *hoe), which translates as "craving," or "hankering," or "whim."* ANTOJOS *are appetizers or hors d'oeuvres of many varieties.* ANTOJITOS, *or "little whims," such as quesadillas are perfect party food for guests at a pre-Christmas posada.* ~
PATRICIA

24 FRESHLY-MADE TORTILLAS (PAGE 152)

1¼ CUPS VEGETABLE OIL

1¼ CUPS LARD

There are two ways to cook quesadillas. To prepare them without oil, start with warm, just-cooked tortillas. Fill with any of the fillings suggested below and fold over, pinching edges shut. After filling each tortilla, immediately return it to the hot comal or skillet and cook briefly, to warm the filling and melt the cheese.

For fried quesadillas, start with raw tortillas, fill, fold over and pinch edges to close. Set quesadillas aside on a damp cloth as you fill them. Heat oil in a deep frying pan. Fry the quesadillas in the hot oil until golden brown. Quesadillas may be prepared ahead of time and reheated in the oven. Serve with Tomatillo-Chipotle Salsa (page 115), Mexican Salsa (page 177), or Chile Ancho Salsa (page 113), served in molcajetes. Or you may serve freshly cooked, pliable tortillas without frying them and guests may fold up their own quesadillas, using the fillings of their choice. **SERVES 8.**

QUESADILLA FILLINGS:

SHREDDED MEAT

2 CUPS COOKED SHREDDED SKIRT STEAK MIXED WITH **1** CUP CHOPPED ONION AND **6** FRESH CHILES SERRANOS OR **3** JALAPEÑOS, STEMMED AND CHOPPED

OR

2 CUPS COOKED SHREDDED CHICKEN SAUTÉED WITH CHOPPED ONION

OR

1 CUP COOKED SHREDDED SKIRT STEAK SAUTÉED WITH CHOPPED TOMATO, ONION, GARLIC AND FRESH CHOPPED CHILE SERRANO OR JALAPEÑO

GROUND MEAT

½ CUP BUTTER OR LARD

1 MEDIUM WHITE ONION, PEELED AND CHOPPED

4 GARLIC CLOVES, PEELED

1 GENEROUS POUND GROUND BEEF OR VEAL (OR SHREDDED MEAT)

3 MEDIUM RIPE TOMATOES, CHOPPED

½ CUP DRY SHERRY OR WHITE WINE

8 OLIVES, CHOPPED

6 ALMONDS, BLANCHED AND CHOPPED

2 TABLESPOONS RAISINS

3 TABLESPOONS TOMATO PASTE

1½ TEASPOONS CUMIN

1½ TEASPOONS GROUND CINNAMON

1 TEASPOON NUTMEG

1 PINCH GROUND CLOVES

SALT TO TASTE

BLACK PEPPER TO TASTE

Heat the oil in a frying pan or wok and brown the onion and garlic cloves. Stir in the beef and tomatoes and cook until beef is browned. Add remaining ingredients, and cook until the mixture has thickened and moisture has evaporated.

CHEESE AND ONION

3   CUPS MOZZARELLA, SOFT GOUDA, MONTEREY JACK OR OTHER MILD CHEESE, GRATED

4   TABLESPOONS CHOPPED WHITE ONION

1   TABLESPOON CHOPPED EPAZOTE

Mix together.

SQUASH BLOSSOM

⅓   CUP OLIVE OIL OR LARD

1   MEDIUM WHITE ONION, PEELED AND CHOPPED

3   GARLIC CLOVES, PEELED AND CHOPPED

1   GENEROUS POUND SQUASH BLOSSOMS, WASHED AND CHOPPED

2   MEDIUM TOMATOES, CHOPPED

2   FRESH CHILES SERRANOS OR 1 JALAPEÑO, STEMMED AND CHOPPED

¾   CUP EPAZOTE OR CILANTRO, CHOPPED

    SALT TO TASTE

    BLACK PEPPER TO TASTE

Heat oil in frying pan. Sauté onion and garlic until brown. Add the squash blossoms, tomatoes, chiles and epazote or cilantro. Season to taste with salt and pepper and cook until moisture evaporates.

CHEESE AND CHILE

2   CUPS MOZZARELLA OR STRING CHEESE, GRATED

2   TO 6 PICKLED CHILES SERRANOS, JALAPEÑOS OR CHIPOTLES, SEEDED AND CUT IN STRIPS, CANNED OR HOMEMADE (PAGE 147-148)

1½ CUPS FETA, FARMER'S OR STRING CHEESE, GRATED

Mix together.

MUSHROOM

¼   CUP LARD

1   POUND MUSHROOMS, WASHED AND CHOPPED

4   GARLIC CLOVES, PEELED AND CHOPPED

7   GREEN ONIONS, CHOPPED

2   TABLESPOONS WHITE WINE

2   TOMATOES, CHOPPED, OR 8 TOMATILLOS, HUSKED AND COOKED 25 MINUTES OR UNTIL TENDER, CHOPPED (OPTIONAL)

4   FRESH CHILES SERRANOS OR 2 JALAPEÑOS, CHOPPED, OR 2 CHILES ANCHOS OR 2 CHIPOTLES, SEEDED AND DEVEINED, LIGHTLY TOASTED AND CRUMBLED

½   CUP CHOPPED EPAZOTE OR CILANTRO (OPTIONAL)

    SALT TO TASTE

Heat the lard in a large skillet. Add the mushrooms and sauté. Add all remaining ingredients, combine and sauté gently till moisture has evaporated. Optional ingredients may be used in addition to or instead of other ingredients. Season to taste.

POTATO AND CHILE

3   TO 4 LARGE POTATOES, COOKED IN SALTED WATER, MASHED WITH A LITTLE LARD, BUTTER OR CHORIZO SAUSAGE

2   TO 4 FRESH CHILES JALAPEÑOS, SEEDED AND DEVEINED, CUT IN STRIPS

2   TO 4 RAW CHILES POBLANOS, SEEDED AND DEVEINED, CUT IN STRIPS

Mix together.

≈

Quesadilla fillings combine deliciously with other dishes. Try them in a skillet-cooked omelet with sliced potatoes and onion, on a toasted sandwich, or combined with cheese and custard in a pastry tart shell for a baked quiche.

For basic quiche custard, combine 1½ cups heavy cream with 3 large eggs and season with nutmeg, salt and pepper. Pour quiche custard and quesadilla fillings into prebaked pie crust and bake in a moderate oven until the filling is set.

QUESADILLA PARTY ≈

Quesadillas are wonderful party food. Make up several fillings and offer them along with fresh tortillas, salsas and garnishes. Guests combine their favorite flavors to create their own quesadillas. At an outdoor party with a barbeque grill, guests can assemble quesadillas and then heat them briefly on the grill.

QUID STYLE QUESADILLAS

QUESADILLAS TICO QUID

In the early 1960s, the Quid Night Club was a famous spot to stop for an ANTOJITO, *(an toe HEE toe)*, or little nibble. These quesadillas, which we prepare for pre-Christmas parties, are similar to ones served at the Quid. ~ MAGO

FOR THE QUESADILLAS

16 TO 24 CORN TORTILLAS, FRESHLY MADE (SEE PAGE 152) OR PURCHASED READY-MADE

1 POUND MILD CHEESE (MONTEREY JACK, MOZZARELLA OR STRING CHEESE), SLICED

⅔ POUND HAM, THINLY SLICED

2½ CUPS LETTUCE, WASHED AND SHREDDED

1 CUP HEAVY WHIPPING CREAM WHISKED WITH ½ CUP SOUR CREAM

FOR THE CHILE SALSA

3 MEDIUM TOMATOES, PEELED OR UNPEELED, FINELY CHOPPED

1 MEDIUM ONION, PEELED AND FINELY CHOPPED

4 FRESH CHILES SERRANOS OR 2 JALAPEÑOS, CHOPPED

SALT TO TASTE

BLACK PEPPER TO TASTE

1 AVOCADO, FINELY CHOPPED

Prepare the tortillas: Heat a comal or skillet. Heat tortillas, turning once. As each one is heated, fill with a slice of cheese and a slice of ham, and fold in half like a turnover.

Prepare the chile salsa: In a glass bowl, mix together the tomato, onion, chile, salt, pepper and avocado.

Prepare the quesadillas: Heat the oil in a frying pan. Fry the quesadillas on both sides until they are crisp and the cheese inside has melted. Drain on paper towels and top with shredded lettuce, cream and salsa. Serve hot. **SERVES 8-12.**

GREEN SALSA WITH CILANTRO

SALSA VERDE CON CILANTRO EN MOLCAJETE

S alsas are an ever-present condiment on Mexican tables — as ubiquitous as the salt and pepper on a North American table. This one is among the most popular in Mexico. It is often served directly from the molcajete.

4 CUPS WATER

12 TOMATILLOS, HUSKED

4 TO 6 FRESH CHILES SERRANOS, STEMMED, WHOLE

½ MEDIUM WHITE ONION, PEELED AND QUARTERED

6 GARLIC CLOVES, PEELED

¼ MEDIUM WHITE ONION, PEELED AND QUARTERED

SALT TO TASTE

30 SPRIGS CILANTRO, CHOPPED

Heat the water in a medium saucepan. Add the tomatillos, chiles, onion and 4 garlic cloves and boil for about 15 minutes. Remove from heat and allow to cool slightly.

Meanwhile, place the remaining 2 raw garlic cloves, raw onion and salt to taste in a molcajete (stone mortar), blender or food processor, and blend. Add chopped cilantro, and gradually add the cooked tomatillos, chiles, onion and garlic. Rectify seasoning. If necessary, add a little cooking water from the vegetables to thin salsa. Garnish with chopped onion and cilantro if desired. **SERVES 8.**

QUID STYLE QUESADILLAS WITH MEXICAN SALSA (PAGE 177) AND A BANK OF POINSETTIAS, NATIVE TO MEXICO.

≈

"The sun is shining like gold,
The moon like silver.
Instead of an oil lamp, a piñata
Of sweets with a treasure."

FROM NOCHEBUENA (CHRISTMAS EVE), A POSADA SONG

MELTED CHEESE AND CHORIZO SAUSAGE

QUESO TOLUQUEÑO

In *Toluca, the capital of the state of Mexico, this dish is prepared with locally-made chorizo sausage. Chorizo sausage, prepared in Toluca since 1564, is famous around the country. This recipe is the perfect* ANTOJITO *for a pre-Christmas party.* ~ PATRICIA

FOR THE CHEESE

⅓ CUP VEGETABLE OIL

1 MEDIUM WHITE ONION, PEELED AND MINCED

4 GARLIC CLOVES, PEELED AND MINCED

2¼ POUNDS TOLUCAN STYLE CHORIZO SAUSAGE, CRUMBLED

2 TO 4 FRESH CHILES SERRANOS OR 2 JALAPEÑOS, MINCED

4 TOMATOES, DICED

¾ CUP CILANTRO, FINELY CHOPPED

1½ POUNDS MILD CHEESE, (FONTINA, MONTEREY JACK OR OTHER), GRATED (COMBINE MORE THAN ONE CHEESE IF DESIRED)

SALT TO TASTE

BLACK PEPPER TO TASTE

FOR THE GARNISH

½ POUND FRIED CHORIZO SAUSAGE

32 FRESHLY MADE CORN TORTILLAS (PAGE 152)

Preheat the oven to 350°F. Heat the oil in a heavy, large skillet. Brown the onion, garlic and chorizo, cooking for about 10 minutes. Then stir in the chiles, tomatoes and cilantro and simmer for 20 minutes over low heat. Add cheese and season to taste with salt. Simmer until the cheese melts. Spoon equal portions of mixture into cazuelitas (little clay bowls) or ramekins. Sprinkle with fried chorizo and bake at 350°F. for 8 minutes or until the cheese melts. Serve hot, accompanied by hot tortillas. **SERVES 8.**

NOTE

For a simpler form of cheese and chorizo, a very popular snack served often with beer or chilled white wine in Mexico City, start with ⅓ cup vegetable oil, 2 cups chorizo, and 12 cups grated morral, manchego, chihuahua, mild white cheddar, Monterey jack or mozzarella cheese. Fry the chorizo in the oil. Place equal portions of cheese in buttered cazuelitas or ramekins and top with chorizo. Bake at 350°F. until cheese has melted. **SERVES 8-10.**

ROAST CROWN OF PORK WITH AVOCADO

CORONA DE PUERCO ROSTIZADA A LA MEXICANA

This *unusual holiday meal combines pork, the gift of Spain to Mexico, with avocados, the gift of Mexico to the world.* ~ MAGO

FOR THE CROWN

16 PORK RIBS, IN A SINGLE SLAB (5½-6½ POUNDS)

FOR THE MARINADE

4 TO 5 GARLIC CLOVES, PEELED AND PURÉED

1 CUP SOY SAUCE

SAUSAGE INTERNATIONAL ≈

Instead of chorizo sausage, Mexican melted cheese hors d'oeuvres may be made with Andouille, a spicy smoked pork sausage, Cajun Andouille — the Louisiana version — or with crumbled hot Italian sausage, Kielbasa Polish sausage, or German sausages.

MEXICAN FIREWORKS ATTACHED TO SPECIAL SCAFFOLDS ACCOMPANY FIESTAS IN EVERY VILLAGE THROUGHOUT THE YEAR.

⅓   CUP WORCESTERSHIRE SAUCE

1   TABLESPOON FRESHLY GROUND BLACK PEPPER

½   TO 1 CUP DRY SHERRY

FOR THE AVOCADO

4   TO 5 AVOCADOS, PEELED AND PURÉED

¼   CUP MILK

3   TO 4 FRESH CHILES SERRANOS, MINCED

¼   CUP CHOPPED CILANTRO

½   CUP CHOPPED PARSLEY

½   CUP OLIVE OR CORN OIL

¼   CUP LIME JUICE

1½   TEASPOONS SALT, OR TO TASTE

FOR THE GARNISH

¾   CUPS CHOPPED GREEN ONION TOPS OR CHIVES

Prepare the marinade: Combine all the ingredients and pour over the crown of ribs. Allow to marinate for 2 hours.

Prepare the meat: Preheat an oven to 450°F. Place ribs on a baking tray. Lower oven temperature to 350°F. and bake ribs for 1½-2 hours, basting regularly with the marinade.

Prepare the avocado purée: Combine all the ingredients in a blender or food processor and purée. Reserve.

To serve: Arrange the slab of ribs standing up. Fill the center with avocado purée and decorate with green onion tops. **SERVES 8.**

VARIATION

Fill ribs with seasoned rice, garnishing with fried chorizo sausage.

The cabbage palm (SABAL PALMETTO), a native of Florida, grows extravagantly in some parts of Mexico, including the state of Veracruz, where it is harvested for the central shoot of the young plant. Each shoot weighs about two pounds. North American cooks are likeliest to find it canned; look for the best quality canned palm hearts you can find, as some are preserved with too much brine and lose their mellow, fresh flavor. A fresh palm heart must be peeled, sliced, soaked in water for an hour, blanched, drained, and simmered for 45 minutes before it is eaten.

HEARTS-OF-PALM SOUP

SOPA DE PALMITO

My mother's mother-in-law taught me how to prepare this Veracruz soup when we celebrated Christmas with the Quintana family. Palms cut fresh in the field were brought to the house so that the hearts could be removed just before preparing. My family always served this soup on Christmas Day. ~ MAGO

FOR THE SOUP

¾   CUP BUTTER

2   GARLIC CLOVES, PEELED

1½ MEDIUM WHITE ONIONS, PEELED AND
    QUARTERED

1   LEEK, SLICED

4   RIBS CELERY, SLICED

2   TENDER PALM HEARTS, FRESH (OR CANNED
    IF FRESH ARE NOT AVAILABLE)
             OR

5   CANS OF PALM HEARTS, APPROXIMATELY
    10 OUNCES EACH (BRAZILIAN ARE BEST)

    SALT TO TASTE

5   CUPS CHICKEN BROTH

6   CUPS MILK, BOILING HOT

2   CUPS CRÈME FRAÎCHE, OR A COMBINATION
    OF HEAVY WHIPPING CREAM AND SOUR
    CREAM

FOR THE GARNISH

16 CHILES DE ÁRBOL OR OTHER HOT DRIED
    SMALL RED CHILES, FRIED IN A SMALL
    AMOUNT OF OIL

6   TABLESPOONS CHIVES OR GREEN ONION
    TOPS

Heat the butter in a saucepan. Add the garlic, onion, leek, celery and palm hearts. Salt to taste and simmer for 25 minutes. Add the chicken broth and cook until the palm hearts are tender. Allow to cool briefly, then purée in a blender or food processor. Strain, and transfer to a medium saucepan. Add the boiling milk, and then gradually incorporate the cream. Stir occasionally while simmering for an additional 20 minutes. Garnish with chiles and chives.
SERVES 8-10.

STEWED PORK WITH APRICOT SAUCE

GUISADO DE CHABACANO

Apricot stew offers a refreshing change from the traditional dishes served at Christmas.

FOR THE PORK

½   CUP VEGETABLE OIL

3⅓ POUNDS PORK LEG OR PORK LOIN, CUT
    INTO CHUNKS

6   SPRIGS THYME

8   WHOLE BAY LEAVES

1   MEDIUM WHITE ONION, SPIKED WITH 8
    WHOLE CLOVES

20 WHOLE BLACK PEPPERCORNS

½   GARLIC HEAD, CUT IN HALF ACROSS THE
    GRAIN

    SALT TO TASTE

8   CUPS WATER

FOR THE APRICOT SAUCE

10 CHILES CHILHUACLES OR 6 CHILES
    MULATOS, WASHED, SEEDED AND
    DEVEINED, ROASTED, AND SOAKED IN
    SALTED WATER

6   CHILES PASILLAS, WASHED, SEEDED AND
      DEVEINED, ROASTED, AND SOAKED IN
      SALTED WATER (SUBSTITUTE DRIED RED
      CHILES CALIFORNIA OR OTHER DRIED RED
      CHILES FOR ALL DRIED CHILES CALLED
      FOR, IF NECESSARY)

1½   CUPS DRIED APRICOTS OR 1 CUP PRUNES,
      PITTED

1½   MEDIUM WHITE ONIONS, PEELED AND
      ROASTED

12   GARLIC CLOVES, PEELED AND ROASTED

20   WHOLE BLACK PEPPERCORNS

8   WHOLE CLOVES

1   CINNAMON STICK, 4 INCHES LONG

1   TABLESPOON OREGANO

½   CUP VEGETABLE OIL OR LARD

      SUGAR TO TASTE

      SALT TO TASTE

Prepare the pork: Heat the oil in a pressure cooker or heavy pot and brown the pork with thyme, bay leaves, onion, peppercorns, garlic and salt to taste. Then add water and cover. Cook for about 45 minutes to 1 hour (or more if not using a pressure cooker).

Remove from heat and allow to cool. Remove pork from broth. Strain broth and retain for another use if desired.

Prepare the sauce: Place the chiles, apricots, onion, garlic, peppercorns, cloves, cinnamon, oregano and a little water in a blender or food processor and purée. In a medium saucepan, heat the oil. Add the blended sauce and season to taste with sugar and salt. Simmer until the mixture releases its fat, approximately 45 minutes. Then add the pork. Continue cooking until the mixture has thickened somewhat, about 30 minutes. **SERVES 8.**

HEARTS OF PALM SOUP ON A BARK PAINTING MADE BY THE HUICHOLES, NORTH OF JALISCO.

STEAMED TURKEY IN ADOBO SAUCE

PAVO ENCHILADO A VAPOR

Steamed turkey in chile sauce suggests the feast aromas of pre-Hispanic cooking. Turkey is native to Mexico and so is chile. In this dish they are flavored with avocado leaves. You may roast the turkey rather than steaming it if you prefer. ~
PATRICIA

FOR THE TURKEY

1   TURKEY (ABOUT **24** POUNDS), FRESH OR FROZEN AND THAWED, WASHED AND DRIED

6   MEDIUM WHITE ONIONS, PEELED AND QUARTERED AND ROASTED

4   GARLIC HEADS, CUT IN HALF

1   BOTTLE WHITE WINE

2   BOTTLES BEER

1½   CUPS LARD OR BUTTER

60   FRESH AVOCADO LEAVES

50   CORN HUSKS OR **6** BANANA LEAVES

6   CUPS WATER

FOR THE ADOBO SAUCE

30   CHILES ANCHOS, WASHED, SEEDED AND DEVEINED AND ROASTED

15   CHILES GUAJILLOS, WASHED, SEEDED AND DEVEINED AND ROASTED (SUBSTITUTE DRIED RED CHILES CALIFORNIA FOR ANCHOS AND GUAJILLOS, IF NECESSARY)

½   CUP VINEGAR

3   CUPS SEMI-SWEET WHITE WINE

3   CUPS WATER

3   CUPS BEER

4   MEDIUM WHITE ONIONS, PEELED AND QUARTERED

8   GARLIC CLOVES, RAW, PEELED

8   GARLIC CLOVES, PEELED AND ROASTED

2   TABLESPOONS OREGANO LEAVES

10   AVOCADO LEAVES, LIGHTLY TOASTED OR 1½ TABLESPOONS GROUND CUMIN SEED

  SALT TO TASTE

1   TABLESPOON GROUND BLACK PEPPER

1½   CUP LARD OR OLIVE OIL

4   SLICES WHITE ONION

FOR THE GARNISH

3   MEDIUM WHITE ONIONS, PEELED AND SLICED

4   RIPE AVOCADOS, SLICED

16   RADISHES, CUT IN THE SHAPE OF A FLOWER AND SOAKED IN ICED WATER

32   LARGE GREEN ONIONS, CUT IN THE SHAPE OF A FLOWER AND SOAKED IN ICED WATER

Prepare the turkey: Place the turkey in a turkey roaster or on a large baking tray and fill with quartered onions and garlic. Drench with wine and beer and marinate for 2 hours in refrigerator.

Prepare the adobo: Soak the chiles in vinegar, wine and water for 30 minutes. Transfer the chiles and soaking liquid to a blender or food processor. Purée with beer, onions, raw and roasted garlic, oregano, avocado leaves, salt and pepper. Purée twice to be sure ingredients are well blended.

Heat the lard in a medium saucepan and brown onion slices. Add chile sauce and simmer for 1½ hours or until the mixture releases its fat.

Spread the turkey with butter. Then carefully lift up skin, and rub with butter and adobo sauce (using about ½ the adobo sauce in total) under skin. Place turkey on the rack of a large steamer or roaster lined with fresh avocado leaves or banana leaves and

STEAMED TURKEY IN ADOBO SAUCE, WRAPPED IN BANANA LEAVES.

ADOBO SAUCE ≈

Adobo is a spicy, rich, cooked red sauce that pairs well with meat and poultry. It can be used to coat chicken breasts or pork chops before roasting or grilling.

AVOCADO LEAVES ≈

Mexican cooks use avocado leaves in moles and stews as a bay leaf might be used, lending a delightful avocado essence. Avocado leaves, if you can obtain them, can be dried in the oven using the heat from the pilot light. They will keep indefinitely in a sealed glass jar.

corn husks, breast down. Add water and cover turkey with more avocado or banana leaves and corn husks. Lay green onions alongside the turkey, then cover with a lid or aluminum foil and steam for 3 to 4 hours or until it is done. Do not overcook. Be careful to check that there is always enough water in the steamer.

To serve: Place cooled turkey on a serving platter on a bed of adobo sauce. Cover with more sauce and garnish with onion slices, avocado, radish and onion flowers, and avocado leaves. Serve additional adobo sauce on the side, along with refried beans and freshly made corn tortillas or a corn torte. You may also shred the steamed turkey for tacos. **SERVES 16.**

GRANDMOTHER'S TURKEY

PAVO DE LA ABUELA

Turkey was called HUEXOLOTL *in Nahuatl, the ancient language of the Aztecs. This bird, native to Mexico, was referred to in several early Aztec writings including the Florentino codice. It was roasted, then prepared with a* PIBIL *or mole sauce.* ~ PATRICIA

FOR THE TURKEY

1	LARGE TURKEY, 15-17 POUNDS
2	CUPS WHITE WINE
2	CUPS AGED TEQUILA

FOR THE MARINADE

10	GARLIC CLOVES, PEELED, ROASTED
10	GARLIC CLOVES, PEELED
2	TABLESPOONS DRIED THYME OR 10 SPRIGS FRESH THYME
2	TABLESPOONS DRIED MARJORAM OR 10 SPRIGS FRESH
8	BAY LEAVES
2	CUPS BUTTER, SOFTENED
1	CUP OLIVE OIL
1½	TABLESPOONS GROUND ALLSPICE
2½	TABLESPOONS SALT
1	TABLESPOON GARLIC SALT
1	TABLESPOON ONION SALT
2	LARGE LEEKS, THINLY SLICED
3	WHITE ONIONS, THINLY SLICED
½	CUP MILK

FOR THE STUFFING

½	CUP OLIVE OIL
½	CUP BUTTER
12	GARLIC CLOVES, PEELED
2	CUPS GRATED ONION
3⅓	POUNDS GROUND MEAT (BEEF, PORK, VEAL, CHICKEN OR HAM)
6	RIPE TOMATOES, FINELY CHOPPED
1	GENEROUS POUND MUSHROOMS, CHOPPED
4	POTATOES, PEELED AND DICED
1	CUP RAISINS OR CURRANTS
2	CUPS PRUNES, PITTED AND FINELY CHOPPED
1½	CUPS CANDIED PINEAPPLE OR CITRON, FINELY CHOPPED
1	CUP STUFFED OLIVES, FINELY CHOPPED
¾	CUP PINE NUTS
¾	CUP ALMONDS, FINELY CHOPPED
2	CUPS CHESTNUTS, FINELY CHOPPED
4	APPLES, PEELED AND FINELY CHOPPED
1	TABLESPOON POWDERED CINNAMON
½	TEASPOON GROUND CLOVES
½	TEASPOON NUTMEG
1	TABLESPOON GROUND BLACK PEPPER
4	BAY LEAVES

3   SPRIGS THYME

3   SPRIGS MARJORAM

1½ CUPS DRY SHERRY OR WHITE WINE

FOR THE SAUCE

LEEKS AND ONIONS THAT TURKEY RESTED
UPON WHILE ROASTING

PAN DRIPPINGS FROM COOKED TURKEY

4   CUPS CHICKEN BROTH

3   TABLESPOONS CORNSTARCH, DISSOLVED IN
    1 CUP WATER

1   CUP DRY SHERRY

½   CUP BURNT SUGAR (MELT IN HEAVY
    SAUCEPAN 6-8 MINUTES TILL CARAMELIZED)

FOR THE GARNISH

4   FRESH POINSETTIA FLOWERS

2   BUNCHES OF GRAPES

2   EGG WHITES, BEATEN

    SUGAR TO TASTE

    CILANTRO

Prepare the turkey: Wash and pat turkey
dry. Mix together the white wine and
tequila and inject turkey, including breast,
legs and the inside cavity, with the liquor.
Set aside.

Prepare the marinade: In a blender or food
processor, purée the roasted and raw garlic,
thyme, marjoram, bay leaves, butter, olive
oil, allspice and salts. Spread this mixture
over the turkey, both outside and inside.
Carefully loosen the turkey's skin and spread
marinade beneath it. Then place the leeks
and onions on a turkey roaster or ovenproof
platter. Place turkey on the leeks and onion
and cover with a dishcloth soaked in milk.
Refrigerate for one day.

Prepare the stuffing: Heat the oil and butter
in a medium saucepan. Brown the garlic
cloves, then remove and discard. Add grated
onion and cook until brown. Add the meat
and cook until it begins to render its fat. Stir
in all the remaining stuffing ingredients and
simmer mixture for 1½ to 2 hours or until it
thickens. Stir regularly to avoid sticking.
Allow mixture to cool, then use to stuff the
turkey.

To cook the turkey: Preheat oven to 400°F.
Place the turkey, still on its bed of leeks and
onion, in a roasting pan. Bake turkey for ½
hour. Cover with aluminum foil and lower
heat to 375°F. Continue baking for another
4-5 hours, depending on the size of the
bird. Baste every 45 minutes and turn from
time to time to insure even cooking. During
the last 45 minutes of cooking, uncover
bird, and baste every 10 minutes to brown
evenly. Prick the legs to see if cooked —
juice should be transparent. When done,
remove from oven and allow to rest for 45
minutes before carving.

Prepare the sauce: Purée the leek and onion
along with pan drippings. Add the chicken
broth and strain mixture. Stir in cornstarch
dissolved in water, sherry and burnt sugar
and simmer for 25 minutes, or until the
mixture thickens slightly.

To serve: Place the baked turkey on a large
round serving platter. Decorate the edges
with poinsettias. Dip the grapes in beaten
egg whites, dredge in sugar and place over
the flowers. On the other sides, garnish
with cilantro. Carve the turkey at the table
just before serving. Serve the sauce on the
side. This dish is delicious with sweet
potatoes or Potato Torte. **SERVES 12-16.**

TURKEY ≈

*Cortez brought the turkey,
a native of Central
America, from Mexico to
Spain in 1519. Europeans
bred the turkey into such a
plump, docile bird that the
first pilgrims settling in
Massachusetts did not
recognize the wild turkey as
the same bird, and
imported domestic turkeys
from Europe.*

POTATO TORTE

TORTA DE PAPA

Potatoes were a favorite vegetable of my grandmother. I prefer the waxy red-skinned ones for this dish. It is a family tradition to serve a potato dish such as this one for Christmas. ~ MARGARITA

10 MEDIUM RED POTATOES

1½ CUP BUTTER

6 EGG YOLKS

1 TABLESPOON BAKING POWDER

2 CUPS PARMESAN CHEESE, GRATED

3 CUPS MILD CHEESE (GOUDA, MONTEREY JACK OR GRUYERE) OR A COMBINATION OF CHEESES

SALT TO TASTE

8 EGG WHITES

Preheat oven to 350°F. Peel the potatoes, and boil in water with a little salt until tender. When done, mash slightly or press through a coarse sieve and transfer to a bowl. Beat the butter until creamy. Gradually add to the potatoes, alternating with the egg yolks. Add the baking powder and beat for about 15 minutes or until light and fluffy. Then stir in cheeses and add salt to taste. In a separate bowl, beat the egg whites until soft peaks form. Fold the egg whites into the potato mixture.
Coat a large ring mold with butter and sprinkle with flour. Spoon potato mixture into mold and bake for 1 to 1½ hours or until golden brown and done. Test with a toothpick. If you prepare the ring ahead of time, reheat for 10 minutes in hot oven before serving. Unmold onto a serving platter. **SERVES 10.**

A GARNISH ≈

Garnish fettuccini with red chiles, lightly fried and tied into bundles with sprigs of cilantro, then sprinkle with chopped cilantro.

An optional garnish for the Potato Torte is shredded lettuce and thinly sliced purple onion. It is also delicious with Chiltomate Sauce (page 221).

FETTUCCINI WITH CILANTRO SAUCE

PASTA AL CILANTRO

Pasta was introduced to Mexico by the Italians in the mid-1800s. This recipe "Mexicanizes" it by the addition of native cilantro. ~ PATRICIA

FOR THE SAUCE

2 CUPS OLIVE OIL

16 GARLIC CLOVES, PEELED AND MINCED

12 TO 14 LARGE CHILES GUAJILLOS, WASHED, SEEDED AND DEVEINED AND CUT IN THIN STRIPS (SUBSTITUTE DRIED RED CHILES CALIFORNIA)

½ TABLESPOON FRESHLY GROUND BLACK PEPPER

SALT TO TASTE

POWDERED CHICKEN BOUILLON TO TASTE

1½ CUPS CILANTRO, CHOPPED

FOR THE PASTA

3 TO 4 QUARTS WATER

1 MEDIUM WHITE ONION

SALT TO TASTE

1 TABLESPOON VEGETABLE OIL

3⅓ POUNDS FETTUCCINI, CAPELLINI OR SPAGHETTI

1 CUP BUTTER, IN CHUNKS AT ROOM TEMPERATURE

1½ CUPS CILANTRO, FINELY CHOPPED

FOR THE GARNISH

½ CUP CHOPPED CILANTRO

Prepare the sauce: Heat the oil in a saucepan. Brown the chopped garlic until golden. Add the chile and cook 6-8 minutes or until it is soft. Season to taste with pepper, salt and powdered bouillon. Be careful when adding salt, since the oil will sizzle. Use salt sparingly. Just before removing from heat, add cilantro. Reheat just before serving the pasta.

Prepare the pasta: Bring the water to a boil in a large stockpot. Add onion, salt and oil. When the water comes to a rolling boil, add pasta. Depending on the freshness of the pasta, it will take between 4 and 12 minutes cooking time. Cook until tender but not mushy — al dente. Drain in a sieve. Transfer the drained pasta to a heated earthenware pot. At the very last moment before serving, gently fold in butter, cilantro and sauce. **SERVES 12-16.**

MARINATED PORK LEG WITH ALMONDS AND PRUNES

PIERNA DE PUERCO

I*n keeping with the ambiance of surprise that comes with Christmas, this recipe gives a new twist to fresh pork by the addition of prunes, almonds, and a Yucatecan sauce.* ~ PATRICIA

FOR THE PORK

6½ POUNDS PORK LEG

1 POUND HAM

1½ CUPS ALMONDS

2 CUPS PRUNES

2 TO 3 PURPLE ONIONS, PEELED AND SLICED THINLY

3 CUPS CHICKEN BROTH

FOR THE MARINADE

12 BLACK PEPPERCORNS

6 WHOLE CLOVES

1 CINNAMON STICK, ABOUT 4 INCHES LONG

12 OREGANO LEAVES

1 TABLESPOON CUMIN

1 TEASPOON CORIANDER

½ GARLIC HEAD, RAW, CLOVES PEELED

½ GARLIC HEAD, ROASTED, CLOVES PEELED

2 CUPS WHITE ONION, PEELED AND ROASTED, CHOPPED

2 CUPS WHITE ONION, PEELED AND THINLY SLICED

2 CUPS SEVILLE ORANGE JUICE OR 1 CUP GRAPEFRUIT JUICE, PLUS ½ CUP ORANGE JUICE AND ⅓ CUP LIME JUICE

½ TABLESPOON POWDERED CHICKEN BOUILLON OR SALT TO TASTE

1 CUP OLIVE OIL

Prepare the meat: Make little holes on the surface of the pork and stud with bits of ham, almonds and prunes. Place in a glass bowl or ovenproof baking dish, and reserve.

Prepare the marinade: Combine all the ingredients and purée in a molcajete, blender or food processor. The mixture should take on a paste-like consistency. Spread over the meat and allow to marinate in refrigerator for 1-2 days.

Bake the meat: Preheat oven to 350°F. Cover meat with purple onion slices and moisten with chicken broth. Then cover with aluminum foil and bake for 1 hour. Remove foil and bake for another 1½ hours or until done. Baste meat regularly with marinade and chicken broth. When tender and done, remove meat from oven and keep covered until serving time. This dish may also be served cold, in which case, chill the pork before serving. **SERVES 12-16.**

OAXACAN MEATBALLS IN CHILE TOMATO SAUCE

ALBONDIGAS ESTILO OAXACA

These are my grandmother's Oaxacan meatballs dressed up for a Christmas party. ~ MARGARITA

FOR THE MEATBALLS

1½ POUNDS GROUND BEEF AND VEAL MIXED TOGETHER

4 GARLIC CLOVES, PEELED AND PURÉED

½ MEDIUM WHITE ONION, PEELED AND CHOPPED

6 MEDIUM, RIPE TOMATILLOS, HUSKED AND CHOPPED

1 TABLESPOON BLACK PEPPER

1 TABLESPOON SALT OR TO TASTE

2 EGGS

3 SLICES WHOLE WHEAT BREAD SOAKED IN MILK

FOR THE SAUCE

⅓ CUP LARD OR VEGETABLE OIL

2 GARLIC CLOVES, PEELED

4 TO 5 LARGE, RIPE TOMATOES

3 GARLIC CLOVES, PEELED

1 MEDIUM WHITE ONION, PEELED AND QUARTERED

4 TO 5 CHILES MORITAS OR CHIPOTLES, WASHED, DRIED AND FRIED LIGHTLY IN A SMALL AMOUNT OF OIL

6 CHILES GUAJILLOS, WASHED, SEEDED AND DEVEINED, AND FRIED LIGHTLY IN A SMALL AMOUNT OF OIL (SUBSTITUTE DRIED RED NEW MEXICO OR CALIFORNIA CHILES)

1½ TABLESPOONS CORN MASA DISSOLVED IN 3-4 CUPS CHICKEN BROTH OR WATER

POWDERED BOUILLON OR SALT TO TASTE

Prepare the meatballs: Combine all the ingredients in a glass bowl. Allow to sit for 20 minutes. Then shape into 1-inch meatballs and set aside.

Prepare the sauce: Heat the lard in a heavy pot. Brown garlic cloves, then remove and discard. Combine the tomatoes, garlic, onion and chiles in a blender or food processor and blend. Strain the mixture, then add to the pot and simmer for 40 minutes or until the sauce releases its fat. Add the corn masa dissolved in the chicken broth and season to taste with bouillon or salt. Add the meatballs to the sauce and simmer an additional 20-30 minutes.

To serve: Serve meatballs in the chile tomato sauce directly from the cooking pot, if using a cazuela. Accompany with white rice or beans and corn tortillas. The meatballs can be used to make tacos or eaten as a main course. For a formal presentation, make tortilla baskets by frying tortillas in a sieve. Spoon meatballs into tortilla baskets on individual plates, decorating with a ribbon of sauce and parsley leaves. **SERVES 8.**

MEXICAN MEATBALLS

≈

Mexican meatballs can be seasoned with various herbs, including spearmint.

Try meatballs as a buffet dish or hot cocktail hors d'oeuvre. Vary their size to suit the occasion and serve from a chafing dish filled with heated sauce.

Cook meatballs in beef broth and use them to stuff tacos. Garnish with Tomatillo-Chipotle Salsa (page 115).

Wrap portions of meatball mixture around halves of hard-cooked egg before cooking them.

OAXACAN MEATBALLS IN CHILE TOMATO SAUCE, SERVED IN A TORTILLA BASKET.

CODFISH WITH POTATOES, OLIVES AND CHILES

BACALAO A LA VIZCAINA

CODFISH WITH POTATOES,
OLIVES AND CHILES,
SERVED WITH A GARNISH
OF CHILES, OLIVES, AND
PARSLEY. THE STEW MAY
ALSO BE SERVED WITH
RICE, FRIED OR FRESH
TORTILLAS, OR BOLILLOS.

*T*he Spanish carried salted, dried cod to
sustain them on their expeditions in the
16th century, and perhaps it was
homesick Spanish sailors who first made
it a traditional Christmas dish in
Mexico. In this classic dish, New World
ingredients — chiles, potatoes and
tomatoes — are combined with codfish in
a superbly flavored spicy fish stew. It is
traditionally served the day after
Christmas. ~ MAGO

FOR THE FISH

4   GENEROUS POUNDS DRIED CODFISH,
     SOAKED OVERNIGHT IN WATER CHANGED 3
     OR 4 TIMES (FRESH POACHED FIRM-
     FLESHED WHITE FISH MAY BE
     SUBSTITUTED; IF SO, DO NOT SOAK)

12   CUPS MILK

FOR THE SAUCE

1   TO 1½ QUARTS OLIVE OIL

20   CLOVES GARLIC, MEDIUM, PEELED

4½   LARGE WHITE ONIONS, PEELED AND FINELY
     CHOPPED

15   LARGE RIPE TOMATOES, ROASTED

1½   MEDIUM WHITE ONIONS, PEELED AND
     QUARTERED

EL ATOLE

3   CUPS WATER

½   POUND FRESH CORN MASA DOUGH OR MASA PREPARED FROM MASA
    HARINA (1 CUP)

5   CUPS MILK

2   TABLESPOONS CORNSTARCH

2   ORANGE LEAVES (OPTIONAL)

3   CINNAMON STICKS, EACH 4 INCHES LONG

1½ CUPS SUGAR OR TO TASTE

Dissolve the masa dough in 1 cup water. Strain the mixture through cheesecloth and transfer to a medium saucepan. Cook about 15 minutes. Add remaining water, milk, cornstarch, orange leaves and cinnamon and cook, stirring regularly with a wooden spoon, till thick, about 30 minutes. When the mixture has thickened, remove from heat and add sugar. Return to heat to melt sugar and cook until the atole is the consistency of heavy cream. If too thick, add milk to achieve preferred consistency. Remove orange leaves and cinnamon stick and serve hot in clay mugs. If desired, add fresh fruit just before serving. SERVES 12.

ATOLE ≈

The indispensable atole (ah TOE leh) is a hot beverage made with ground corn, or masa. It is prepared with milk or water, sweetened with refined sugar or piloncillo, and flavored with cinnamon, fruit, almonds or chocolate. It is served with breakfast, dinner, or as a snack, and is always served with the traditional King's Cake on All Kings Day. Atole has the consistency of heavy cream.

---

6   GARLIC CLOVES, PEELED

     A PINCH OF SALT

2   CUPS PARSLEY, FINELY CHOPPED

1½   POUNDS BABY POTATOES, BOILED AND
     PEELED

2   CUPS OLIVES, STUFFED WITH PIMIENTO

½   CAN PICKLED CHILES GÜEROS OR CANNED
     JALAPEÑOS OR OTHER HOT PEPPERS
     (8 OUNCES)

FOR THE GARNISH

8   OUNCES CANNED RED PIMIENTO

1   CAN PICKLED CHILES GÜEROS
     (8 OUNCES)

1   CUP OLIVES, STUFFED WITH PIMIENTO

¾   CUP PARSLEY, FINELY CHOPPED

Prepare the fish: After soaking the fish, drain, reserving the water. Soak the fish in the milk for about 2 hours. Then remove fish and clean, discarding skin and bones. Finely shred the fish and set aside.

Prepare the sauce: Heat the oil in a saucepan. Brown the garlic in oil, then remove and reserve. Add onion to oil and brown lightly. In a blender or food processor, place the roasted tomatoes, raw white onion, garlic and reserved fried garlic cloves. Purée well, then strain. Add strained mixture to hot oil (with browned onion) and simmer for about 2-3½ hours, or until it thickens and has a caramelized aroma. Rectify seasoning, being careful not to oversalt. Add parsley, shredded fish, boiled potatoes, olives and chiles güeros, with a little chile juice. Simmer mixture for another hour. This dish is even more delicious reheated. SERVES 8-12.

TO SOAK SALT COD ≈

Immerse the pieces of washed salt-cured codfish in clean, cold water and allow to soak for a minimum of 24 hours, changing the water three or four times. This will remove the saltiness from the fish. Then continue with your recipe as indicated.

EMILIA'S COOKIES

GALLETAS ESTILO EMILIA

My grandmother prepared for each Christmas with a wide variety of special, homemade cookies. These were, by far, my favorite. They melt in your mouth. They are even more delicious when prepared with homemade blackberry preserves (page 195). ~ EMILIA

1½ CUPS BUTTER, AT ROOM TEMPERATURE

⅓ CUP SUGAR

3 CUPS ALL-PURPOSE FLOUR

1½ TEASPOONS VANILLA EXTRACT

4 EGG YOLKS

4 TO 5 EGG WHITES

½ TO ¾ CUP SUGAR

THE JUICE OF 1 LIME

2½ CUPS BLACKBERRY OR APRICOT PRESERVES

½ CUP GRAN MARNIER

½ CUP CONFECTIONERS' SUGAR

¾ CUP CHOPPED WALNUTS

With an electric beater mix the butter, sugar and flour until well blended. Then add the vanilla and egg yolks and mix with the fingers until you can shape a large ball. Knead the dough for about 4 minutes, then sprinkle with flour, and refrigerate for 30 minutes to an hour.

Meanwhile, preheat oven to 350°F. and grease 2 baking trays. Beat the egg whites until stiff. Lower speed and gradually add sugar and lime juice and beat for 1 minute until mixture is shiny.

On an extended, floured surface, roll out the dough. Transfer to a buttered baking tray, and continue to roll out until very thin. Beat the preserves and liqueur together, then spread over the extended dough. Cover with the egg white mixture, and sprinkle with confectioners' sugar and chopped nuts. Bake in preheated oven for 45 minutes to 1½ hours (depending on the oven), or until the egg whites are golden brown and crisp, the dry texture of meringue, and the pastry is fully baked. Remove from oven and allow to cool, then cut into squares. **MAKES APPROXIMATELY 2½ DOZEN COOKIES.**

SESAME-SEED CANDY

PEPITORIA DE LA HUASTECA

We used to make this sweet on the Chapopote ranch, where we served it in baskets layered with banana leaves. ~ PATRICIA

2 CUPS WATER

2 GENEROUS POUNDS DARK PILONCILLO OR DARK BROWN SUGAR

1⅓ POUNDS SESAME SEED, CLEANED AND LIGHTLY TOASTED

OIL OR BUTTER

Place the water in a copper or enamel pot. Add the piloncillo and simmer until the mixture forms a heavy syrup. Test by placing a drop of the syrup in a glass of cold water. It will form a ball when ready. Remove from heat and stir in sesame seeds. Line a baking tray with banana leaves or grease it well with oil or butter. Place by the tablespoonful onto prepared tray and allow to cool at room temperature. When the candy has hardened, arrange on a serving platter decorated with a banana leaf (optional). **SERVES 8.**

SESAME SEEDS ≈

The tiny cream-colored seeds of SESANMUM INDICUM *has a mild pleasant flavor intensified by toasting. It is rich in polyunsaturated oil. The sesame plant is a native of Central Asia. Toast seeds quickly in an open skillet over moderate heat or in a moderate oven in a single layer for 10-15 minutes.*

CHRISTMAS PUNCH

PONCHE NAVIDEÑO

Hot *fruit punch is always associated with* POSADAS *and Christmas festivities. If the tropical tejocotes and guavas are not available, substitute the fruit of your choice. Hibiscus flowers impart a lovely red color to the punch along with a slightly dry, pleasant taste. If you cannot get them, rose petals will color your punch.* ~ MARGARITA

- **6** QUARTS WATER
- **1** CUP PRUNES, PITTED AND CHOPPED
- **2¼** POUNDS TEJOCOTES OR DRIED APRICOTS, WASHED AND OPENED SLIGHTLY WITH A CROSS CUT
- **16** GUAVAS, CUT IN QUARTERS
- **1½** CUPS HIBISCUS FLOWERS, WASHED (SOLD DRY IN MEXICAN MARKETS)
- **6** SUGAR CANE STICKS, PEELED AND CUT INTO QUARTERS
- **1** BOTTLE WHITE WINE
- **2** PILONCILLO CONES OR TO TASTE (SUBSTITUTE **2** CUPS DARK BROWN SUGAR)
- **2** CUPS APPLES, CHOPPED
- **2** CUPS PEARS, SEMI-RIPE, CHOPPED
- **½** CUP RAISINS
- **2** ORANGES, EACH SPIKED WITH **10** WHOLE CLOVES
- **4** CINNAMON STICKS, **6** INCHES LONG
- **2** CUPS LIGHT OR DARK RUM TO TASTE

Place the water in a large saucepan or stockpot. Add the prunes and tejocotes and cook for about 20 minutes or until the fruit softens. Then add the guava, hibiscus flower, sugar cane, white wine, piloncillo, apples, pears, raisins, oranges and cinnamon sticks. Simmer for 1 hour. Serve punch hot, being sure to ladle fruit into each mug. Add rum at the last minute. **SERVES 16.**

CHRISTMAS PUNCH.

ALMOND-PUMPKIN SEED CANDY

QUESO DE ALMENDRA Y PEPITA

When we traveled through the state of San Luis Potosi, we always stopped to buy almond-pumpkin seed candy which my grandmother Margarita would bring to all my aunts and uncles in Monterrey, particularly around Christmastime. Very rich paste-like candies such as this suggest the influence of the Spanish nuns of the colonial period, who in turn had been influenced by the Arab taste for such sweets. ~ MAGO

FOR THE ALMOND CANDY

2 CUPS WATER

4 CUPS SUGAR MINUS 2 TABLESPOONS

1 CINNAMON STICK, 6 INCHES LONG

12 EGG YOLKS, BEATEN

½ POUND ALMONDS, BLANCHED, SOAKED OVERNIGHT AND GROUND

FOR THE PUMPKIN SEED CANDY

4 CUPS SUGAR MINUS 2 TABLESPOONS

2 CUPS WATER

12 EGG YOLKS, BEATEN

1 POUND HULLED, TOASTED PUMPKIN SEEDS, GROUND

FOR THE GARNISH

CONFECTIONERS' SUGAR, TO TASTE

Prepare the almond candy: Line a 9 x 9-inch cake tin with waxed paper and butter the paper. Place water and sugar in a medium saucepan. Stir with a wooden spoon to dissolve, then add the cinnamon stick. Cook over medium heat until the syrup reaches the hard ball stage (250°-266°F.). Allow to cool and then return to the heat. Gradually pour syrup into beaten egg yolks. Return to saucepan. Add ground almonds and simmer until you can see the bottom of the pan when the mixture is separated with a spoon. Allow to cool a little. Then process until creamy in a food processor. Spread the almond candy in the prepared cake tin.

Prepare the pumpkin seed candy: Repeat the same procedure used for the almond candy, substituting pumpkin seeds for almonds and omitting cinnamon. Once the syrup is cool and has been processed in a food processor, spread over the almond candy.

Place the cake tin in a large pan filled with hot water to unmold. Unmold the candy on a serving platter, then garnish with the powdered sugar. Cut into wedges. **SERVES 8.**

CANDIED WALNUTS

NUECES GARAPIÑADAS

Wonderful walnuts grow high in the mountains of Monterrey. They are coated with a scented sugary glaze in this Christmas sweet. ~ MARGARITA

2 CUPS WALNUTS

1¾ CUPS SUGAR

1 TEASPOON INSTANT COFFEE

¼ TEASPOON POWDERED CINNAMON

BUTTER

Heat a heavy skillet over high heat. Add the walnuts, sugar, water, instant coffee and cinnamon and reduce heat. Stir constantly, simmering ingredients until the sugar is melted and has evenly coated the nuts. The sugar should take on a brown color.

Butter a glass baking dish. Drop the candy on the prepared surface by the teaspoonful. Once the candy has hardened, peel off carefully and arrange on a platter. Serve as a snack, to accompany coffee or tea, or as a light dessert. **SERVES 8.**

PINE NUT BALLS

BOLITAS DE PIÑON

This is a perfect candy to toast with at a Christmas Eve dinner party. The combination of pine nuts and almonds makes a very elegant sweet. ~ EMILIA

4 CUPS SUGAR

2½ CUPS WATER

2½ CUPS PINE NUTS, GROUND

2 CUPS ALMONDS, BLANCHED AND GROUND

10 EGG YOLKS

⅓ CUP SHERRY

CONFECTIONERS' SUGAR OR SUGAR TO TASTE

Place the sugar and water in a medium saucepan, preferably a copper pot. Cook until it reaches the soft ball stage (234°-240°F.). Then remove from heat and allow to cool briefly. Combine ground pine nuts, almonds and egg yolks. Then add to syrup and return to heat. Cook until you can see the bottom of the pot when you separate mixture with a spoon. Remove from heat, add sherry and allow to cool until the mixture can be formed into balls. Shape 1-1 ½ inch balls and then roll in confectioners' sugar or sugar. (If desired, stamp balls with a mold.) Arrange in petit four paper cups on a serving dish or in a basket and serve with a glass of wine or champagne. You may also wrap the candies in tissue paper and tie with ribbons, or twist paper ends shut. **MAKES 60 CANDIES.**

RAISIN AND NUT CAKE

PASTEL CON PASITAS Y NUEZ

In Mexico, most cakes are made with almonds; the influence of my family's international background calls for the use of raisins and nuts instead. My mother used to make this cake for Christmas. It is perfect with a cup of coffee or tea at twilight after a day of bustling holiday activity. ~ PATRICIA

FOR THE CAKE

1¼	CUP BUTTER, AT ROOM TEMPERATURE
¾	CUP SUGAR + 1 TABLESPOON
¾	CUP PILONCILLO, GRATED, + 1 TABLESPOON OR BROWN SUGAR
6	EGG YOLKS
1½	CUPS FLOUR, SIFTED TWICE
1½	CUPS WHOLE WHEAT FLOUR
1½	TEASPOONS CINNAMON
1½	TEASPOONS GROUND CLOVES
1½	CUPS WALNUTS, CHOPPED COARSELY
2	CUPS RAISINS
½	CUP RUM
6	EGG WHITES

FOR THE GARNISH

CONFECTIONERS' SUGAR TO TASTE

Preheat oven to 350°F. Butter and flour a 10-inch ring mold or a loaf pan.

With an electric beater, beat the butter for 8 minutes. Gradually add the sugar and piloncillo and beat for another 8 minutes until soft and fluffy. Add the egg yolks, flours, cinnamon and cloves, alternating eggs and dry ingredients. Once the ingredients are well mixed, add the nuts and raisins with rum and beat for 6 minutes.

In a separate bowl, beat the egg whites until they form soft peaks. Fold into the cake batter. Spoon batter into the prepared baking pan and bake in preheated oven for 45 minutes to one hour, or until done (test with a toothpick). Remove from oven and cool on a rack for 20 minutes. Then unmold. Sprinkle with confectioners' sugar.

BAKED PLANTAINS

PASTEL DE PLÁTANO MACHO

My grandmother made this dish using the abundant plantains of our Veracruz ranch, near Tierra Blanca. She learned to prepare baked plantains from her mother, Emilia. Although the plantains are no longer picked fresh from the tree since we all live in the capital, it is still delicious! ~ MARGARITA

FOR THE PRUNE FILLING

6	CUPS PRUNES, PITTED
1	CUP SUGAR
1	CUP ORANGE JUICE
1½	CUPS DRY SHERRY
1½	TABLESPOON POWDERED CINNAMON
½	TEASPOON GROUND CLOVES

FOR THE PLANTAINS

4	CUPS VEGETABLE OIL
10	PLANTAINS, RIPE (ALMOST BLACK) SLICED LENGTHWISE INTO ¼-INCH THICK STRIPS
	SUGAR FOR SPRINKLING
2	EGGS, BEATEN

PLANTAINS

≈

Many varieties of bananas are sold in Mexican markets. The plantain distinguishes itself as a banana for cooking. Compared to its yellow cousin, much more common in the U.S., it is thicker, coarser, and larger. Fully ripe, it darkens to brownish-black. Ripening may take several days. After ripening at room temperature, you may refrigerate for several days. Plantains may be fried, boiled or baked, sliced or whole; for easy slicing, slice with the skin still on, then remove it before frying. Their pleasant flavor marries well with that of meat, especially pork. A fried plantain has a dense, almost bread-like texture and a clean, not-too-sweet flavor that is wonderful with breakfast or lunch dishes too. You may also slice into thin rounds and deep-fry for "chips." For a superb, low-fat version of cooked plantains, charbroil very ripe plantains, still in their skins, over an outdoor grill, peel and serve along with barbequed meats or poultry.

FOR THE GARNISH

1½ CUPS HEAVY WHIPPING CREAM, FROZEN
FOR ½ HOUR

1½ CUPS CRÈME FRAÎCHE OR LIGHT SOUR
CREAM, FROZEN FOR ½ HOUR

½ CUP SUGAR OR TO TASTE

1 TABLESPOON VANILLA

2 CUPS FRESH COCONUT, GRATED FINELY

Prepare the prune filling: Place the pitted prunes in a glass bowl. Add the sugar, orange juice, sherry, cinnamon and cloves and mix together until the ingredients resemble a heavy marmalade. Set aside.

Prepare the plantains: Heat the oil in a large skillet. Fry the plantain strips until golden brown. Remove and drain on several layers of paper towels. Place a layer of fried plantains in a buttered 8-inch round cake pan lined with buttered waxed paper. Sprinkle with a little sugar and beaten egg and cover with a layer of prune filling. Repeat a second layer of plantains, beaten egg, sugar and prune filling until all ingredients are used. Bake in a preheated oven (350°F.) for 45 minutes or until a toothpick inserted in the dish comes out clean. Cook for 45 minutes.

Meanwhile prepare the garnish: Mix together the frozen creams and beat until they form peaks. Then add the sugar and vanilla. When the plantain dish is cool, unmold on a serving platter. Garnish with shredded coconut and cream and serve the cream on the side. **SERVES 8.**

PIGGY COOKIES

PUERQUITOS

Puerquitos, *translated as "little piggies," are a crisp, caramel-flavored cookie typical of Mexico. Lorenza Caraza taught me how to prepare this wonderful recipe. ~ Patricia*

3½ CUPS ALL-PURPOSE FLOUR

½ TEASPOON SALT

1½ TEASPOONS BAKING SODA

1½ CUPS LARD OR VEGETABLE SHORTENING

3 MEDIUM EGGS

1½ PILONCILLO CONES OR 1½ CUPS DARK
BROWN SUGAR

1 CUP WATER

1 CINNAMON STICK, ABOUT 2½ INCHES
LONG

4 EGG WHITES

Prepare the cookies: Sift the flour with the salt and soda. Place in a medium mixing bowl and add lard or vegetable shortening. Work the lard into the flour with your fingers. Add the eggs. In a saucepan, combine the piloncillo, water, cinnamon stick and egg whites. Cook until the mixture forms a syrup. Let cool, then add to batter, kneading until the mixture forms a smooth dough. If the dough is too sticky, add flour.

Refrigerate dough for 1½ hours. Preheat oven to 350°F. Butter two baking trays. Remove dough from refrigerator and roll out on a floured surface, until the dough is ¼ inch thick. Cut cookies with a cookie cutter in the shape of a little pig (or any favorite cookie cutter). With the help of a spatula, place on prepared baking sheets. Bake for 20-25 minutes or until golden brown. Remove from oven and allow to cool.
MAKES ABOUT 2 DOZEN COOKIES.

≈ *Circling the Family* ≈

WEDDINGS
AND BIRTHDAYS

BODAS Y CUMPLEAÑOS

I n Mexico, as throughout the world, the bonding of two lovers is celebrated by *"echando la casa por la ventana,"* or — literally — "throwing the house out the window." The open-handedness associated with the feast is evidenced from the moment the suitor presents himself to the parents of the bride. When his petition is accepted, a family toast is made. Soon after, thoughts turn to planning the viands and sweets to delight the guests at the wedding feast, whether it will occur in a grand hall or — as most often — in the parental home of the bride or the groom.

If the wedding takes place in a hacienda in the center of the Republic, it may preserve the flavor of rural Mexico, expressed with an aristocratic

ALMOND WEDDING CAKE, DECORATED WITH WHITE
CHOCOLATE LEAVES.

touch, as the bride and groom dress in turn-of-the-century costumes, he as a *charro,* a Mexican cowboy of the past, and she as an *adelita* or *soldadera,* a brave camp follower or female soldier of the revolution. The bride travels from her parental home to the church in a carriage festooned with flowers, and the groom is mounted on horseback on a silver saddle.

CHOCOLATE LEAVES ≈

Any waxy leaf can serve as the mold for dark or white chocolate leaves. The chocolate is melted, tempered by beating, then brushed over the leaf. When the chocolate has cooled and hardened, the leaf is gently peeled away.

When they arrive at the hacienda, the courtyard is aflutter with decoratively cut colored tissue paper, like flocks of exotic birds moving in the breeze. In place of the family escutcheon hangs a heart-shaped wreath of gardenias with the initials of the bridal pair.

Now comes the chief delight, the wedding feast, whose aromas, colors and flavors are a just celebration of love, both in the flesh and in the spirit. Guests will partake of a puebla-style mole, a *zacahuil* (a six-foot tamal), scented broth, cactus paddles, white, red, green or yellow rice, roasted meats, savory beans, mocajetes filled with fresh salsas, dark and light beers on tap, tequila, mexcal, pulque, and charanda, and the wedding cake, sliced to the joyous accompaniment of mariachi music, laughter and shouts of VIVA! for the bridal pair.

Likewise, the pulsing of the big guitar, the cry of the trumpet, the sweet strains of the violin, and the wild sweetness of the singing voices will break the silence of the dawn with *Las Mañanitas* to announce the beginning of a birthday celebration. Snatched from sleep, the celebrated one comes to the window, surprised and moved, to receive the affectionate homage.

Of course, there is no limit to the choice of food for the birthday dinner. The menu is planned with consideration for the tastes and preferences of the guest of honor, who may prefer stuffed chiles, pickled meats, torte de tamal or roast leg of pork, to be accompanied by Mexican table wines.

The happy commotion that surrounds the conjugal event and the birthday observation is the music of the private fiesta, a constant in the life of Mexico. Like the daily feast that appears on every table, low or high, it is the natural and sustaining accompaniment to the circling of the family.

ALMOND WEDDING CAKE

PASTEL DE ALMENDRA DE BODA

Since almonds symbolize the seed from which happiness grows, an almond cake is perfect for a wedding. Dress up the cake with white chocolate leaves.

FOR THE CAKE BATTER

- 12 EGG YOLKS
- 1½ CUPS SUGAR
- 1 CUP BUTTER, MELTED, STILL WARM
- 3 CUPS ALMONDS, PEELED AND GROUND
- ¾ CUP CONFECTIONERS' SUGAR
- 12 EGG WHITES
- PINCH OF SALT
- ¾ CUP FLOUR, SIFTED
- 1 TABLESPOON VANILLA
- 1 TEASPOON ALMOND EXTRACT

FOR THE RUM SYRUP

- 2 CUPS SUGAR
- 1½ CUPS WATER
- 1½ CUPS RUM

FOR THE BUTTERCREAM FROSTING

- 12 EGG YOLKS
- 1¼ CUPS SUGAR
- ⅔ CUP WATER
- 2 CUPS BUTTER
- 1 TEASPOON ALMOND EXTRACT

FOR THE ALMOND PASTE

- 2 CUPS ALMONDS
- 2½ CUPS CONFECTIONERS' SUGAR
- 2 SMALL EGG WHITES, BEATEN LIGHTLY
- ½ TEASPOON ALMOND EXTRACT

FOR THE CHOCOLATE LEAVES

- 3⅓ POUNDS WHITE CHOCOLATE, GRATED
- 30 TO 50 CAMELLIA LEAVES OR OTHER WAXY, NON-POISONOUS LEAVES
- CONFECTIONERS' SUGAR

Prepare the batter: Preheat oven to 350°F. Butter and flour two 9-inch square or round cake molds. Line with waxed paper cut to fit bottoms and butter paper. Beat the egg yolks and sugar together until they are a lemony color and have doubled in volume. Add the melted butter while it is still hot and continue beating until mixture thickens. Pulverize the almonds with the confectioners' sugar until they combine in a fine powder. Gradually add almond-sugar powder to the egg-sugar-butter mixture and beat until blended well. In a separate bowl, beat the egg whites with a pinch of salt until soft peaks form. Gently fold 4 tablespoons of beaten egg whites into the egg-sugar-butter mixture by hand. Then fold in flour, vanilla and almond extract. Fold in remaining beaten egg whites. Spoon batter into prepared cake molds and bake in preheated oven for 45 minutes or until golden brown. Remove from oven and unmold.

Prepare the rum syrup: In a medium saucepan, combine the sugar, water and 1 cup rum. Cook for 8 minutes on medium heat and then remove from heat and add remaining rum. While syrup is warm, brush generously over tops and sides of the unmolded cakes.

SIMPLE SYRUP ≈

Brown sugar, white sugar or piloncillo can be used to make a flavored syrup for cakes, stewed fruits, fritters, or other desserts. For thickest syrup use one part sugar to one part water, for medium syrup 2 parts water, and for thin syrup 1 part water. Combine in a heavy saucepan, bring to a boil, stirring, and cook until all the sugar is dissolved, approximately 5 minutes. Flavor with the addition of sherry, fruits, rum, cinnamon sticks, cloves, anise seed, or other ingredients.

Prepare the buttercream frosting: Beat the egg yolks well. In a small saucepan, combine the sugar and water and cook until the syrup reaches the soft ball stage (234°-240°F.). Gradually add syrup to the egg yolks and beat until the mixture cools. Gradually add butter and almond extract. Set aside. If your kitchen is very warm, refrigerate frosting.

Prepare the almond paste: Place almonds in a medium saucepan. Cover with water and boil for 10 minutes. Allow to cool, then remove skins. Dry on a baking tray for 10 minutes. (If you are using blanched almonds, omit this step.) Grind in a food processor or spice mill along with the confectioners' sugar until the mixture forms a thick paste. Add egg whites and spread paste on wax paper sprinkled with confectioners' sugar. Shape into a square or circle.

Make the chocolate leaves: Melt chocolate in a double boiler, stirring constantly. Remove pan from heat when chocolate has melted, and beat until chocolate is shiny, about 8 minutes. Brush the underside of each leaf with a thin layer of chocolate, shaking to remove excess. Place on a baking sheet to harden. Harden at room temperature or in the refrigerator for 2 hours. Peel the leaves gently away from the chocolate, leaving behind the chocolate leaves.

Assemble the cake: Place one cake on a serving plate. Spread a layer of buttercream frosting over top and sides of cake. Top with the other cake, then frost top and sides. Sprinkle with confectioners' sugar. Invert circle of almond paste over cake, then peel off wax paper. Cover almond paste with a thin layer of remaining buttercream. Garnish with overlapping white chocolate leaves around edges to form a flower. Sprinkle with powdered sugar. **SERVES 12-16.**

ORANGES ≈

The three basic orange types are eating oranges, juice oranges and bitter oranges. Bitter oranges such as the Seville, known as NARANJA AGRIA, *or sour orange, in Mexico, are best for marmalade and some sauces and are often used in Yucatecan cooking. Seville oranges are also used in making liqueurs such as Cointreau, Grand Mariner, Triple Sec and curaçao. The oranges grown in Monterrey are sweet and large, similar to navel oranges.*

STUFFED CORNISH HENS IN ORANGE SAUCE

GALLINITAS RELLENAS DE ARROZ DE LOS ABUELOS CON SALSA DE NARANJA

When *my mother traveled to Monterrey to visit my Aunt and Uncle Fernández every year, she used to look forward to this succulent dish, made with the large, sweet, seedless oranges grown in the area. The recipe hints at the Sephardic Jewish influence that is present in Monterrey regional cooking.* ~ MAGO

FOR THE CORNISH HENS

6 CORNISH HENS, ABOUT ½ POUND EACH

6 GARLIC CLOVES, PEELED AND PURÉED

1½ MEDIUM WHITE ONIONS, PEELED AND GRATED

1 TABLESPOON FRESHLY GROUND BLACK PEPPER

1 TABLESPOON GROUND CINNAMON

½ TEASPOON GROUND CLOVES

1½ TABLESPOONS POWDERED BOUILLON OR SALT

1½ CUPS ORANGE JUICE

1½ CUPS TANGERINE JUICE

⅓ CUP OLIVE OIL

½ CUP BUTTER, AT ROOM TEMPERATURE

3 CUPS COOKED RICE, PREPARED WITH ALMONDS, RAISINS AND PINE NUTS

⅓ CUP BUTTER, CUT IN PIECES

FOR THE SAUCE

4 TABLESPOONS BUTTER

1 MEDIUM WHITE ONION, PEELED AND GRATED

1   TEASPOON FRESHLY GROUND BLACK PEPPER

1   CINNAMON STICK, ABOUT 4 INCHES LONG

6   WHOLE CLOVES

6   WHOLE ALLSPICE

3   BAY LEAVES

6   CUPS ORANGE JUICE

2   CUPS TANGERINE JUICE

2   CUPS CHICKEN BROTH, REDUCED TO ⅔ CUP

1   CUP PILONCILLO OR BROWN SUGAR
      SALT TO TASTE

1½ TO 2 TABLESPOONS CORNSTARCH, DISSOLVED IN ½ CUP WATER OR BROTH

8   TABLESPOONS BUTTER

FOR THE GARNISH

4   ORANGE PEELS, FRUIT REMOVED AND PEELS CUT INTO "BASKETS"

4   ORANGES, PEELED AND SECTIONED

½   CUP ALMONDS, BLANCHED AND SLICED ON THE DIAGONAL

2   BUNCHES SPEARMINT

4   CUPS COOKED RICE, PREPARED WITH ALMONDS, RAISINS AND PINE NUTS

Prepare the Cornish hens: Place the hens in a large glass bowl. Add garlic, onion, pepper, cinnamon, cloves, bouillon, orange juice, tangerine juice, olive oil and butter. Marinate a minimum of 4 hours at room temperature, or in the refrigerator. Stuff the marinated hens with the prepared rice. Preheat oven to 450°F. Butter a baking tray. Place the hens on the baking tray and spoon remaining marinade over them. Scatter pieces of butter over hens and bake in preheated oven for about ½ hour. Then lower heat to 350°F. and continue baking hens for another half hour or until crispy, basting occasionally. When hens are done, remove from oven and cover with aluminum foil, allowing to set for about 20 minutes. Remove the pan drippings.

Prepare the sauce: Place pan drippings in a saucepan. Add butter, onion, pepper, cinnamon stick, cloves, allspice, bay leaves, orange and tangerine juices, chicken broth, piloncillo and salt. Stir well, then simmer to reduce to half. Add the cornstarch, dissolved in water or broth, and simmer sauce until it thickens and becomes translucent. Stir in the butter. Keep the sauce hot until serving time in a double boiler.

To serve: Arrange the hens on a large serving platter. Drench with sauce. If necessary, reheat hens in a hot oven, covering them with aluminum foil so that they will not dry out. Serve rice on the side. Garnish with orange baskets, filled with orange sections and decorated with almonds and spearmint sprigs. Spoon additional sauce over hens just before serving. Serve remaining sauce on the side. SERVES 12.

≈

Nardos are as essential to Mexican weddings as are orange blossoms to traditional weddings in North America. Their distinctive perfume fills the festooned aisles of churches prepared for weddings. In addition to the wedding ring, the groom at a traditional Mexican wedding gives to his bride a handful of gold coins signifying that, throughout life's vicissitudes, their fortunes are joined together.

≈

Chocolate Bags may be made in any size. Use sweet, bittersweet or white chocolate and fill with any treat from scoops of ice cream to candies or small cakes.

CHOCOLATE BAGS

BOLSAS DE CHOCOLATE

"*P*aper sacks" *made of chocolate are a delightful surprise for a party table. The bag may be made with any type of chocolate, including white chocolate. If it is to be used only for decoration, you may coat it with chocolate once, and leave the paper sack in place on the inside. If you wish to eat the bag, coat three times with chocolate and remove the paper sack from the inside.* ~ PATRICIA

10	OUNCES BITTERSWEET CHOCOLATE, GRATED
10	OUNCES SEMI-SWEET CHOCOLATE, GRATED
1	PAPER BAG, 5 BY 7 INCHES
2	LARGE EMPTY CANS

Prepare a double boiler, bringing water to a simmer. Melt the two chocolates together in the double boiler, stirring occasionally with a spoon. Remove from heat and beat vigorously to temper the chocolate. Open the bag and fill with two empty cans, to keep it in an upright position. Holding the bag from the inside, brush the outside with a complete coat of chocolate. Refrigerate. When the chocolate has hardened, brush with a second layer of chocolate, being careful to coat evenly (it will be necessary to melt remaining chocolate first and beat it to temper it again). Again refrigerate, and then apply a third coat of chocolate. When hardened, carefully remove cans and peel the paper bag away from the inside. Place on a serving dish and fill with chocolates, candies or fruit.

≈

*"How lovely is the morning
On which I come to greet you.
We have all come with pleasure,
Singing in your honor.*

*On the day of your birth
All the flowers were born
And at your baptism
The nightingales sang."*

FROM LAS MAÑANITAS (THE EARLY MORNINGS), A WELL-KNOWN BIRTHDAY SONG

LIME SOUP

SOPA DE LIMA ESTILO YUCATECO

This soup is typical of the Yucatán peninsula, where limes grow abundantly. The limes of Yucatán (CITRUS LIMETTA) are round and sweetish-tart in flavor rather than sour. ~ PATRICIA

FOR THE BROTH

6	QUARTS WATER
1	CHICKEN BREAST, WHOLE, WITH BONE, OR 2 SPLIT CHICKEN BREASTS
1	WHOLE STEWING CHICKEN
10	GIZZARDS, CLEANED
10	CHICKEN LIVERS, CLEANED
20	GARLIC CLOVES, PEELED
2	MEDIUM WHITE ONIONS, PEELED AND ROASTED
1	HEAD OF GARLIC, ROASTED
1	TABLESPOON FRESH OREGANO LEAVES
20	WHOLE ALLSPICE
2	TABLESPOONS SALT OR TO TASTE
2	LARGE LIMES OR LEMONS, LIGHTLY GRATED AND CUT OPEN WITH A CROSSCUT

FOR THE SOUP BASE

4	TABLESPOONS LARD OR VEGETABLE OIL
1½	CUPS FINELY CHOPPED GREEN ONIONS
6	GARLIC CLOVES, PEELED, ROASTED AND PURÉED
2	MEDIUM, RIPE TOMATOES, ROASTED, PURÉED AND STRAINED
	SALT TO TASTE
½	TEASPOON FRESHLY GROUND BLACK PEPPER OR TO TASTE

FOR THE GARNISH

20	THIN TORTILLAS
1	CUP VEGETABLE OIL
1½	CUP WHITE ONION, PEELED AND FINELY CHOPPED
¼	CUP FRESH CHILE HABANERO, CHILE SERRANO OR BANANA PEPPER, SEEDED, DEVEINED AND FINELY CHOPPED
20	LIME SLICES, CUT THINLY
½	CUP FRESH OREGANO LEAVES

Prepare the broth: Place the water in a medium saucepan. Add the chicken, gizzards, livers, garlic, roasted onion, roasted garlic, oregano, allspice and salt. Simmer ingredients for 25 minutes, then skim. Remove chicken breast and reserve. Add the limes and cook for an additional 25 minutes. Remove from heat and allow to cool. Then remove chicken, gizzards and livers. Chop gizzards and livers. Bone and shred stewing chicken and reserved chicken breast. Strain broth.

Prepare the soup base: Heat the lard in a medium saucepan. Brown the chopped onion and puréed garlic. Then add the strained tomato purée. Season to taste with salt and pepper and simmer for 20 minutes or until the mixture begins to thicken and release its fat. Stir in the strained broth and cook for 20 minutes more, rectifying seasoning.

Prepare the garnish: Cut the tortillas into thin strips. Heat the oil and fry the tortilla strips. Drain on paper towels.

To serve: Heat the soup. Add the shredded chicken and chopped gizzards and livers. Transfer to a soup tureen. Arrange the garnishes in individual bowls and serve on the side. Ladle the soup into individual soup bowls at the table. As each soup bowl is filled, squeeze in a drop or two of lime juice for the fragrance. **SERVES 10.**

≈

Another way to serve Lime Soup is to ladle it into warmed bowls containing crisp, lightly fried tortilla strips, then garnish with paper-thin slices of lime.

≈

The Yucatecan fruit used to make Lime Soup is not the Persian lime familiar to North American cooks, but a fruit called LIMA AGRIA, *or "sour lemon." To approximate its flavor you can use a combination of lime juice and lemon juice, or lime juice with a touch of grapefruit rind, or use the juice of common Persian or Key limes. All will result in a delicious soup.*

WHITE CEVICHE

CEVICHE BLANCO

*C*eviche *(seh VEE cheh) is one of the most common fish cocktails in Mexico, although it has its origins in Peru. It arrived in Mexico via Acapulco, where tomatoes were added to prepare red ceviche. My version is white, without tomatoes, but you may add them if desired, to make a colorful variation.* ~
PATRICIA

FOR THE FISH

2   GENEROUS POUNDS SIERRA OR RED SNAPPER, CUT IN 1X2 INCH PIECES

1½ CUPS CIDER OR WHITE WINE VINEGAR OR LIME JUICE

1¼ CUPS WATER

THE JUICE OF 6 LIMES OR BITTER ORANGES

2   MEDIUM WHITE ONIONS, PEELED AND PURÉED

4   GARLIC CLOVES, PEELED, ROASTED AND PURÉED

3   BAY LEAVES

1   SPRIG THYME

1   SPRIG MARJORAM

FOR THE SAUCE

12 BLACK PEPPERCORNS, CRUSHED

2   TABLESPOONS OREGANO

½ TABLESPOON THYME

5   FRESH CHILES SERRANOS OR 2 FRESH CHILES JALAPEÑOS WASHED, CHOPPED FINELY

½ TABLESPOON CORIANDER SEED

4   GARLIC CLOVES, PEELED

½ TABLESPOON CUMIN SEED

½ CINNAMON STICK, 2 INCHES LONG

1½ CUPS CORN OR OLIVE OIL

FOR THE GARNISH

1 GENEROUS POUND MUSHROOMS, WASHED AND SLICED

1½ CUPS CILANTRO, FINELY CHOPPED

½ CUP ITALIAN PARSLEY, FINELY CHOPPED

2 CUPS STUFFED OLIVES, FINELY CHOPPED

¾ CUP CAPERS

SALT TO TASTE

3 TABLESPOONS CILANTRO, FINELY CHOPPED

Prepare the fish: Place the fish in a large glass bowl. Add vinegar, water, lime juice, onion, garlic, bay leaf, thyme and marjoram. Marinate in refrigerator overnight or for a minimum of 12 hours.

Prepare the sauce: Place all the ingredients in a glass bowl. Mix well. Then pour over the fish. Three hours before serving, add the mushrooms, cilantro, parsley, olives and capers. Season with salt and pepper. Refrigerate.

To serve: Spoon the ceviche into individual bowls, cocktail cups, or halved, seeded avocados. Garnish with chopped cilantro and olives. Serve with a variety of crackers. **MAKES 16 LARGE SERVINGS.**

VARIATION

Add to the sauce 4 large ripe tomatoes, finely chopped, or 2 large ripe avocados, peeled and chopped.

ACHIOTE PASTE

PASTA DE ACHIOTE

The seed of the annatto tree (BIXA ORELLANA) *is customarily used in Yucatecan cooking. The beautiful dark red seed is used to color many dishes, and is also prepared in a paste to be added to meat, poultry and fish dishes. The paste is prepared with bitter orange, onion, garlic and other local ingredients such as fresh oregano, and steamed or cooked over an open fire to give it added flavor. You may find it at Hispanic grocery stores. Or, if you are able to obtain the seed, here is a recipe for the paste. Achiote, or annatto, paste will keep indefinitely in the refrigerator.*

1½ CUPS ANNATTO SEEDS

2 TO 3 CUPS SEVILLE ORANGE JUICE OR GRAPEFRUIT OR ORANGE JUICE WITH A SPLASH OF VINEGAR

3 MEDIUM HEADS OF GARLIC, PEELED AND ROASTED (ALMOST CHARRED)

2 MEDIUM WHITE ONIONS, PEELED AND ROASTED (ALMOST CHARRED)

2 TABLESPOONS GROUND BLACK PEPPER

1 TABLESPOON CUMIN SEED

1 CINNAMON STICK, ABOUT 3 INCHES LONG

1½ TABLESPOONS DRIED OREGANO LEAVES

SALT TO TASTE

Place the annatto seeds in a glass bowl. Add juice and allow to soak 1 hour to soften. Heat mixture until the seeds begin to dissolve. Transfer to a spice mill or processor and add remaining ingredients. Process to make a paste. If achiote paste is purchased ready-made, it may be mixed with additional spices to give it a better flavor. **MAKES 3 CUPS.**

ACHIOTE PASTE ≈

A typical use for Achiote Paste is to spread ¾ cup of the spicy red paste on 4 chicken breasts, drizzle with olive oil and cover with thinly sliced purple onion. Season to taste with salt and chicken broth and roast 30 minutes or until done in a moderate oven. Serve whole or shred chicken meat for a taco filling. Achiote Paste is also an interesting basting and marinating medium for pork, chicken or beef in preparation for the barbeque grill. See page 19 for a source for achiote.

ANNATTO COLOR ≈

The seed of the annatto tree is used as a safe commercial food coloring; it is commonly used to color cheddar cheese.

PICKLED CHILES STUFFED WITH GUACAMOLE

CHILES ANCHOS CURTIDOS RELLENOS DE GUACAMOLE

Chiles, piloncillo, garlic, onion, and avocados combine in this very unusual, exceptionally good appetizer. In Mexico the large elephant garlic is called MACHO *(meaning "male") garlic. Either elephant garlic or regular garlic may be used in the recipe.* ~ PATRICIA

"I have cut the flower of the avocado/ Mixed with parsley./ When the moon is tender/ I will ask you to marry me. . ."

FREE VERSE, SALMORAL (VERACRUZ), 1958, ORAL TRADITION

FOR THE CHILES

2 CUPS WHITE WINE VINEGAR

2 CUPS RED WINE VINEGAR

4 CUPS WATER

4 TO 5 PILONCILLO CONES (6½ OUNCES EACH), CUT IN PIECES OR 3-4 CUPS BROWN SUGAR, OR TO TASTE

⅓ CUP CORN OIL

⅓ CUP OLIVE OIL

   SALT TO TASTE

6 ELEPHANT GARLIC CLOVES (1 ELEPHANT GARLIC CLOVE IS ABOUT 4 TIMES THE SIZE OF A REGULAR GARLIC CLOVE, BUT HAS A SUBTLER FLAVOR), CUT INTO STRIPS OR 5 LARGE GARLIC HEADS, CUT IN THIN RINGS

5 MEDIUM WHITE ONIONS, PEELED AND SLICED THINLY

20 BAY LEAVES

20 SPRIGS THYME

2 TABLESPOONS BLACK PEPPER

2 TABLESPOONS WHOLE ALLSPICE

16 MEDIUM DRIED CHILES ANCHOS, WASHED, SLIT OPEN, SEEDED, AND DEVEINED (SUBSTITUTE LARGE DRIED RED CALIFORNIA CHILES)

FOR THE FILLING

5 RIPE AVOCADOS, PEELED AND FINELY CHOPPED

2 MEDIUM WHITE ONIONS, PEELED AND FINELY CHOPPED

¾ CUP FRESH CILANTRO, FINELY CHOPPED

3 FRESH SMALL CHILES SERRANOS OR 1 SMALL JALAPEÑO, FINELY CHOPPED

   THE JUICE OF 2 LIMES

   SALT TO TASTE

4 TABLESPOONS OLIVE OIL

Prepare the chiles: Bring the vinegars and water to a boil in a large saucepan. Add the piloncillo, oils and salt. Heat until the piloncillo melts. Add the garlic, onion, bay leaves, thyme, pepper and allspice. Cook approximately 8 minutes. Remove from heat and add oil and chiles. Let the chiles marinate for a minimum of 3 hours (preferably one day) at room temperature.

Prepare the filling: Just before serving, mash the avocado with a fork, stirring in the onion, cilantro, chiles, lime juice, salt and olive oil.

To serve: Stuff the chiles with the filling. Arrange on a serving platter and drench with lukewarm marinade. Decorate with marinated onion, garlic, peppercorns, allspice and herbs. Serve with hard french rolls or crackers. **SERVES 16.**

VARIATION

Fill with shredded crab, shrimp, or refried beans, or squash blossoms sautéed with onion, garlic and corn kernels.

FISH IN PUFF PASTRY

BOMBA DE PESCADO A LA VERACRUZANA

*T*his *is a twist on a typical Veracruz fish dish. It uses the customary ingredients but combines them in a contemporary presentation, perfect for a special occasion such as a wedding. ~*
PATRICIA

FOR THE FISH BROTH

3 QUARTS WATER

3 CUPS WHITE WINE

1 FISH HEAD

2 FISH TAILS

1 MEDIUM WHITE ONION, PEELED AND QUARTERED

8 LARGE GARLIC CLOVES, PEELED

4 RIBS CELERY

4 CARROTS, PEELED

10 SPRIGS PARSLEY

1 TEASPOON BLACK PEPPERCORNS

1 TEASPOON WHOLE ALLSPICE

½ TABLESPOON OREGANO LEAVES

4 BAY LEAVES

2 SPRIGS FRESH THYME

2 SPRIGS FRESH MARJORAM

SALT TO TASTE (USE SPARINGLY)

FOR THE SAUCE

1 CUP OLIVE OIL

6 GARLIC CLOVES, PEELED

4 LARGE TOMATOES, ROASTED AND PURÉED

6 MEDIUM TOMATOES, GRATED AND PURÉED

2 MEDIUM WHITE ONIONS, PEELED, QUARTERED AND PURÉED

8 MEDIUM OR 4 ELEPHANT GARLIC CLOVES, PEELED AND PURÉED

1 CUP OLIVES STUFFED WITH PIMIENTOS, FINELY CHOPPED

½ CUP CAPERS

4 TO 6 BAY LEAVES

4 SPRIGS FRESH THYME

2 SPRIGS FRESH MARJORAM

½ CAN (8-10 OUNCES) PICKLED CHILES GÜEROS OR OTHER CANNED MILD CHILES, DRAINED

SALT TO TASTE

FOR THE BABY SHARK OR LOBSTER

1¼ CUPS OLIVE OIL

4 LARGE GARLIC CLOVES, PEELED

1 MEDIUM WHITE ONION, PEELED AND FINELY CHOPPED

2 LARGE RIPE TOMATOES, FINELY CHOPPED

1½ GENEROUS POUNDS BABY SHARK, LOBSTER OR SOAKED DRIED COD, POACHED IN WATER WITH BOUQUET GARNI (BAY LEAF, THYME, MARJORAM AND PARSLEY)

¾ CUP PARSLEY, FINELY CHOPPED

FOR THE FISH

8 FISH FILLETS, 4½ OZ EACH

1 LEEK, SLICED THINLY, WITH TOP

2 MEDIUM WHITE ONIONS, SLICED THINLY

4 ELEPHANT GARLIC CLOVES, PEELED AND SLICED

30 FRESH EPAZOTE LEAVES

SALT TO TASTE

FRESHLY GROUND BLACK PEPPER TO TASTE

4 CUPS WATER

4 CUPS WHITE WINE

TO SERVE FISH IN PUFF PASTRY ≈

Spoon sauce onto plates, arrange bombas over sauce and garnish with olives, almonds, chiles and bay leaves. Photograph on page 24.

MAKING STOCKS AND BROTHS ≈

Many Mexican recipes call for the cooking of meat or poultry in water. The meat is then shredded and combined with cooked sauces. When preparing meat to shred for various recipes, you may be left with cooking liquid or broth not needed for the recipe. Leftover broth is extremely useful for making soups, thinning sauces and stews, or as a flavorful medium in which to simmer vegetables or rice. Leftover broth keeps very well in airtight containers in the freezer.

Also very valuable to the cook are the crusty bits and pan juices left after cooking meat in a skillet or pan. They can be diluted (or deglazed) with water, stock, or wine to make a quick and delicious sauce.

TO FLAVOR STOCK ≈

Add green onion, cilantro, mint, chiles, oregano, garlic, leeks, bay leaves, marjoram, or thyme. For a quick but rich soup, reduce 6-8 cups of broth to intensify its flavor, then whisk in 2-3 tablespoons of butter and chile purée to taste.

FOR THE FILLING

3   PLUM TOMATOES, SLICED AND WELL DRAINED

    SALT

1½ CUPS EPAZOTE OR CILANTRO, FINELY CHOPPED

½   CUP FRESH CHILE JALAPEÑO, THINLY SLICED

FOR THE DOUGH

1   PACKAGE PHYLLO PASTRY OR 3½ TO 4 POUNDS PUFF PASTRY

2   CUPS CLARIFIED BUTTER

1   EGG YOLK

1½ CUPS SESAME SEEDS, CLEANED

FOR THE GARNISH

24 BLANCHED ALMONDS

24 OLIVES, STUFFED WITH PIMIENTOS

8   CANNED PICKLED CHILES GÜEROS OR ANY PICKLED CHILE SUCH AS BANANA PEPPERS

24 BAY LEAVES

Prepare the fish broth: Heat the water in a large stockpot or saucepan. Add the wine, fish head, fish tails, onion, garlic, celery, carrots, parsley, black pepper, allspice, oregano, bay leaves, thyme and marjoram. Season to taste with salt sparingly (since fish may be salty) and bring to a boil. Reduce to medium heat and cook for 1½ hours. Then strain broth and cook for an additional 2 hours or until the broth is reduced to 2 cups.

Prepare the sauce: Heat the oil in a medium saucepan. Add the garlic cloves and brown. Remove and discard. Add the puréed tomato, onion and garlic and simmer until the mixture begins to release its fat. Then add the olives, capers, bay leaf, thyme, marjoram, chiles and salt to taste. Cook for

about 1½ hours or until the mixture thickens and you can see the bottom of the pan when stirring with a spoon. If necessary, add a little more fish broth. Keep at room temperature.

Prepare the baby shark or lobster: Heat the oil in a medium saucepan. Brown the garlic cloves, remove and discard. Add the chopped onion and brown slightly. Then stir in tomatoes, shredded baby shark, lobster or cod, and parsley. Season lightly with salt and cook for 1½ hours or until the mixture has rendered its fat and thickened.

Prepare the fish: Preheat oven to 400°F. Place fish in a poacher or ovenproof pan. Sprinkle with leek, onion, garlic, epazote, salt, pepper, water and wine. Bake for 8-12 minutes. Remove from oven and allow to cool. Flake the fish.

Prepare the dough: Butter two baking trays with clarified butter. Lightly butter 12 5-inch bowls or tart molds (or, if desired, butter only 6 and prepare half the recipe at a time).

If using phyllo pastry: Unroll the packaged sheets of phyllo pastry and lay out flat, stacked as they come from the package. Cut the stack of pastry sheets in half across the narrow dimension of their rectangular shape, so that you have two stacks of pastry sheets that are approximately square. You will need four of these square sheets for each bomba. Brush the entire surface of the top pastry sheet with melted butter, then gently lift it and place it in one of the prepared bowls. Repeat with 3 more sheets. Fill the bottom of the pastry-lined bowl with plum tomato slices. Sprinkle with salt, epazote and thinly sliced chiles jalapeño. Spoon in baby shark mixture, then flaked fish. Gather together the edges of the pastry and press shut at the top, forming a little "purse." Repeat for remaining bombas.

If using packaged (frozen) puff pastry: Prepare puff pastry according to package directions. Cut pastry into 12 circles approximately 6 inches in diameter and 12 circles approximately 7 inches in diameter. The smaller circle will form the bottom crust of the bomba and the larger one the top crust. For each bomba, line a small buttered bowl with the smaller circle of pastry, fill as directed for phyllo bombas (immediately above), and top with the larger circle of pastry. Crimp the edges shut carefully all around and seal with a small amount of egg yolk whisked with water or milk. Then gently press the top to flatten slightly. Refrigerate for 25 minutes before baking.

Continue with the bombas: Very carefully, remove the bombas from the bowls or tart molds that were used to support them during the filling process, and place them on the buttered baking sheets. Brush tops with remaining butter whisked with egg yolk (using the mixture to seal the bombas where you have pressed the pastry shut), and sprinkle with sesame seeds. Bake in a preheated 400° oven 45 minutes or until golden brown. **SERVES 12.**

SQUASH BLOSSOM SOUP

CREMA DE FLOR DE CALABAZA

Flowers *have been used in Mexican food and drink since pre-Hispanic times. If squash blossoms are not readily available, perhaps you can obtain them from a gardening friend, or ask for them in a local farmers' market.*

5	TABLESPOONS BUTTER
½	CUP OLIVE OIL
1½	MEDIUM WHITE ONIONS, PEELED AND QUARTERED
4	GARLIC CLOVES, PEELED
4	LARGE TOMATOES, ROASTED
2¼	POUNDS SQUASH BLOSSOMS, WASHED AND CUT IN HALF
2	CARROTS, PEELED AND DICED
3½	CUPS CORN KERNELS
12	CUPS CHICKEN BROTH
	SALT TO TASTE
4	TABLESPOONS BUTTER
½	MEDIUM WHITE ONION, PEELED AND GRATED
3	GARLIC CLOVES, PEELED AND PURÉED
1½	CUPS CORN KERNELS
2	CHILES POBLANOS, ROASTED, SWEATED AND PEELED, SEEDED AND DEVEINED, DICED
1½	CUPS HEAVY WHIPPING CREAM
	SALT TO TASTE
	BLACK PEPPER TO TASTE
1	CUP CHOPPED CILANTRO

Prepare the soup: Preheat a large skillet and add olive oil and butter. Add onion and garlic and sauté. Add tomatoes, squash blossoms, carrots, and corn and cook for 25 minutes. Add 6 cups chicken broth and cook 20 minutes more. Salt to taste. Remove from heat and allow to cool. Transfer to a blender or food processor and blend. Heat a large saucepan. Add butter. Add onion, garlic, corn, and chiles poblanos and sauté until tender. Salt to taste. Add puréed mixture to the pan and thin with remaining 6 cups chicken broth. Add cream and heat gently until slightly thickened. Season to taste with salt and pepper. Garnish with chopped cilantro. **SERVES 16.**

≈

"With flowers you write/ Oh Giver of Life!/ With songs you give color,/ With songs you shade/ those who must live on the earth."

PRE-HISPANIC NAHUATL POEM

MEAT AND SHRIMP FONDUE, MEXICAN STYLE

FONDUE DE CARNE Y CAMARON A LA MEXICANA

Although fondue is of Swiss origin, I adapted it to Mexican cooking by offering various little cazuelitas (clay bowls) or molcajetes (stone mortars) filled with typically Mexican sauces and garnishes. The fondue pot is filled with hot oil, and diners skewer their own shrimp and meat, cook it in the oil, then season it with the salsas of their choice. This is a perfect dish for a birthday celebration.

FOR THE FONDUE

4½ POUNDS LEAN BEEF FILLET, CUT IN SMALL CHUNKS

2 GENEROUS POUNDS SHRIMP, DEVEINED AND PEELED

FOR THE MARINADE

6 GARLIC CLOVES, PEELED AND PURÉED

2 TABLESPOONS BLACK PEPPER

4 TABLESPOONS WORCESTERSHIRE SAUCE

1 CUP OLIVE OIL

2 TEASPOONS POWDERED CHICKEN BOUILLON

FOR THE FONDUE POT

¾ CUP CLARIFIED BUTTER

2 CUPS OLIVE OIL

Prepare the marinade: Mix together the garlic, pepper, Worcestershire sauce, olive oil and bouillon. Pour over meat and shrimp and marinate 3 hours in the refrigerator.

Remove meat and shrimp and arrange on a platter. Prepare fondue pot by filling the warming device with alcohol and lighting a flame. Place butter and olive oil in the pot. Keep covered with a lid so that the oil does not splatter. Provide each diner with a plate and a long fork or skewer. Arrange various sauces on the table and allow diners to garnish to taste. **SERVES 12.**

VARIATION

After marinating meat, fry it with green onion slices, fresh chiles serranos seeded and cut in half, and bacon.

After marinating the shrimp, fry in olive oil with peeled, seeded and deveined chiles pasilla, ancho, or Anaheim and garnish with aged cheese.

CHILE ANCHO SALSA

SALSA DE CHILE ANCHO

8 CHILES ANCHOS, WASHED, SEEDED AND DEVEINED, ROASTED, DICED OR CUT INTO STRIPS

1 MEDIUM ONION, PEELED AND FINELY CHOPPED

4 GARLIC CLOVES, PEELED AND PURÉED

½ CUP OLIVE OIL

½ CUP RED VINEGAR

¾ CUP FETA CHEESE, CRUMBLED

1 TEASPOON CRUSHED OREGANO LEAVES

SALT TO TASTE

Combine all ingredients in a bowl and marinate for 2 hours.

CHILE DE ÁRBOL SALSA

SALSA DE CHILE DE ÁRBOL

¼ CUP OLIVE OIL

8 TO 12 CHILES DE ÁRBOL OR OTHER HOT DRIED RED CHILES, WASHED, SEEDED AND DEVEINED

2 TO 3 MEDIUM GARLIC CLOVES, PEELED AND ROASTED

½ MEDIUM WHITE ONION, PEELED AND QUARTERED

½ CUP GRAPEFRUIT JUICE OR WATER

1 TEASPOON SALT

Heat a heavy skillet, add oil, and stir-fry the chiles. Transfer the chiles and oil to a molcajete or processor and grind. (If using a processor, be careful not to overblend.) Add garlic, onion and grapefruit juice and grind to blend. Add salt to taste. This is a very hot salsa.

MEAT AND SHRIMP FONDUE, MEXICAN STYLE.

CHILE ORIGINS ≈

Chiles belong to the genus CAPSICUM *and are closely related to tomatoes, tobacco, jimson weed, potatoes and eggplants. They were first called "chilli peppers" as the result of an error made by Christopher Columbus, who mistook them for the native Asian peppercorn (greatly valued in the early spice trade). The first part of their name he took from the Nahuatl* CHILLI. *Columbus took chiles, or, as he called them, chilli peppers, back to the Old World. Soon they spread to Africa, India, Thailand, Indonesia, and Szechuan China, where they are still integral to the cuisines. One variety became well established in Hungary — in its ground form, U.S. cooks know it as paprika.*

DRIED CHILES CALIFORNIA ≈

The dried red chile called California has begun to be widely available in U.S. supermarkets. In its fresh state, it is a long green pepper, ripening to red. It may be called the Anaheim, Colorado, New Mexico, or California pepper or chile. Dried, it may vary from mild to hot, depending on the cultivar and the growing conditions. This is the chile that is ripened on the plant and strung together to dry in a "ristra," commonly seen in the Santa Fe area and other parts of the American Southwest. In its green form, it is canned by Ortega, Old El Paso and other processors and sold in the Mexican food section of supermarkets.

DRUNKEN SALSA

SALSA BORRACHA

6	CHILES PASILLAS, WASHED, SEEDED AND DEVEINED, LIGHTLY FRIED (SUBSTITUTE DRIED RED CHILES CALIFORNIA)
6	CHILES MULATOS, WASHED, SEEDED AND DEVEINED, LIGHTLY FRIED (SUBSTITUTE DRIED RED CHILES CALIFORNIA)
1½	TEASPOONS SALT, OR TO TASTE
2	MEDIUM WHITE ONIONS, PEELED AND CHOPPED, SAUTÉED FOR 5 MINUTES IN ⅓ CUP OIL
2	MEDIUM WHITE ONIONS, PEELED AND CHOPPED (RAW)
¾	CUP BEER, PULQUE, SPARKLING WINE OR 1 TABLESPOON TEQUILA, OR TO TASTE
2	TABLESPOONS OLIVE OIL
½	CUP FINELY CHOPPED WHITE ONION
½	CUP QUESO FRESCO CRUMBLED

Grind all ingredients except olive oil and ½ cup chopped onion in a food processor or blender and season to taste with salt (be careful not to overprocess.) Add more liquor if desired. At the last moment before serving, stir in the oil and onion.

CHILE SALSA WITH ORANGE JUICE

SALSA CON JUGO DE NARANJA

¼	CUP OLIVE OIL OR VEGETABLE OIL
4	CHILES PASILLAS OR ANCHOS, OR DRIED RED CALIFORNIA OR MILD NEW MEXICAN CHILES, WASHED, SEEDED AND DEVEINED
2	MEDIUM GARLIC CLOVES, PEELED
1	TEASPOON SALT
¾	CUP ORANGE JUICE

Heat oil in a heavy skillet. Add chiles and stir-fry them. Place fried chiles, garlic, salt and orange juice in a processor and blend. If the salsa is too thick, add more orange juice. Season to taste with salt.

DRIED CHILE SERRANO SALSA

SALSA DE CHILE SERRANO SECO

1	TEASPOON SALT OR TO TASTE
2	GARLIC CLOVES, PEELED
½	MEDIUM ONION, PEELED AND QUARTERED
7	TO 15 DRIED CHILES SERRANOS, WASHED AND DRIED, STEMMED, WHOLE, LIGHTLY ROASTED
2	LARGE TOMATOES, ROASTED
½	TO ⅔ CUP WATER, OR TO TASTE

Grind the salt, garlic and onion in a molcajete or processor, then add the chiles and ⅓ cup of the water and blend. Last, add the tomatoes, the remainder of the water and salt to taste. This salsa has a smooth consistency.

FRESH TOMATO SALSA

SALSA DE JITOMATE CRUDA

4	MEDIUM TOMATOES, DICED
1	MEDIUM WHITE ONION, DICED
8	GREEN ONIONS, FINELY CHOPPED
12	SPRIGS CILANTRO, FINELY CHOPPED
3	TO 6 FRESH CHILES SERRANOS OR 2 JALAPEÑOS, MINCED
	SALT TO TASTE
⅓	CUP GRAPEFRUIT OR LIME JUICE
1	MEDIUM AVOCADO, DICED
1	TEASPOON FRESH OREGANO, CRUMBLED
½	CUP CRUMBLED FRESH CILANTRO, CHOPPED

Combine all ingredients. If prepared ahead of time, combine all the ingredients except the avocado, which should be added just before serving.

TOMATILLO-CHIPOTLE SALSA

SALSA DE TOMATE AL CHIPOTLE

1   TEASPOON SALT OR TO TASTE

2   GARLIC CLOVES, PEELED

4   TO 6 CHILES CHIPOTLES OR MORITAS,
    ROASTED, SEEDED AND DEVEINED IF DESIRED,
    SOAKED IN HOT WATER 10 MINUTES OR 2
    CANNED PICKLED CHILES CHIPOTLES

1½ CUPS TOMATILLOS, HUSKED AND BOILED IN
    WATER

½   MEDIUM WHITE ONION, COOKED WITH
    TOMATILLOS

10 CILANTRO SPRIGS

⅓   MEDIUM WHITE ONION, CHOPPED

⅓   TO ½ CUP WATER

¾   CUP FRESH CILANTRO, CHOPPED

If you are using the classic stone mortar,
grind salt and garlic first before adding other
ingredients so that their flavors will
permeate all the other ingredients. If you
are using a food processor, you can still add
the ingredients in this order, but it is
extremely important to pulse as quickly as
possible when blending so that ingredients
will retain a coarse, chunky texture. Garnish
with cilantro.

BRICKLAYER'S SALSA

SALSA DE ALBAÑILES

1   MEDIUM, ONION, PEELED AND QUARTERED

2   SMALL GARLIC CLOVES, PEELED

1½ TEASPOONS SALT OR TO TASTE

8   SPRIGS FRESH CILANTRO, CHOPPED

12 FRESH CHILES SERRANOS OR 6
    JALAPEÑOS, STEMMED AND ROASTED
    WHOLE

1½ CUPS TOMATILLOS, HUSKED, ROASTED OR
    BOILED IN WATER

⅓   TO ½ CUP WATER

1   PINCH SUGAR

1   TEASPOON SALT OR TO TASTE

1   CUP FRESH CILANTRO, MINCED

¾   CUP WHITE ONION, PEELED AND MINCED

Add onion, garlic and salt to a mortar or
food processor. If using a mortar, grind
well. If using a processor, pulse once very
quickly. It is very important not to
overprocess or the texture of the salsa will
suffer. Add cilantro and pulse again, very
quickly. Add chiles, tomatillos and water and
pulse again. Season to taste. Garnish with
chopped cilantro and onion. To prepare
without a mortar or processor, mince all
ingredients extremely finely and combine.

THE VERSATILE SALSA

≈

*The fresh, piquant sauce
called a salsa can be served
as thick or thin as you
wish (thin with beer, broth,
tequila, or water). Try it
with shish-ke-babs, poached
fish, pasta, cold shrimp,
beans, barbequed or grilled
pork chops, chicken, or
meats. Whisk salsa into
cream for a piquant sauce
for crepes or omelets.
Spoon salsa onto an open-
faced melted cheese
sandwich (with an
additional bottom layer of
refried beans), you have a
MOLLETE. And of course,
serve it with any selection
of Mexican ANTOJITOS.*

SALSAS FOR THE FONDUE:
CHILE ANCHO SALSA,
LEFT, AND CHILE DE
ÁRBOL SALSA.

TENDERLOIN IN BAY LEAF SAUCE

FILETE AL LAUREL

Marinating a fillet with bay leaves gives it wonderful flavor. Mexican bay leaves are smaller and slightly more delicate than the bay leaf familiar to North American cooks. Either may be used in this recipe. ~ PATRICIA

FOR THE MEAT

4½ POUNDS TENDERLOIN FILLET (CHATEAUBRIAND)

½ STICK BUTTER, CUT IN PIECES

¼ CUP OLIVE OIL

FOR THE MARINADE

3 GARLIC CLOVES, PEELED AND PURÉED

1 TABLESPOON GROUND ALLSPICE

4 BAY LEAVES (OR 8 MEXICAN BAY LEAVES)

1 TABLESPOON DRIED OREGANO LEAVES

1 TABLESPOON THYME

½ CUP STEAK SAUCE OR SOY SAUCE

½ CUP WORCESTERSHIRE SAUCE

½ CUP OLIVE OIL

THE JUICE OF 3 LIMES

TO COMPLETE THE SAUCE

2 TEASPOONS CORNSTARCH

¾ CUP WATER

1 CUP REDUCED CHICKEN OR BEEF BROTH

½ CUP BUTTER, CUT INTO PIECES

⅓ CUP COGNAC

SALT TO TASTE

Prepare the meat: Place the meat in a deep baking dish, if necessary cutting it into portions to fit the dish. Combine all ingredients for marinade and pour over meat. Marinate in refrigerator, preferably overnight. The next day, drain the meat, reserving the marinade. Heat a large, heavy skillet for 15 minutes. Add the butter and olive oil to the skillet and bring back to full heat (approximately 2-3 minutes). When the skillet is hot again and the butter and oil well heated, add the meat. Brown for approximately 7½ minutes, rocking the meat back and forth gently with tongs to keep it from sticking. Then turn and brown the other side 7-8 minutes, again rocking with the tongs. Then turn the meat one-quarter turn so that one uncooked edge will have direct contact with the hot skillet and brown for 5 minutes. Turn so that the opposite edge can brown, again approximately 5 minutes (total cooking time for the cut of meat will be about 25 minutes). When meat is cooked, immediately remove from skillet and wrap closely in aluminum foil so that it will reabsorb its cooking juices and stay moist. It should rest for about 10 minutes before being cut or pierced.

Complete the sauce: While the meat is resting and the skillet with remaining butter, oil and pan juices is still hot add water to skillet and stir. Add the reserved marinade. Simmer 5 minutes. Then whisk the cornstarch into the broth and add to the skillet. Simmer until the mixture forms a syrupy glaze. Transfer sauce to a double boiler if you do not plan to serve it immediately. At the last moment, just before serving, whisk in butter, cognac, and salt to taste. Pour the sauce over the cooked fillet, then slice with a very sharp knife. Spoon additional sauce onto each serving. Serve with Onions stuffed with Mushrooms, page 119. **SERVES 8-10.**

COLD PICKLED VEAL RUMP

CUETE FRIO EN ESCABECHE

T*his is among my favorite main courses. It's a great recipe since the meat lasts long and is easy to store — if you're lucky enough to have leftovers! The veal rump is first marinated overnight, then baked in an herb-scented sauce, then allowed to marinate again in a delicious pickling sauce. ~ MARGARITA*

FOR THE VEAL

4 POUNDS VEAL RUMP OR EYE OF THE ROUND

½ CUP OLIVE OR CORN OIL

¾ CUP BUTTER OR MARGARINE

FOR THE MARINADE

1 MEDIUM WHITE ONION, PEELED AND QUARTERED

3 GARLIC CLOVES, PEELED

1 TABLESPOON GROUND BLACK PEPPER

THE JUICE OF ONE GRAPEFRUIT

THE JUICE OF ONE LIME

THE JUICE OF ½ ORANGE

OREGANO TO TASTE

"I want to give you/ a cloak of lace/ sea foam/ with which to cover yourself/ like a bridal veil/ and may white sand/ scattered over your hair/ be the wedding rice."

FROM A POPULAR SONG, LA VIDA ES MÁS SABROSA.

TENDERLOIN IN BAY LEAF SAUCE, SERVED WITH SAUTÉED SCALLIONS, ONIONS STUFFED WITH MUSHROOMS (PAGE 119) AND AN ONION STUFFED WITH THE SPICY BLACK CORN FUNGUS CUITLACOCHE.

FOR THE SAUCE

8 TO 10 CUPS WATER

2 TO 3 BAY LEAVES

1 SPRIG FRESH THYME

1 SPRIG FRESH MARJORAM

2 CELERY TOPS, CHOPPED

1 TURNIP, PEELED AND QUARTERED

2 CARROTS, PEELED AND SLICED

½ LEEK, SLICED, WITH GREEN TOP

12 WHOLE BLACK PEPPERCORNS

2 CUPS DRY SHERRY OR WHITE WINE

FOR THE PICKLING SAUCE

2 CUPS OLIVE OR CORN OIL

12 GARLIC CLOVES, PEELED

5 CARROTS, PEELED AND CUT INTO THIN SLICES

2 MEDIUM WHITE ONIONS, SLICED THINLY

3 BAY LEAVES

3 SPRIGS FRESH THYME

3 SPRIGS FRESH MARJORAM

12 WHOLE BLACK PEPPERCORNS

1 TABLESPOON OREGANO

3 CUPS WHITE WINE VINEGAR

1 TEASPOON SUGAR

   SALT TO TASTE

1 CUP MEAT BROTH

FOR THE GARNISH

1½ CUPS STUFFED OLIVES

2 CANS PICKLED CHILES GÜEROS OR JALAPEÑOS, WHOLE

3 RIPE AVOCADOS, PEELED AND SLICED

2 TO 3 WHITE ONIONS, SLICED THINLY

2 CUPS PICKLED CANNED CHILES JALAPEÑOS, CUT INTO STRIPS

Prepare the marinade: Purée onion in a blender or food processor. Pour into a glass bowl, adding all the ingredients for the marinade. Stir well. Place meat in a glass or enamel baking dish and pour marinade over. Marinate in the refrigerator overnight. The following day, drain the meat, setting aside the marinade.

Prepare the sauce and cook the meat: Heat the oil and butter or margarine together in a large skillet. Brown the rump. Remove the rump to a roaster. Mix together ingredients for the sauce in a glass bowl, then pour this mixture over the rump. Cover roaster with lid and cook in a medium oven for about 2½ to 3 hours, or until the meat is tender. Remove from the pan and allow to cool for a minimum of 4 hours. (The meat can be prepared a day ahead.) Set aside 1 cup broth and strain. Cut rump into thin slices using a very sharp knife.

Prepare the pickling sauce: In a saucepan, heat the oil. Add garlic cloves and brown lightly. Stir in carrots, onion, herbs, spices, vinegar, sugar and broth. Simmer over low heat for about 25 minutes. Correct seasoning and allow sauce to cool. Pour over sliced meat and allow the meat to absorb the sauce for a minimum of three hours at room temperature before serving.

To serve: Carefully arrange meat on a serving platter. Garnish with olives, chiles, avocado slices, onion slices and jalapeños. Serve cold or at room temperature.
SERVES 8-12.

ONIONS STUFFED WITH MUSHROOMS

CEBOLLITAS RELLENAS DE HONGO

*T*he noble onion pairs with the earthy magic of the mushroom in a side dish that can accompany any meat, chicken, or fish main course. Try it with Tenderloin in Bay Leaf Sauce. ~
PATRICIA

FOR THE ONIONS

8	CUPS WATER
3	TABLESPOONS BUTTER
4½	TEASPOONS SALT
16	SMALL FRESH BOILING ONIONS

FOR THE FILLING

SEE THE MUSHROOM GARNISH FOR POACHED EGGS IN FRITTERS, PAGE 131

4	TABLESPOONS BUTTER

FOR THE GARNISH

⅓	CUP OLIVE OIL
16	CULTIVATED OR WILD MUSHROOMS
2	TEASPOONS MINCED GARLIC
2	TABLESPOONS FRESH CILANTRO, CHOPPED
	SALT TO TASTE
	BLACK PEPPER TO TASTE
16	CHILES DE ÁRBOL (OR OTHER SMALL DRIED HOT CHILE), FRIED WHOLE
16	FRESH PARSLEY SPRIGS

Prepare the onions: Bring the water to a boil in a medium saucepan. Add the butter, salt and onions and cook until tender. Do not overcook or the onions will become mushy and difficult to fill. Drain off water and refresh in iced water for 1 minute. Drain off water and remove the central part of each onion, leaving only the outer layers in the form of a shell.

Prepare the filling: Prepare the mushroom garnish as indicated in the recipe for Poached Eggs in Fritters. Fill the onions with the mushroom mixture. Heat the butter in a medium frying pan and carefully add stuffed mushrooms. Cover with a lid and simmer for 20 minutes.

Prepare the garnish: Heat the olive oil in a frying pan. Add mushrooms, garlic and cilantro. Season to taste with salt and pepper. Stir and add the chiles de árbol, cooking for about 10 minutes.

To serve: Spoon the garnish on individual dinner plates and place the stuffed onions on the bed of garnish.

STUFFED ONIONS
≈

Prepare onions for stuffing as suggested above and then fill them with any of a number of succulent or spicy mixtures, for example:

Chorizo Sausage (page 143), sautéed with chopped onion.
Quesadilla Fillings (page 72).
Squash Blossoms, Chiles and Corn filling for crepes (page 188).
Sautéed sweet corn kernels, chopped onion and roasted chile strips.
Quintoniles or Spinach with Chile (page 201).
Minced Potatoes with Pepper and Garlic (page 207).
Tinga (page 241).

TOURNEDEAU WITH MORELS IN A CHILE-CREAM SAUCE

TOURNEDEAU CON MORILLAS A LA CREMA Y CHILE VERDE

Years of research in Mexican cuisine and the combination of indigenous ingredients have resulted in a repertoire of recipes which I serve at special feasts. This delicious meat dish is a fine main course at a wedding dinner. ~ PATRICIA

TOURNEDEAU WITH MORELS IN CHILE-CREAM SAUCE, SERVED OVER A BED OF SAUCE AND DECORATED WITH WHOLE COOKED RESERVED MORELS, SLICED SAUTEED ZUCCHINI AND TWO GARNISHES.

BEVERAGES WITH MEXICAN FOOD ≈

Good, earthy red wines, especially Mexican, Chilean, Portuguese and Eastern European wines, pair well with Mexican dishes. Cold Mexican beer is also a good choice. A typical luncheon beverage is a refreshing glass of Mexican lemonade, iced water with a squeeze of lemon or lime and a touch of sugar.

FOR THE MARINADE

4 GARLIC CLOVES, PEELED

1 MEDIUM WHITE ONION, PEELED AND QUARTERED

1 TABLESPOON FRESHLY GROUND BLACK PEPPER

4 FRESH CHILES SERRANOS OR **2** JALAPEÑOS, FINELY CHOPPED

⅓ CUP WHITE WINE VINEGAR

¾ CUP OLIVE OIL

FOR THE MEAT

12 PORTIONS FILLET MIGNON, EACH **4** OUNCES

9 TABLESPOONS OLIVE OIL

3 TABLESPOONS BUTTER

SALT TO TASTE

BLACK PEPPER TO TASTE

¾ CUP WHITE WINE

1 CUP REDUCED BEEF STOCK

FOR THE SAUCE

⅓ CUP OLIVE OIL

1 CUP BUTTER

½ MEDIUM WHITE ONION, PEELED AND MINCED

2 LARGE GARLIC CLOVES, PEELED AND MINCED

3⅓ POUNDS FRESH MORELS OR OTHER MUSHROOM, WASHED AND DRAINED SALT AND PEPPER TO TASTE

12 OUNCES CREAMY GRUYERE OR SEMI-SOFT CHEESE

10 OUNCES PORT SALUT OR MILD CHEESE, CUBED

1½ CUPS WHIPPING CREAM

1½ CUPS SOUR CREAM OR CRÈME FRAÎCHE

⅓ CUP OLIVE OIL

2 TABLESPOONS BUTTER

6 GARLIC CLOVES, PEELED AND MINCED

1 WHITE ONION, PEELED AND MINCED

3 FRESH CHILES SERRANOS OR **2** JALAPEÑOS, MINCED

2 BAY LEAVES

2 SPRIGS FRESH THYME

¾ CUP WHITE WINE

½ TEASPOON POWDERED CHICKEN BOUILLON OR SALT TO TASTE

FOR THE GARNISH

⅓ CUP OLIVE OIL

½ CUP BUTTER

14 GREEN ONIONS, SLICED THINLY

6 CHILES DE AGUA OR FRESH ANAHEIM, OR BANANA PEPPERS, WASHED, SEEDED AND DEVEINED, SLICED LENGTHWISE INTO NARROW SLIVERS

6 CHILES CARIBE, ANAHEIM, OR BANANA, PREPARED AS ABOVE

SALT AND PEPPER

⅓ CUP OLIVE OIL

⅓ CUP BUTTER

24 LARGE SQUASH BLOSSOMS, WASHED AND DRIED

SALT AND PEPPER

2 ZUCCHINI, COOKED UNTIL TENDER IN SALTED WATER, DRAINED AND SLICED THINLY

Prepare the marinade: Place the garlic and onion in a blender or food processor and blend. Transfer to a medium glass bowl. Add remaining ingredients and stir well. Pour over the meat and allow to marinate in refrigerator overnight.

Prepare the sauce: Heat a large skillet. Add oil and butter, then add onion and garlic and sauté. Add mushrooms and sauté until liquid has evaporated. Season to taste with salt. Remove 36 mushrooms and set aside for the presentation. Place the remainder of the

COOKING MEAT ≈

Have meat and poultry at room temperature before cooking. After washing, pat dry thoroughly for better browning. Allow roasted meats to stand, covered with foil, for 15 minutes before carving so that they reabsorb their juices and do not lose them to the carving board. After cutting meat or vegetables on the cutting board, add them to the dish by scraping them off the board with the back of the knife, not the blade.

sautéd mixture in a food processor. Add the cheeses and creams and blend until smooth. Heat a large, heavy saucepan. Add oil and butter. Add garlic, onion, chiles, bay leaves, thyme and sauté. Add white wine and allow to reduce to half over medium heat. Add the puréed mushroom mixture to the saucepan. Cook 35 minutes over low heat until sauce has thickened. Season with salt or powdered bouillon. Thin with broth if necessary.

Prepare the garnish: Heat a wok or a heavy skillet with deep sides. Add oil and butter. Add onion and very quickly stir-fry. Add chiles and stir-fry briefly until slightly wilted. Season to taste with salt and pepper and set aside. Heat the wok or skillet again and add oil and butter. Add the squash blossoms to the hot wok and very quickly stir-fry. Season with salt and pepper and set aside. Keep onion garnish and squash blossom garnish warm, or re-warm before using.

Prepare the meat: Remove meat from marinade and drain. Preheat a heavy skillet. Add approximately 3 tablespoons oil and 1 tablespoon butter and heat thoroughly. Add 4 fillets to the skillet. Cook 3-4 minutes, then turn with tongs and cook another 3-4 minutes, then put aside. Sprinkle with salt and pepper to taste. Reheat skillet, add the same amounts of oil and butter, and cook 4 more fillets. Repeat with the remaining 4 fillets. Adding a small amount of meat to the skillet allows it to retain its heat, thus searing the meat so that its juices are retained. When all 12 fillets are cooked set them aside, add wine to pan drippings and reduce to a syrupy liquid. Add beef stock and cook 10 minutes. Transfer the resulting sauce to the large saucepan containing the mushroom-cheese-cream sauce that you prepared earlier. Heat through and season to taste. **SERVES 12.**

MUSHROOM TOMATILLO SAUCE WITH CHILE MORITA, SERVED WITH PASTA.

MUSHROOM TOMATILLO SAUCE WITH CHILE MORITA

HONGOS DE TEMPORADA AL MIL TOMATE CON CHILE MORITA

Dozens of varieties of mushrooms grow in Mexico, ranging from tiny to huge in size, subtle to strong in flavor. This recipe may be prepared with any variety of mushroom available. ~ **PATRICIA**

4 CUPS WATER

1½ POUNDS MIL TOMATES (TINY TOMATILLOS) OR 1½ POUNDS REGULAR TOMATILLOS, HUSKED

½ MEDIUM WHITE ONION, PEELED AND QUARTERED

4 CLOVES GARLIC, PEELED

MEXICAN PASTA ≈

Pasta can combine deliciously with many Mexican sauces and fillings. Try garnishing with chopped cilantro or crumbled feta cheese. Here are a few possibilities:

Seashell pasta with Chile Ancho Salsa (page 113).

Lobster ravioli with Tomato and Chile de Arbol Salsa (page 113).

Tortellini stuffed with spinach or ricotta and served with Salsa Mexicana (page 177).

Canneloni stuffed with Tinga (page 241) and topped with Chile Strips in Cream (page 146).

Angel hair pasta with White Ceviche (page 106).

Wide egg noodles with Oaxacan Meatballs in Chile Tomato Sauce (page 87).

1	POUND TOMATILLOS, RIPE, ALMOST YELLOW, HUSKED AND ROASTED
½	MEDIUM WHITE ONION, PEELED AND ROASTED
4	CLOVES GARLIC, PEELED AND ROASTED
5	TO 8 CHILES MORITAS OR CHIPOTLES, ROASTED WHOLE AND SOAKED IN HOT WATER 10-15 MINUTES (SUBSTITUTE CANNED CHIPOTLES OR OTHER SMALL HOT CHILES, FRESH OR DRIED)
1	MEDIUM WHITE ONION, PEELED AND QUARTERED
⅔	CUP VEGETABLE OIL
4	CLOVES GARLIC, PEELED
1¼	TO 1½ POUNDS MUSHROOMS, WASHED AND SLICED
	SALT TO TASTE

Place water in a medium-sized saucepan. Bring to a rolling boil. Add mil tomates, onion and garlic and cook 15 minutes. Place boiled ingredients plus 1 cup cooking liquid in a blender or food processor along with roasted tomatillos, roasted onion, roasted garlic and roasted chiles moritas. Add quartered raw onion and blend well. If necessary, purée in batches. Meanwhile heat oil in a medium-sized saucepan. Add 4 cloves of garlic and brown. Stir in mushrooms and sauté. Add prepared mil tomate sauce and season with salt to taste. Simmer until the mixture renders its fat, about one hour.

To serve with pasta (cooked al dente), add ½ cup butter as you combine the pasta with the sauce. Decorate with fried chiles morita. To serve as a taco filling, serve with freshly made blue-corn tortillas. To thin the sauce, add water or chicken broth. Kept thick, the sauce is also a good filling for quesadillas or omelets. **SERVES 8.**

TO CAPTURE MUSHROOM FLAVOR ≈

After reconstituting dried mushrooms, save the soaking liquid for a flavorful addition to many dishes; it contains the earthy goodness of the mushrooms. Strain carefully by pouring the liquid through a coffee filter inserted in a wire-mesh sieve.

CREAM OF WALNUT SOUP

CREMA DE NUEZ

My great-grandmother Emilia used to prepare this recipe at the turn of the century. It can be made with any nut, although she always favored walnuts. ~ EMILIA

FOR THE CHICKEN BROTH

6   QUARTS WATER
½   STEWING CHICKEN
4   CHICKEN LEGS (DRUMSTICK AND THIGH)
½   POUND VEAL
3   WHOLE CARROTS, PEELED
1   WHOLE LEEK, WASHED, WITH GREEN TOP
½   CUP CELERY, WITH LEAVES, WASHED
2   MEDIUM WHITE ONIONS, PEELED AND HALVED
½   GARLIC HEAD, CUT IN HALF ACROSS THE GRAIN
1   SMALL TURNIP, PEELED
3   BAY LEAVES
1   SPRIG FRESH THYME OR ½ TEASPOON DRIED THYME
1   SPRIG FRESH MARJORAM OR ½ TEASPOON DRIED MARJORAM
10 WHOLE BLACK PEPPERCORNS
10 WHOLE ALLSPICE
    SALT OR POWDERED BOUILLON TO TASTE

FOR THE VELOUTE SAUCE

5   TABLESPOONS BUTTER, AT ROOM TEMPERATURE
¼   CUP RICE FLOUR OR CORNSTARCH
¼   CUP ALL-PURPOSE FLOUR
½   MEDIUM WHITE ONION, PEELED AND QUARTERED

2   RIBS CELERY
½   LEEK, SLICED LENGTHWISE
3   CUPS WALNUTS OR PECANS, GROUND FINE IN A SPICE MILL OR FOOD PROCESSOR
2   CUPS WHIPPING CREAM
1   TEASPOON NUTMEG
    SALT TO TASTE

FOR THE GARNISH

1   CUP WALNUTS, GROUND (OPTIONAL)
½   CUP PARSLEY OR CHIVES, FINELY CHOPPED (OPTIONAL)
    POMEGRANATE SEEDS (OPTIONAL)

Prepare the chicken broth: Heat the water in a large saucepan or stockpot. Add chicken, veal, carrots, leek, celery, onion, garlic, turnip, bay leaves, thyme, marjoram, peppercorns, allspice and salt. Bring to a boil, skim, reduce to simmer and cook for 1½ hours. Skim off fat. Strain and reserve broth, reserving chicken and veal for another use if desired. Or begin with previously made chicken broth.

Prepare the veloute sauce: Heat the butter in a large saucepan or stockpot. Stir in rice flour and all-purpose flour and cook, stirring, until the flour begins to brown. Stir in chicken broth (12 to 14 cups) gradually with a whisk, being sure that the mixture is smooth. Wrap the onion, celery and leek in cheesecloth and place in broth. Simmer for 20 minutes. Remove cheesecloth bag with vegetables. Add nuts, cream and nutmeg. Simmer an additional 20-25 minutes. If soup thickens too much, add a little broth or milk.

To serve: This soup may be served from a hollowed-out pumpkin or squash. Garnish as desired. **SERVES 12.**

CREAM OF WALNUT SOUP, DECORATED WITH POMEGRANATE SEEDS.

THE POMEGRANATE ≈

A native of Western Asia, the pomegranate traveled to the Mediterranean, and probably hence, via the Spanish, to Mexico. It is mentioned in the Bible and in the songs of Homer and was used in pagan fertility rites. Its brilliantly red pulp is comprised of numerous sparkling seeds with a mild nutty taste. The fruit will keep whole several days in a cool, dry place, or if you wish, you can remove the seeds, keeping them dry, and refrigerate them in an airtight container for up to a month.

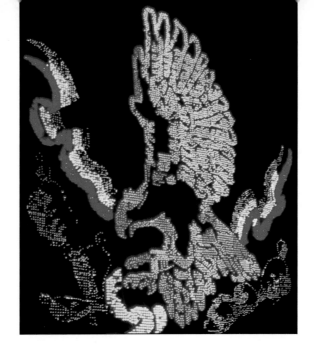

≈ *The Ordering of Life* ≈

BREAKFAST, PORTABLE FEASTS, INDEPENDENCE

DESAYUNOS, ITACATE, SEPTIEMBRE

Morning. Life within the home begins to make itself felt. The family, hurrying, voices still touched with sleep, prepares to start the day. The house, little by little, becomes fragrant with the sharp odor of black coffee and the soft aroma of warm tortillas, inseparable companions of the food that will appear on the breakfast table: eggs, chilaquiles with cheese, dobladas in chile sauce, or beans and chorizo sausage. Grandparents and grandchildren, parents, uncles and aunts, brothers and sisters take their places around the table to share the first food of the day.

SALSAS ARE THE CONSTANT AND VIVID COMPANION OF MEXICAN CUISINE. HERE THEY ARE PRESENTED IN THE MOLCAJETES, OR MORTARS, IN WHICH THEY ARE MADE.

In Mexico there is a popular saying: "Don't make an important decision without first having eaten." Mexicans heed this advice. The breakfast ritual is observed in the family setting, and also in restaurants of all kinds where people meet with the double aim of breaking bread together and of taking up matters of the most varied kind. Businessmen and women, tradespeople, industrialists, politicians, now follow the custom of combining the day's first work session with breakfast.

Another widely observed custom among the natives in all parts of the country is that of taking breakfast in the market. This does honor to Father Diego de Durán who said, in his *Historia de las Indias,* "Let me see the market first, I'll go to heaven later." There is no Mexican market without a special area for food stands where the hungry buyer may sample the great range of regional and popular dishes that make up Mexican cuisine. From the pre-dawn hours of the morning until nearly midday, cooks and waiters scurry to attend the many people who come to their booths to enjoy a dish of fruits, a main course, coffee black or with hot milk, sweet rolls or regional specialties.

For many of those who will not take the midday meal at home, the tradition of the *itacate* still prevails. The custom originates in the countryside, where the husband, departing for work in a faraway field, is given a packet of food by his wife. It has long been a familiar sight to see peasants carrying a bandana, its four corners knotted up, or a woven bag filled with sustaining food. Afterwards the custom spread to schoolchildren as well and from there to their homes when some special meal or celebration was shared. To this day, it is a way of praising the food when a departing guest requests, half jokingly, half seriously, to be given an *itacate* with bits of what was left from the meal.

The fact is that one of the characteristics of the Mexican is his enjoyment of eating away from home, particularly during a celebration such as the patriotic holidays commemorating the nation's independence. On September 15 and 16, Mexico is one immense fiesta. People flood the streets to celebrate amidst the joyousness of streamers and confetti, bugles, noisemakers, balloons, revolutionary costumes of huge palm leaf hats, ponchos and other native dress, mariachi music, and shouts of Viva Mexico! that ascend like the rockets and fireworks illuminating the Mexican night. Amidst all this celebration is another substantial festivity — the tumultuous world of the booths of food. Everything that tickles the palate is sold hot or cold on corners, in the middle of the street, or in the doorways of tenement houses. Likewise, the restaurants and eateries are packed with entire families enjoying the dishes that on this occasion more than any other delight the populace: green enchiladas, enchiladas with mole, garnachas, bean gorditas, picaditas, fried tortillas filled with barbecued goat meat, tacos and molotes.

The celebration of Independence Day is a vivid and passionate peak in the gentler cycle of the ordered life — the waking and sleeping, the working and resting, and the daily ritual of sustenance which supports both the life of the body and the life of the spirit.

POACHED EGGS IN FRITTERS

HUEVOS POCHE EN BUÑUELO

Buñuelos are Spanish in origin. Here they are incorporated into an otherwise very Mexican breakfast. You could also serve the eggs in tortilla baskets.

~ PATRICIA

FOR THE BUÑUELOS

PREPARE ACCORDING TO RECIPE ON PAGE 71.

FOR THE FILLING

⅓ CUP OLIVE OIL

⅓ CUP BUTTER

4 GARLIC CLOVES, FINELY CHOPPED

2 CUPS GREEN ONIONS, THINLY SLICED

2 CUPS SPINACH LEAVES OR WATERCRESS, COOKED UNTIL TENDER IN A SMALL AMOUNT OF SALTED WATER

6 CHILES POBLANOS, ROASTED, SWEATED AND PEELED, SEEDED AND DEVEINED, AND SOAKED IN 2 CUPS WATER, ⅓ CUP VINEGAR AND SALT FOR 25 MINUTES, THEN CUT INTO THIN STRIPS

FOR THE CILANTRO SAUCE

2 CUPS CRÈME FRAÎCHE OR 1¼ CUPS HEAVY CREAM WHISKED WITH ¾ CUP SOUR CREAM

1 CUP HEAVY WHIPPING CREAM

2½ CUPS CILANTRO

1 MEDIUM WHITE ONION, PEELED AND QUARTERED

3 GARLIC CLOVES, PEELED

½ CUP REDUCED CHICKEN BROTH

1 TEASPOON CORNSTARCH

½ CUP BUTTER

SALT TO TASTE

BLACK PEPPER TO TASTE

FOR THE CHIPOTLE SAUCE

2½ CUPS CRÈME FRAÎCHE OR 1½ CUPS HEAVY CREAM WHISKED WITH 1 CUP SOUR CREAM

1 CUP HEAVY WHIPPING CREAM

4 CHILES CHIPOTLES, STEMMED, WHOLE, STIR-FRIED AND SOAKED IN WATER FOR 20 MINUTES

1 MEDIUM WHITE ONION, PEELED AND QUARTERED

3 GARLIC CLOVES, PEELED

2 CANNED PICKLED CHILES CHIPOTLES

½ CUP REDUCED CHICKEN BROTH

1 TEASPOON CORNSTARCH

½ CUP BUTTER

SALT TO TASTE

BLACK PEPPER TO TASTE

FOR THE EGGS

6 CUPS WATER

4 BAY LEAVES

2 SPRIGS THYME

2 SPRIGS MARJORAM

SALT TO TASTE

¼ CUP VINEGAR

2 TABLESPOONS VEGETABLE OIL

24 EGGS AT ROOM TEMPERATURE

FOR THE MUSHROOM GARNISH

⅓ CUP OLIVE OIL

⅓ CUP BUTTER

6 SMALL GARLIC CLOVES, PEELED AND FINELY CHOPPED

1 MEDIUM WHITE ONION, PEELED AND FINELY CHOPPED

POACHED EGGS IN FRITTERS WITH CILANTRO SAUCE, CHIPOTLE SAUCE AND MUSHROOM GARNISH.

POACHED EGGS ≈

Poached Eggs with Mexican sauces and garnishes can also be served on a toasted waffle or English muffin, on toasted pita or pocket bread, or with fried corn tortillas or toasted flour tortillas. To toast flour tortillas, arrange them on a cookie sheet and bake in a preheated oven at 350° for 15-20 minutes or until golden and crisp. You may wish to brush first with seasoned butter.

3 FRESH CHILES SERRANOS OR 1 JALAPEÑO, FINELY CHOPPED

1 POUND MUSHROOMS, WASHED AND FINELY CHOPPED

½ CUP CILANTRO, FINELY CHOPPED

½ CUP EPAZOTE, FINELY CHOPPED

SALT TO TASTE

BLACK PEPPER TO TASTE

Prepare the buñuelos: Prepare ¼ the recipe for buñuelos on page 71, the equivalent of 12 buñuelos (or prepare entire recipe and freeze the rest for another occasion). Form 5- to 6-inch buñuelos and fry in oil until golden brown. Reserve.

Prepare the filling: Heat the oil and butter in a medium saucepan. Brown the chopped garlic, then add green onions and cook until light brown. Add spinach and sauté for 5 minutes. Stir in chile strips and cook 20 minutes more. Season to taste with salt and pepper.

Prepare the cilantro sauce: Place the creams, cilantro, onion and garlic in a blender or food processor and purée. Stir in reduced chicken broth and cornstarch and transfer to a saucepan. Simmer until thick, remove from heat and place in a double boiler. Whisk in butter. Season to taste with salt and pepper. Keep warm.

Prepare the chipotle sauce: Place creams, fried chiles, onion, garlic and canned chiles in a processor or blender and purée. Stir in chicken broth and cornstarch and transfer to a saucepan. Simmer until thick, remove from heat and place in a double boiler. Whisk in butter. Season to taste with salt and pepper. Keep warm.

Prepare the eggs: Place the water in a medium saucepan. Add bay leaves, thyme, marjoram, salt, vinegar and oil. Bring to a boil and reduce heat. Cook the first egg only to test the water. Break the egg into a glass without breaking the yolk, then carefully transfer to the barely boiling water using a large cooking spoon to assist. Gently fold egg whites over the yolk as it begins to cook. Cook for about 3-4 minutes, being careful not to overcook. (Reduce water temperature slightly after egg begins to cook.) With a spoon, carefully remove from water and repeat procedure for remaining eggs. Eggs can be cooked ahead of time and kept warm in warm water. Drain before using.

Prepare the garnish: Heat the oil and butter in a medium saucepan. Sauté garlic cloves and onion until light brown. Add chile and mushrooms and simmer for 35 minutes or until the moisture evaporates. During the last 20 minutes of cooking time, add the cilantro and epazote. Season to taste with salt and pepper. Keep hot in a double boiler.

To serve: Place buñuelos in the centers of individual plates. Cover with about 2 tablespoons of filling, and flatten slightly. Place two poached eggs on top. Then spoon cilantro sauce over one egg and chipotle sauce over the other egg. Carefully spoon mushrooms in the middle. Serve immediately.

CILANTRO OMELET

OMELETTES AL CILANTRO

T *his hearty breakfast recipe was published in my monthly column in the Mexican edition of* VOGUE. *It is a contemporary alternative to scrambled or fried eggs.* ~ PATRICIA

FOR THE FILLING

⅓ CUP OLIVE OIL

⅓ CUP BUTTER

6 GARLIC CLOVES, PEELED AND MINCED

2 MEDIUM WHITE ONIONS, PEELED AND FINELY CHOPPED

4 TO 6 FRESH CHILES SERRANOS, FINELY CHOPPED

2¼ POUNDS FRESH MUSHROOMS, FINELY CHOPPED

SALT TO TASTE

BLACK PEPPER TO TASTE

½ CUP CILANTRO OR EPAZOTE, CHOPPED

FOR THE CORN GARNISH

⅓ CUP VEGETABLE OIL

½ CUP BUTTER

2 MEDIUM WHITE ONIONS, PEELED AND FINELY CHOPPED

8 EARS OF CORN, KERNELS REMOVED

4 FRESH CHILES SERRANOS, MINCED

½ CUP CILANTRO OR EPAZOTE, CHOPPED

SALT TO TASTE

FOR THE OMELET

20 EGGS (ABOUT 2½ EGGS PER OMELET), BEATEN

4 TABLESPOONS CREAM

SALT TO TASTE

BLACK PEPPER TO TASTE

½ CUP BUTTER

½ CUP VEGETABLE OR OLIVE OIL

FOR THE GARNISH

32 CILANTRO OR EPAZOTE LEAVES

8 CILANTRO OR EPAZOTE SPRIGS

Prepare the filling: Heat the oil and butter in a medium saucepan. Brown the garlic, onion and chile. Add mushrooms and cook for 45 minutes or until the mixture thickens. Add salt and pepper to taste and cilantro or epazote and reserve filling.

Prepare the corn garnish: Heat the oil and butter in a medium saucepan. Add the onion, corn and chiles, and cover saucepan with lid. Simmer for 35 minutes or until the liquid evaporates. Add cilantro or epazote and salt to taste, and reserve.

Prepare the omelets: Beat eggs with cream, salt and pepper. Heat an omelet pan. Add a little butter and oil and add about 2½ eggs to pan. Let eggs set, stirring with a fork, and rotating pan. When eggs set, place 2 tablespoons of filling on one side, and fold omelet. Turn over with the help of a spatula and cook for 2-3 minutes, or until light brown. Transfer to a plate, and repeat procedure for remaining omelets, adding butter and oil as necessary.

To serve: Place omelets on individual serving plates and garnish with mounds of mushroom filling on one side and corn filling on the other side. Decorate with cilantro or epazote leaves and sprigs. SERVES 8.

HERB OMELETS ≈

Herb omelets, Mexican style, can include fresh mint or oregano instead of cilantro. Try them with classic fresh salsas, such as the Mexican Salsa (page 177).

EGGS POACHED IN TOMATO-CHILE SAUCE

HUEVOS EN RABO DE MESTIZA

*H*earty breakfasts are a tradition in Mexico where lunch is usually eaten between two and four in the afternoon and dinner around ten at night. My Aunt Vasseur combined French techniques with Mexican ingredients and came up with this dish — poached eggs in tomato sauce laced with chile poblano strips, local cheeses and cilantro.

FOR THE SAUCE

6   RIPE TOMATOES (ABOUT 2½ POUNDS)

1½ MEDIUM WHITE ONIONS, PEELED AND QUARTERED

4   GARLIC CLOVES, PEELED

3   CUPS WATER

½   CUP OLIVE OIL

2   SLICES WHITE ONION

     SALT TO TASTE

FOR THE EGGS

½   CUP VEGETABLE OIL

1½ MEDIUM WHITE ONIONS

6   CHILES POBLANOS, ROASTED, SWEATED AND PEELED, SEEDED AND DEVEINED, SOAKED IN SALTED WATER FOR 10 MINUTES, THEN CUT IN THIN STRIPS

16   EGGS

8   SLICES MOZZARELLA, OAXACAN OR STRING CHEESE, ABOUT 1½ OUNCES EACH

FOR THE GARNISH

½   CUP CHOPPED CILANTRO OR PARSLEY

Prepare the sauce: Place the tomatoes, onion, garlic and water in a blender or food processor and purée. Strain mixture. Heat oil in a frying pan. Brown the onion slices, then remove and discard. Transfer the strained tomato mixture to the frying pan and simmer until semi-thick, about 40 minutes. Season to taste with salt.

Prepare the eggs: Heat oil in a saucepan. Sauté onion slices until soft and transparent. Then add the chile strips and cook for about 8 minutes. Season to taste with salt. Transfer the onions and chile to the tomato sauce and bring to a boil. Add 1 to 1½ cups water or chicken broth if the sauce thickens too much. It should be relatively thin for successful poaching. Then lower heat to a very slow simmer. Break eggs into the sauce very gently, taking care not to break yolks. You may wish to break each egg into a large serving spoon, then slide it into the sauce. Cover saucepan and continue cooking until the egg white is cooked, about 8 minutes. Add the cheese slices just before removing from heat, to melt them. If you wish, you may poach eggs in water instead. Drain, then add them to the sauce.

To serve: Serve directly from saucepan so as not to break egg yolks. Garnish with chopped cilantro or parsley. Accompany this dish with black beans (page 230), for breakfast or white rice for lunch. Serve with hot tortillas. **SERVES 8.**

DOBLADAS IN CHILE SAUCE

DOBLADAS ESTILO CHOLULA

My mother used to make dobladas regularly on our Chapopote Ranch. She learned to prepare them on a trip we took to Puebla to buy livestock. The mixture of dried chiles, cheese and cream make this a rich dish, perfect for breakfast or brunch. ~ MAGO

FOR THE SAUCE

12 CHILES PASILLAS, WASHED, SEEDED AND DEVEINED (SUBSTITUTE DRIED RED MILD NEW MEXICAN OR CALIFORNIA CHILES)

2 CHILES CHIPOTLES, WASHED, SEEDED AND DEVEINED

6 GARLIC CLOVES, PEELED

2 MEDIUM WHITE ONIONS, PEELED

2 POUNDS RIPE TOMATOES

2 CUPS WATER

⅔ CUP VEGETABLE OIL

2 SLICES WHITE ONION

SALT TO TASTE

FOR THE DOBLADAS

2 CUPS VEGETABLE OIL

36 MEDIUM CORN TORTILLAS

3 CUPS MUNSTER, STRING CHEESE, FRESH MOZZARELLA OR OTHER MILD CHEESE, GRATED

3 CUPS FRESH FETA OR FARMER'S CHEESE, DICED, GRATED OR CRUMBLED

¾ CUP GREEN ONIONS, CHOPPED

FOR THE GARNISH

¾ CUP HEAVY CREAM WHISKED WITH ¾ CUP SOUR CREAM

Prepare the sauce: Heat an ungreased skillet. Add the chiles and toast gently, turning with tongs. Soak chiles in salted water for about 20 minutes to reduce piquancy. Add the garlic, onion and tomatoes to the skillet and roast. Place chiles, garlic, onion and tomatoes in a blender or food processor with water and blend well.

Heat the oil in a frying pan. Brown the onion slices, then stir in ½ cup blended tomato sauce. Allow it to sizzle a moment, then add remainder of sauce. Simmer ingredients, stirring occasionally, for about 40 minutes or until the sauce has thickened. Season to taste with salt and thin with water or broth if necessary.

Prepare the dobladas: Preheat oven to 350°F. Heat the oil in a frying pan. Fry the tortillas briefly, turning once. Remove and drain on paper towels. Then dip tortillas in the chile sauce and fill with cheeses and chopped onion. Fold tortillas in half, then fold again to form triangular wedges. Place on a shallow baking tray or ovenproof dish and bake 20-25 minutes or until thoroughly hot. Remove from oven and drench with chile sauce. Sprinkle with remaining chopped onion, cheese and cream. **SERVES 8.**

MACHACA WITH EGGS, SONORA STYLE

MACHACA ESTILO SONORA

In northern Mexico, several kinds of meat are sun-dried with salt for later use with eggs, main courses, and snacks such as tortas and tacos. Dried beef is usually served with wheat flour tortillas, more typical of the region than are corn tortillas. This recipe from the state of Sonora was one of my grandmother's favorites for dried meat. ~ MARGARITA

1⅓ POUNDS DRIED BEEF OR SKIRT STEAK

¾ CUP VEGETABLE OIL

2 CUPS WHITE ONION, PEELED AND FINELY CHOPPED

3 LARGE, RIPE TOMATOES, ABOUT 1½ POUNDS, FINELY CHOPPED

6 FRESH CHILES, JALAPEÑOS OR SERRANOS, FINELY CHOPPED

SALT TO TASTE

8 EGGS, BEATEN

Prepare the beef: Shred the dried meat finely. Heat oil in a medium saucepan. Fry the onion until light brown, then add the dried beef. Add tomatoes, chile and season to taste (use salt sparingly if using dried beef). Cook for 25 minutes or until the mixture thickens. Then add the eggs and cook briefly, or until the eggs set. Do not overcook. Serve hot, accompanied with wheat tortillas and beans. **SERVES 8.**

NOTE

A substitute for machaca is cooked flank steak, finely shredded and dried in the microwave oven. Sauté with onion and oil before using.

CHILAQUILES WITH CHICKEN, SAUSAGE AND CHEESE

CHILAQUILES CON CHORIZO Y POLLO, ESTILO METEPEC

Chilaquiles (chee la KEE lez) are a Mexican favorite prepared with tortilla wedges or strips that are fried until crisp, then bathed with a sauce. Additional ingredients vary. This recipe calls for a typical Tolucan sausage and chicken. Other versions include eggs, cream, cheese, or a red sauce instead of a green sauce. ~ MAGO

FOR THE SAUCE

4 CUPS WATER

20 TOMATILLOS, HUSKED

1½ MEDIUM WHITE ONIONS, PEELED

6 LARGE RIPE TOMATOES (2½ GENEROUS POUNDS, APPROXIMATELY)

4 CHILES CHIPOTLES, LIGHTLY ROASTED AND SOAKED IN HOT WATER 5-10 MINUTES, OR FRESH SERRANOS, WASHED AND STEMMED, WHOLE

6 GARLIC CLOVES, PEELED AND PURÉED

½ CUP VEGETABLE OIL

1½ MEDIUM WHITE ONION, GRATED

SALT TO TASTE

FOR THE CHILAQUILES

3 CUPS VEGETABLE OIL

40 SMALL TORTILLAS, CUT INTO WEDGES

3 CHICKEN BREASTS, BOILED FOR 20 MINUTES WITH ONION, GARLIC, CELERY, CARROTS, BAY LEAF AND OREGANO AND SALT, THEN SHREDDED

2 CUPS CHORIZO SAUSAGE, FRIED

3 CUPS OAXACA, MONTEREY JACK, FRESH MOZZARELLA OR OTHER MILD, SOFT CHEESE, GRATED

1½ CUPS CRÈME FRAÎCHE

Prepare the sauce: Bring the water to a boil in a medium saucepan. Add the tomatillos and onion, and boil for about 25 minutes. Then place in a blender or food processor with 1-2 tablespoons cooking water and the tomatoes, chiles, and garlic. Purée, then strain and reserve.

Heat the oil in a medium frying pan. Sauté the grated onion, then add the strained tomatillo sauce. Simmer the mixture for about 35 minutes or until it thickens. Season to taste with salt.

Prepare the chilaquiles: Heat the oil in a medium frying pan. Fry the tortilla wedges until crisp, then remove from oil and drain on paper towels.

Preheat oven to 350°F. Butter a deep baking dish. Place a layer of fried tortillas on the bottom. Cover with half the tomatillo sauce. Cover with a layer of shredded chicken, fried chorizo sausage, cheese and cream. Repeat with a second layer of tortillas, sauce, chicken, chorizo, cheese and cream.

Bake the dish for about 40-45 minutes or until hot. Serve immediately, accompanied with refried beans. You may also prepare as individual servings by layering into individual baking dishes. If you prefer, you may reserve some of the sauce and serve individual unmolded casseroles on a bed of sauce, topped with melted cheese. **SERVES 8.**

PARROQUIA COFFEE

3 CUPS BOILING WATER

14 TABLESPOONS FRESHLY GROUND COFFEE (ESPRESSO)

8 CUPS SCALDING HOT MILK

SUGAR TO TASTE

Bring the water to a boil in a medium saucepan. Add all the coffee at once and stir. Then turn off heat and allow coffee to steep for 10 minutes. Strain coffee and serve about 1 inch of coffee in each glass or mug. Top with hot milk and serve immediately. **SERVES 8.**

PARROQUIA COFFEE ≈

To offer Parroquia Coffee in the style of the famous Parroquia Cafe at a brunch, set up an espresso maker where guests can help themselves to coffee, then pass a tray with scalded milk and sugar.

MEXICAN SCRAMBLED EGGS

HUEVOS REVUELTOS A LA MEXICANA

My grandmother Margarita taught my mother how to prepare this Mexican classic. She used to prepare it almost every day, since we were always in a hurry to get to school on time. ~
MARGARITA

FOR THE EGGS

16 TABLESPOONS OIL

1½ MEDIUM WHITE ONIONS, PEELED AND FINELY CHOPPED

6 MEDIUM RIPE TOMATOES, FINELY CHOPPED

4 TO 8 FRESH CHILES SERRANOS, FINELY CHOPPED

SALT TO TASTE

12 EGGS, BEATEN

FOR THE GARNISH

8 TORTILLA BASKETS OR CHIPS

BLACK BEANS

½ CUP CHOPPED CILANTRO

Prepare the eggs: Heat the oil in a large frying pan for about 3 minutes. Add 1 tablespoon of chopped onion and brown slightly. Then add the rest of the chopped onion, tomatoes and chiles and cook over high heat. Season with salt when ingredients begin to change color. Add eggs. Do not stir until the eggs set. Once they set, stir with a spoon or fork once, then finish cooking until the consistency of scrambled eggs. Remove frying pan from heat and stir eggs gently.

To serve: Serve the eggs in tortilla baskets (a tortilla set inside a mesh sieve and fried until crisp), or with tortilla chips and black beans. Garnish with chopped cilantro.
SERVES 8.

SIEVED BLACK BEANS WITH CHILE AND EPAZOTE

FRIJOLES ESTILO YUCATECO COLADO

This simple bean dish is at the heart of country cooking in the Yucatán peninsula. Epazote and chile give a lively twist to the flavor.

1   POUND BLACK BEANS, WASHED AND SORTED

WATER

1½   MEDIUM WHITE ONIONS, PEELED AND QUARTERED

4   EPAZOTE SPRIGS

2   CHILES HABANEROS OR FRESH JALAPEÑOS, WHOLE

SALT TO TASTE

FOR THE GARNISH

10   EPAZOTE LEAVES

3   FRESH CHILES HABANEROS OR FRESH JALAPEÑOS, CHOPPED COARSELY

Place beans in a large saucepan or cazuela (clay pot). Cover with three times their volume in water and soak overnight. The next day, drain beans and place in a large pot with water to cover. Cook beans with the onion, epazote and chile for 1½ hours or until very tender. Season to taste with salt. Remove whole chiles. Allow beans to cool, then pass through a sieve. Blend the beans and pass through a sieve again. Reheat beans with epazote and chiles until they thicken, then serve directly from the cazuela. **SERVES 8.**

EGGS BETWEEN TORTILLAS

HUEVOS MONTEJO ENTRE TORTILLAS

I had this dish for the first time in the Garcia Ponce home near the lovely Paseo del Montejo Avenue in Merida. I thought it a clever idea to break an egg directly into a split tortilla and cook the two together.

FOR THE EGGS

8   FRESHLY MADE CORN TORTILLAS (PACKAGED TORTILLAS CANNOT BE SUBSTITUTED)

8   EGGS

SALT TO TASTE

BLACK PEPPER TO TASTE

CHILTOMATE SAUCE, PAGE 221

2   CUPS SAFFLOWER OR CORN OIL

TOOTHPICKS

FOR THE GARNISH

¾   CUP AGED CHEESE OR FETA CHEESE, CRUMBLED

8   CHILES HABANEROS

Prepare the eggs: Prepare fresh tortillas (page 152). As you cook them on the comal or skillet, watch carefully. When they puff up, quickly make a small slit in the side and slide in a raw egg. Close with a toothpick. Heat oil in skillet. Sprinkle tortillas with salt and pepper to taste. Fry tortillas filled with eggs for 3-4 minutes, turning once. Remove from oil and drain on paper towels when done. Remove toothpick.

To serve: Drench with Chiltomate Sauce (page 221). Garnish with crumbled cheese and a chile habanero or other hot chile, or with epazote leaves. **SERVES 8.**

EPAZOTE ≈

The pungent wild herb so integral to Mexican bean cookery is called epazote (EP AH ZO TAY), wormseed, goosefoot, or Mexican tea. Its camphor-scented serrated leaves grow copiously on a tough woody-stemmed perennial plant that may arrive at 3 to 5 feet in height. Long a peasant's comfort, the herb is added to beans during the last 15 minutes of cooking and is said to make them more digestible as well as more delicious. Though seldom available fresh in North American markets, epazote grows quickly and easily from seed. In cold climates it will die back in winter but it is extremely hardy and enthusiastically self-propagating.

SEASHELL PASTRIES

CONCHAS

Pastries, which reflect both Spanish and native tastes, are a basic part of the Mexican breakfast. ~ PATRICIA

FOR THE YEAST

3   ENVELOPES DRY YEAST

9   TABLESPOONS LUKEWARM WATER

¾   CUP ALL-PURPOSE FLOUR

MEXICAN COFFEE

4 QUARTS WATER

4 STICKS CINNAMON, ABOUT 5 INCHES LONG

⅔ CUP PILONCILLO OR DARK BROWN SUGAR

2 CUPS MEDIUM-GRIND COFFEE, FRESHLY GROUND

Put the water in a pot and bring to a boil. Add cinnamon and sugar and boil 20 minutes. Add coffee and return to a boil, then remove from heat and cover. Steep 5 minutes. Return to heat and bring to a boil again, then remove from heat, cover and steep 5 minutes. Return to heat, boil, remove and steep one last time. Strain if not serving immediately.

MEXICAN COFFEE ≈

Coffee is grown in the southeastern highlands of Mexico. Prepared in the traditional manner, it has a very distinctive flavor. In the cold months it is often laced with rum or cognac and served to top off a heavy meal. Sometimes it is flavored with a clove or two, or with a twist of orange peel.

FOR THE DOUGH

4 CUPS ALL-PURPOSE FLOUR

1¼ TEASPOONS SALT

½ CUP LARD OR VEGETABLE SHORTENING

1 CUP BUTTER

1⅓ CUPS SUGAR

7 LARGE EGGS PLUS 2 EGG YOLKS

FOR THE TOPPING

1 CUP ALL-PURPOSE FLOUR

1 CUP SUGAR

1½ CUPS LARD OR VEGETABLE SHORTENING

4 EGG YOLKS

Prepare the yeast: Dissolve the yeast in lukewarm water. Add flour and blend slightly until the mixture forms a ball. Cover with a cloth and set aside in a draft-free spot for 10 to 30 minutes, or until the dough doubles in volume.

Prepare the dough: Sift the flour and salt on a flat surface. Add the lard and butter and knead. Work in sugar and eggs, then add yeast starter. Knead until the dough is smooth, slightly elastic and no longer sticky.

Sprinkle in a little extra flour if necessary. Shape into a ball and place in a bowl. Grease hands with butter or lard and smooth over ball so that the dough does not dry out. Cover dough and let stand in a draft-free spot for 2½ hours. Transfer to bottom shelf of refrigerator and let rest 12 hours.

Remove from refrigerator. Butter 2 or 3 baking trays and preheat oven to 350°F. Knead the dough 5-8 minutes, then divide into 20 equal portions. Place on prepared baking trays.

Prepare topping: Combine the flour, sugar, lard and egg yolks in a medium bowl, mixing with the hands. Once well mixed, divide the mixture into 20 equal portions and shape into little pancakes. Place a sugar pancake on top of each ball, and score with a knife or special concha scorer both lengthwise and widthwise. Set aside and allow the conchas to rise again until doubled. Bake in preheated oven for 40 minutes or until the shells are very light brown. Do not overbake or they will harden. Remove from oven and cool. Serve with hot chocolate or coffee. Marmalade may be served on the side. **MAKES 20 PASTRIES.**

SEASHELL VARIATIONS ≈

Concha dough may be shaped into a cone, brushed with egg yolk and milk, then sprinkled with sugar to make a little volcano. You may also add 1½ to 2½ tablespoons of ground cinnamon or cocoa to the dough.

SEASHELL PASTRIES WITH COFFEE. BELOW, THE CONCHA SCORERS USED TO SCORE THE TOPS OF THE PASTRIES.

EGGS IN GREEN SAUCE

HUEVOS EN SALSA VERDE

When I was a child, this traditional breakfast dish was prepared at home and on the Chapopote Ranch, although it always seemed to taste better on the ranch, probably because the ingredients were fresher and it was prepared on a firewood stove. Whether it is made with freshly laid eggs or not, it is a sure hit for breakfast. ~ PATRICIA

FOR THE SAUCE

8	CUPS WATER
24	TOMATILLOS, MEDIUM, HUSKED
1	MEDIUM YELLOW OR WHITE ONION, PEELED
8	GARLIC CLOVES, PEELED
8	FRESH CHILES SERRANOS OR 4 CHILES JALAPEÑOS, STEMMED, WHOLE
40	CILANTRO SPRIGS
1	MEDIUM YELLOW OR WHITE ONION, PEELED AND QUARTERED
6	GARLIC CLOVES, PEELED
6	FRESH CHILES SERRANOS OR 4 CHILE JALAPEÑO, STEMMED, WHOLE
	SALT TO TASTE
⅔	CUP VEGETABLE OIL
2	ONION SLICES
1½	CUPS WATER
	SALT AND PEPPER TO TASTE

FOR THE EGGS

⅔	CUP VEGETABLE OIL
18	EGGS
1	TEASPOON SALT OR TO TASTE

FOR THE GARNISH

⅔ CUP CHOPPED CILANTRO

⅔ CUP CHOPPED WHITE ONION OR A COMBINATION OF YELLOW AND WHITE ONION

Prepare the sauce: Bring the water to a boil in a medium saucepan. Add the tomatillos, onion, garlic, chiles and cilantro. Cook for about 8 minutes. Then remove boiled ingredients with a slotted spoon and transfer to a blender or food processor along with the raw onion, raw garlic, chiles and salt. Add 1 to 2 cups cooking water. Purée. Strain half the mixture.

Heat the oil in a medium frying pan. Brown the onion slices, then remove and discard. Transfer the strained and unstrained tomatillo sauce to the frying pan. Cook for about 35 minutes or until the sauce releases its fat. Then add tomatillo cooking water and cook until sauce is medium-thick. Rectify seasoning.

Prepare the eggs: Add oil to a large frying pan and heat thoroughly. Meanwhile, beat the eggs with salt. Pour eggs into the preheated frying pan and cook until set, as if preparing an omelet. Turn and cook for an additional 5 minutes. Then break cooked eggs into pieces with a spoon. Pour green sauce over the eggs and simmer about 20 minutes.

To serve: Serve eggs hot, garnished with chopped cilantro and onion and accompanied with corn tortillas, beans and Mexican coffee (page 141). **SERVES 8.**

CHORIZO SAUSAGE, PITIC STYLE

CHORIZO ESTILO PITIC

Chorizo, *a Mexican version of Spanish sausage, is a basic ingredient in Mexican cooking. It is served with everything from scrambled eggs to main courses, taco fillings and quesadillas.* ~ MARGARITA

2 GENEROUS POUNDS GROUND PORK, WITH A LITTLE FAT

⅔ CUP LARD

6 CHILES ANCHOS OR CALIFORNIA, WASHED, SEEDED AND DEVEINED, ROASTED, SOAKED IN WATER AND PURÉED

1½ TABLESPOONS SALT OR TO TASTE

1½ TABLESPOONS SUGAR OR TO TASTE

10 GARLIC CLOVES, PEELED AND PURÉED

1½ TEASPOONS DRIED OREGANO

1½ TEASPOONS GROUND CINNAMON

1 TEASPOON FRESHLY GROUND BLACK PEPPER

¼ TEASPOON GROUND CLOVES

¾ CUP VINEGAR

VEGETABLE OIL

4 WHITE ONION SLICES, THICK

Combine in a large bowl the meat, lard, chiles, salt, sugar, garlic, oregano, cinnamon, pepper, cloves and vinegar. Mix well and refrigerate for 2 days. Pack the meat into cleaned, dry tripe or sausage casings and hang in a cool airy room for 3 days or until well dried, then refrigerate for long storage. If you wish, you may pack the chorizo in plastic bags instead and freeze for later use. In this case, freeze immediately after packing. To cook, add oil to a frying pan, brown onion slices in the oil, then remove and discard. Add chorizo and brown. **SERVES 8.**

EGGS IN GREEN SAUCE WITH PARROQUIA COFFEE (PAGE 137) AND FRESH TORTILLAS.

CHORIZO ≈

The Mexican version of the Spanish sausage chorizo may be added to scrambled eggs, poultry stuffing, beans, lentil soup, cornbread muffins, biscuits, quiche (page 73), meatloaf, or other dishes. To reduce fat, lightly fry it, then drain it thoroughly on paper towels before adding it to the dish. "Pitic" is the name of the place in Hermosillo, Sonora, where this chorizo was first made.

EGGS IN GREEN SAUCE WITH PARROQUIA COFFEE (PAGE 137) AND FRESH TORTILLAS.

BAKED CHILE-TOMATO CREPES

CREPAS DE RAJAS Y SALSA DE JITOMATE

My Aunt Vasseur used to prepare this delicious dish. My grandmother eventually learned to make it since we enjoyed it so much. It is particularly suitable for a brunch or late breakfast. ~ EMILIA

FOR THE CREPES

24 CREPES (PAGE 45)

FOR THE FILLING

½ CUP OLIVE OIL

⅓ CUP BUTTER

½ MEDIUM WHITE ONION, PEELED AND SLICED ON THE DIAGONAL

8 CHILES POBLANOS OR CHILACAS, ROASTED AND SWEATED, PEELED, SEEDED AND DEVEINED, SOAKED IN WATER AND VINEGAR FOR **20** MINUTES, CUT IN THIN STRIPS (SUBSTITUTE ANAHEIM OR BANANA PEPPERS)

4½ CUPS CORN KERNELS, COOKED (PREFERABLY BOILED ON THE COB IN SALTED WATER FOR **8** MINUTES)

SALT TO TASTE

FOR THE SAUCE

6 LARGE, RIPE TOMATOES (2½ POUNDS APPROXIMATELY)

1¼ MEDIUM WHITE ONIONS, PEELED AND QUARTERED

4 GARLIC CLOVES, GROUND

4 FRESH CHILES SERRANOS OR **2-3** FRESH CHILES JALAPEÑOS, STEMMED, WHOLE

1½ CUPS WATER

½ CUP VEGETABLE OIL

2 SLICES WHITE ONION

SALT AND PEPPER

1 POUND CHIHUAHUA, FONTINA, STRING, MONTEREY JACK OR OTHER SEMI-SOFT MILD CHEESE, GRATED

Prepare crepes according to the recipe, making them very thin.

Prepare the filling: Heat the oil and the butter in a saucepan. Add onion, chile strips, and corn. Season to taste with salt and cook 10 minutes over low heat until the mixture thickens.

Prepare the sauce: Place tomatoes, onion, garlic, chiles and water in a blender or food processor and purée. Strain. Heat the oil in a frying pan, add the sliced onion and brown. Stir in tomato purée (it should sizzle when it hits the skillet) and simmer, stirring occasionally, about 40 minutes or until thick. Season to taste with salt and pepper.

Assemble the crepes: Preheat oven to 350°F. Butter a shallow baking dish. Fill each crepe with chile mixture and fold in half. Fold once again into the shape of a triangular wedge. Crepes may also be rolled if you prefer. Overlap on a prepared baking tray. Cover with tomato sauce and sprinkle with grated cheese. Bake for about 40 minutes. Serve hot, accompanied with green salad.
SERVES 8.

VARIATION

Add cream to the tomato sauce (1½ cups heavy cream and 1 cup sour cream); garnish platter with cream.

RICE AND CHILE CASSEROLE

BUDÍN DE ARROZ CON RAJAS DE CHILE POBLANO

This souffle-like casserole is exquisite. My mother learned to prepare it from my grandmother. It is a good dish for a brunch buffet. ~ MAGO

FOR THE RICE

6 CUPS WHITE RICE, COOKED

FOR THE SAUCE

½ CUP CORN OIL

4 GARLIC CLOVES, PEELED

2 LARGE WHITE ONIONS, PEELED AND SLICED DIAGONALLY

12 CHILES POBLANOS, ROASTED, SWEATED AND PEELED, SEEDED AND DEVEINED, SOAKED IN SALTED WATER FOR 20 MINUTES TO REMOVE PIQUANCY, CUT INTO STRIPS

6 LARGE RIPE TOMATOES

1 MEDIUM WHITE ONION, PEELED AND QUARTERED

3 GARLIC CLOVES, PEELED

SALT TO TASTE

BLACK PEPPER TO TASTE

FOR THE CREAM

2 CUPS CRÈME FRAÎCHE OR 1 CUP HEAVY WHIPPING CREAM WHISKED WITH 1 CUP SOUR CREAM

2 CUPS YOGURT, NATURAL FLAVOR

½ TEASPOON SALT

½ TEASPOON FRESHLY GROUND BLACK PEPPER

2 CLOVES GARLIC, PEELED AND PRESSED

2½ CUPS FRESH MOZZARELLA, OAXACA OR STRING CHEESE

2 CUPS CREAMY MONTEREY JACK, GRUYERE OR CHIHUAHUA CHEESE

FOR THE TOPPING

5 EGG WHITES

¼ TEASPOON SALT

4 EGG YOLKS, BEATEN LIGHTLY

Cook rice and reserve.

Prepare the sauce: Heat the oil in a medium saucepan. Brown the garlic cloves, then remove and discard. Sauté the onion slices in the same oil until transparent. Stir in chile strips and cook for an additional 5 minutes. In a blender or food processor, grind the tomatoes with the raw onion and garlic. Strain the tomato mixture and stir into the sautéed chile strips. Season to taste with salt and pepper and continue cooking over a low heat for an additional 30 minutes or until the sauce thickens.

Prepare the cream and cheese: Stir together cream and yogurt. Season with salt, pepper and garlic. Set aside. Grate cheese and set aside.

Prepare the topping: Beat egg whites with salt until stiff. Then carefully fold in egg yolks.

Assemble the casserole: Preheat oven to 350°F. Butter a deep baking dish. Spoon half the rice into the dish and cover with half the tomato-chile sauce. Then place a layer of half the cream on top. Sprinkle half the grated cheese over dish. Repeat a second layer of rice, using remaining rice. Repeat layers of sauce, cream and grated cheese until all the ingredients are incorporated. Cook for 25 minutes. Then spread the prepared topping over the casserole and bake for 45 minutes or until the topping is golden brown. Serve immediately. SERVES 8-12.

CHILE FLAVORING ≈

Fresh, chopped or roasted chiles are extremely versatile. They may flavor cornbread, creamed corn, vinaigrettes, chicken consommé, mayonnaise, fried potatoes, rice, cheese sauce, sautéed mushrooms, cream soups, potato salad or other salads and many other dishes.

BRUNCH BUFFET ≈

FRESH FRUIT

RICE AND CHILE CASSEROLE

PICKLED SHRIMP WITH OLIVES AND CHILES
Page 196.

CILANTRO OMELETS
Page 133.

CRISP, FRIED TORTILLAS
Page 152.

FRESH SALSAS
Pages 114 and 115.

NAOLINCO BREAD WITH PUMPKIN SEED BUTTER
Page 215.

LENTEN TURNOVERS
Page 193.

TORITOS
Page 172.

COFFEE

CHILE STRIPS WITH CREAM

RAJAS CON CREMA

½   CUP BUTTER

⅓   CUP OLIVE OIL

1   TABLESPOON GARLIC, MINCED

4   MEDIUM WHITE ONIONS, PEELED AND
    SLICED ON THE DIAGONAL

14   CHILES POBLANOS, ROASTED, SWEATED
    AND PEELED, SEEDED AND DEVEINED,
    SOAKED IN SALTED WATER FOR 20 MINUTES
    AND CUT INTO STRIPS

1¼   CUP HEAVY WHIPPING CREAM WHISKED
    TOGETHER WITH 1¼ CUP SOUR CREAM

    SALT TO TASTE

    BLACK PEPPER TO TASTE

Heat the butter and oil in a medium saucepan. Sauté minced garlic until light brown. Add onion and chiles and sauté for 8 minutes. Stir in creams and season to taste with salt and pepper. Cook until the mixture thickens, about 40 minutes. **SERVES 8.**

USING PICKLED CHILES

≈

Use pickled chiles to:

Garnish a tostada (a fried tortilla topped with beans, shredded meat, shredded lettuce and avocado).

Season a Puebla-style semita — a round hard roll with goat cheese, avocado, pickled carrots and a drizzle of olive oil.

Add to beans or rice.

Flavor a chicken broth.

Tuck inside a quesadilla.

Combine with cream cheese and spread on toasted tortillas.

Add to a fresh leafy salad with vinaigrette.

Place on the table as an everyday condiment.

Serve with all egg dishes, and add to omelets.

Make enfrijoladas — caramelized onions topped with refried beans and pickled chiles.

Add to a creamy dip for fried tortillas.

PICKLED OAXACAN CHILE PASILLAS

CHILES PASILLAS OAXAQUEÑOS ENCURTIDOS

The Oaxacan marketplace looks folkloric with its mountains of colored chiles lining the market stalls. There you will find the chile pasilla of Oaxaca, a lightly smoked chile whose taste differs from others of its type in Mexico. Oaxacan chiles pasillas are commonly pickled in pineapple vinegar and served at any meal — breakfast, lunch, or dinner. This pickle may be made with any favorite chile. ~ PATRICIA

1½   POUNDS OAXACAN CHILE PASILLAS,
    WASHED, CHOPPED AND SOAKED FOR 2
    HOURS IN SALTED WATER (SUBSTITUTE
    OTHER DRIED RED MEDIUM-HOT CHILES)

6   MEDIUM WHITE ONIONS, PEELED AND
    SLICED THINLY

60   GARLIC CLOVES, PEELED (6 HEADS)

40   SPRIGS THYME

2   TEASPOONS CLOVES

2   TABLESPOONS BLACK PEPPERCORNS

    SALT TO TASTE

2   TABLESPOONS WHOLE ALLSPICE

4   QUARTS FRUIT VINEGAR OR WINE VINEGAR,
    PREFERABLY PINEAPPLE VINEGAR, OR TO
    COVER

Sterilize a 4-quart jug or jar or 4 quart jars. Layer the chiles, onion, garlic, thyme, cloves, peppercorns, allspice and salt in the jar until all are used. Bring the vinegar to a boil, then pour over chiles and spices. Cover tightly. Allow the mixture to marinate 4-5 days minimum at room temperature. (To sterilize jars, immerse them in boiling water 15-20 minutes.) **MAKES 4 QUARTS.**

PICKLED ONIONS, CARROTS AND CHILES

CEBOLLAS, ZANAHORIAS Y CHILES ENCURTIDOS

This piquant condiment is a familiar companion to tacos, tortas, egg dishes, beans and rice. It adds a toothsome touch to a picnic, being easy to transport and a zesty addition to any main course. In some outdoor Oaxacan restaurants guests nibble on a little dish of pickled onions, carrots and chiles as they sip a cold beer and watch the passersby.

6½　POUNDS WHITE ONIONS, PEELED AND QUARTERED OR CUT ON THE BIAS

4½　POUNDS CARROTS, PEELED AND SLICED THINLY

3⅓　POUNDS FRESH CHILES SERRANOS OR JALAPEÑOS, WASHED, WHOLE (JALAPEÑOS WILL BE MORE PIQUANT)

40　BLACK PEPPERCORNS

4　TABLESPOONS OREGANO

12　SPRIGS MARJORAM

12　SPRIGS THYME

15　BAY LEAVES

80　GARLIC CLOVES, PEELED

2　TABLESPOONS SALT OR TO TASTE

3　QUARTS LIGHT VINEGAR OR TO COVER

1¼　CUPS OLIVE OIL, SPANISH STYLE

In a large bowl or gallon glass jar, combine all the ingredients except vinegar and oil. Heat vinegar to boiling, then remove from heat and whisk in oil. Pour this mixture over the chiles and other ingredients and stir well. Part of the vinegar may be substituted with water to make a lighter pickling sauce. Allow vegetables to marinate for a minimum of 5 days at room temperature. Then refrigerate for longer storage. **MAKES 4 QUARTS.**

NOTE

The vegetables may be lightly sautéed in olive oil, then brought to a boil with vinegar, before marinating.

CHILE DE AGUA STRIPS AND LIME

RAJAS DE CHILE DE AGUA Y LIMÓN

My grandmother prepared chile de agua — grown locally in Oaxaca — in strips, marinated in lime juice, for family picnics. She would soak the chiles at least a day before the outing, so that they took on a tangy flavor. She served the chiles with the snack or main course she had made for the occasion, which might range from fish to poultry or meat. This recipe is an easily portable substitute for a chile sauce, and may also be served alone with large tortillas (blanditas) and guacamole. ~ MARGARITA

12　CHILES DE AGUA OR ANAHEIM OR POBLANOS, ROASTED, SWEATED AND PEELED, SEEDED AND DEVEINED, CUT IN THIN STRIPS

1　LARGE WHITE ONION, PEELED AND SLICED ON THE BIAS

　THE JUICE OF 3 LIMES

1　TEASPOON DRIED OREGANO OR TO TASTE

　SALT TO TASTE

Combine the chiles, onion and lime juice in a glass bowl. Season to taste with oregano and salt and marinate for 3 hours or overnight. Before serving, sprinkle with oregano. **SERVES 8.**

CHILES

CHILE FIRE ≈

Capsaicin is the alkaloid in chiles that gives them their fire. It is concentrated primarily in the interior ribs or veins and secondarily in the seeds that cling to the veins. For a milder dish, thoroughly remove veins and seeds, parboil chiles briefly, or soak in water mixed with 1-2 tablespoons vinegar. Or use fewer chiles.

LOVERS OF CHILE FIRE ≈

Frequent chile eaters seem to develop an immunity to the piquance of chiles, but they can lose their immunity over a period of blander eating. To cool a chile-fired mouth, do not drink liquids (which spread the capsaicin to other taste buds) but enjoy a bite of tortilla, rice or bread, and salt.

PICKLED SMOKED CHILES

CHIPOTLES A LA POBLANA

Chipotle chiles are small jalapeño or serrano chiles that have been sun-dried and smoked. Although they vary from region to region, they all share a slightly smoky and pungent flavor. They are delicious pickled in vinegar with piloncillo sugar, garlic and herbs. You can control the bite of the chiles by the amount of seeds you leave in — the more, the hotter. ~ PATRICIA

1	CUP OLIVE OR VEGETABLE OIL
6	GARLIC HEADS, CUT IN HALF ACROSS THE GRAIN
6	MEDIUM WHITE ONIONS, PEELED AND QUARTERED
2	GENEROUS POUNDS OF CHILES CHIPOTLES OR FRESH JALAPEÑO CHILES (OR CHILES MORITAS OR MECO) PRICKED WITH A NEEDLE, WASHED AND SOAKED IN SALTED WATER FOR 1½ DAYS
40	SPRIGS THYME
40	SPRIGS MARJORAM
20	BAY LEAVES
1	TABLESPOON OREGANO
2	TABLESPOONS WHOLE ALLSPICE
1	TABLESPOON PEPPERCORNS
20	LARGE CARROTS, OR 30 SMALL, PEELED AND CUT IN SLICES
	SALT TO TASTE

14 CUPS FRUIT OR WINE VINEGAR

8 CUPS WATER

3 CUPS PILONCILLO SUGAR OR DARK BROWN
SUGAR, OR TO TASTE

Heat the oil in a large pot. Add garlic and
sauté for 10 minutes. Then add onion and
sauté. Stir in chiles, thyme, marjoram, bay
leaves, oregano, allspice, peppercorns and
carrots and cook for 20 minutes.

In a separate saucepan, heat the vinegar,
water and piloncillo. Bring to a boil and heat
until the piloncillo has melted. Then add to
the chiles and bring to a boil three times,
lowering heat after each boil. Stir chiles
occasionally with a wooden spoon. Rectify
seasoning. Then remove from heat and
allow to cool. When cool, transfer to one or
more large sterile glass jars and cover
tightly. As the chiles age, they become
more flavorful. Keep at room temperature
or refrigerate. MAKES ABOUT 3 QUARTS.

VARIATION

To make pickled chiles adobados, add 6
chiles anchos, a cinnamon stick, cloves and
pepper. These ingredients should be fried in
⅓ cup olive oil, seasoned to taste, and
added to chiles.

TELERAS FILLED WITH
REFRIED BEANS,
SHREDDED LETTUCE,
CHEESE AND CREAM,
SERVED AT A PICNIC.

HARD ROLLS

BOLILLOS Y TELERAS

*W*heat flour has become almost as important as corn in today's Mexican diet. This recipe comes from LA COSA ESTA DEL COCOL Y OTROS *(Museo Nacional de Culturas Populares.)*

4½ CUPS FLOUR

1 TABLESPOON (1⅔ OUNCE) FRESH COMPRESSED YEAST OR 1 TABLESPOON (⅓ OUNCE) DRIED YEAST

2 TABLESPOONS SUGAR

½ TEASPOON SALT OR TO TASTE

⅔ CUP LARD OR VEGETABLE SHORTENING

1½ CUPS PLUS 4 TABLESPOONS WATER OR MORE, DEPENDING ON THE FLOUR

5 TEASPOONS SALT

Combine 2 cups flour and yeast in a bowl. Add sugar and ½ teaspoon salt. Heat the lard or shortening and water in a medium saucepan until warm. Add this mixture to flour and yeast and beat with the kneading attachment of a food processor or by hand. Gradually add remaining flour, scraping sides of bowl with a rubber spatula. Beat dough until it is smooth, elastic and glossy, and no longer sticky. Generously butter a baking tray. Shape the dough into a ball and place on the tray, rolling slightly to butter. Sprinkle with flour and cover dough with a cloth. Allow to stand in a draft-free spot for 2 hours or until it doubles in volume.

Preheat oven to 350°F. Divide the dough into 12 equal portions.

For bolillos, shape each portion into an oblong shape and stretch the edges slightly to make two pointed tips. Holding the two tips, roll the dough in the air, as if you were wringing it. Place on prepared baking tray and make an incision on the top. Repeat same procedure for remaining rolls. Allow to set for 45 minutes.

If preparing teleras, shape each portion of dough into an oblong shape and place on the prepared baking tray. Press slightly to flatten dough and score twice on top. Repeat procedure for remaining dough and allow to set for 45 minutes.

Dissolve salt in water and use to brush tops of rolls. Bake in preheated oven for 30-45 minutes or until golden brown.
MAKES 1 DOZEN ROLLS.

BOLILLOS Y TELERAS
≈

The Mexican version of French bread is versatile and ubiquitous. Serve bolillos:

Spread with a layer of refried beans and topped with melted cheese and Salsa Mexicana (page 177).

With poached eggs and Chile Strips in Cream (page 146) or Chiltomate Sauce (page 221).

Cubed and toasted to garnish a soup.

With Oaxacan Meatballs and sauce (page 87) as an open-faced sandwich.

CLASSIC CORN MASA ≈

Begin with two pounds of dried hominy corn kernels. Place them in a large stockpot with approximately 3 quarts water. Stir in 2 tablespoons powdered lime. Simmer over medium heat, stirring regularly, for approximately 40 minutes or until the skins of the kernels can be removed easily. Remove the pot from the heat and allow to stand for one day. Next day, skin the kernels by rubbing them against one another between your hands. Also remove the "eye" at the base of each kernel. Wash very thoroughly, using several changes of water. Drain and grind the kernels, using a hand grinder and metate or a food processor.

CORN TORTILLAS

TORTILLAS

Tortillas (tor TEE yahz) are to Mexican cuisine what the sun is to the day and the moon to the night. They are served to accompany breakfast, lunch and dinner, and are combined with a variety of fillings for a small tasty bite or a sumptuous main course. There is always an abundance of tortillas in my family's kitchen. To vary our menu we sometimes serve white, sometimes yellow (the most common in Mexico City), blue or purple corn tortillas. Either we buy them ready made, or make them from scratch. They are eaten in many sizes — from 2 inches in diameter, for tiny crepes, to 4 or 5 inches (the most widely used in the metropolitan area), to 8 or even 12 inches, the size of the TLAYUDAS or BLANDITAS. Their thickness and shape vary as well. Sometimes they are prepared paper-thin, and other times they are made thick. They may be served with toppings (GORDITAS), filled with beans like "pita" pockets (PANUCHOS) or fried (TOTOPOS). Although most tortillas are round, some are shaped ovally to make HUARACHES or TLACOYOS.

A tortilla that is filled and folded in half like a turnover is called QUESADILLA. One that is fried, served flat and topped with beans or meat and garnishes is called a TOSTADA. When stuffed and rolled up, tortillas are referred to as TACOS, which means "rolled." Tacos that are drenched in a cream, tomato or tomatillo sauce are called ENCHILADAS. Tortillas are easy to make and the fresh corn aroma of the silky dough is a pleasure to experience. Look for a tortilla press and a comal (a special griddle for toasting tortillas) in specialty kitchen shops such as Williams Sonoma, or in Hispanic markets, some health food stores, and gourmet shops. Tortilla-making is a daily ritual in the Mexican kitchen. You will quickly acquire the "feel" for it if you try it; after a very little experience, it will become fast and natural. It also provides the opportunity for a party with friends. Invite them to join you in the kitchen making tortillas, fillings and salsas, then sit down to a wonderful feast.

Here are three easy ways to prepare masa dough for tortillas.

MASA FROM MASA HARINA

2 CUPS DRY QUAKER'S MASA HARINA OR MASECA BRAND DRIED MASA (THESE ARE PACKAGED MIXES MADE FROM DRIED GROUND LIMED CORN NOW WIDELY SOLD IN THE FLOUR SECTION OF U.S. SUPERMARKETS)

⅓ CUP FLOUR

½ TEASPOON SALT

1½ TO 1¾ CUPS WARM WATER

CORN FLOUR MASA

2 CUPS CORN FLOUR (NOT CORN MEAL), WHITE OR BLUE, (SOLD ESPECIALLY FOR MAKING TORTILLAS, AVAILABLE IN HISPANIC AND SPECIALTY MARKETS)

½ CUP ALL-PURPOSE FLOUR

½ TEASPOON SALT

1½ TO 1¾ CUPS WARM WATER, APPROXIMATELY

FRESH MASA DOUGH

1 POUND FRESH MASA (FRESH DOUGH MADE FROM DRIED HOMINY CORN KERNELS SOAKED IN WATER WITH POWDERED LIMESTONE, THEN HULLED AND GROUND, AVAILABLE IN SOME HISPANIC AREAS)

WARM WATER

Masa harina is the most widely available ingredient for making tortillas in the U.S. However, whichever set of ingredients you are using, first place dry ingredients in a large bowl, then add warm water. Turn the dough out on a flat surface. Knead the dough with dampened hands for 5-10 minutes until it forms a smooth, silky mass that is not sticky. Texture should be soft and moist, so that a pinch of dough presses flat easily between two fingers. Allow the dough to rest as you heat the comal or griddle. After resting, it may need the addition of a small amount of warm water. Heat a large ungreased griddle or comal until it is very hot. Line a tortilla press with two squares of plastic. Pinch off enough dough to make a 1 to 1½-inch ball. Place the ball of dough between the plastic squares in the tortilla press and apply pressure to the lever to flatten the dough. Remove carefully, peeling away the plastic squares (return them to the press for the next tortilla). Toss the tortilla back and forth a few times between your hands to aerate it slightly. If dough is moist enough, it will spread evenly in the press and the edges will be smooth and silky. If edges crack when the dough is pressed, dough may be too dry. Slide the tortilla onto the hot skillet, comal or griddle and bake 30 seconds. Turn with a fork or your fingers and cook 1 minute. Turn again and finish cooking, about 15-30 seconds. Tortillas will puff up slightly, then deflate a little. If the tortilla colors very unevenly in "hot spots," the griddle may be too hot. A freshly cooked tortilla will have a richly colored, slightly glossy patina. If tortillas stick, you may need to wipe the griddle with a touch of oil applied to a paper towel. Griddles used for tortillas will cure over time and should be reserved for tortilla-making if possible. Repeat with remaining dough. Keep tortillas warm, wrapped in a cloth so they don't become brittle. Makes approximately 12 tortillas. Tortillas may be used immediately or cooled, wrapped closely and kept in the refrigerator for up to a week. Reheat on a griddle or comal before using.

MASA HARINA ≈

Because ground limed corn (masa) sours easily, it is dried into a powdered substance called masa harina, sold in packages in the flour section of supermarkets. Masa harina can easily be reconstituted with water to create masa dough for tortillas. Two common brands are Quaker's Masa Harina and Maseca brand dried masa (masa + "seca," or "dried" = Maseca).

CORN AND LIME ≈

From the very early days, Indian cultures that depended on corn processed the kernels with the help of an alkaline substance. Mayans and Aztecs used wood ashes or powdered limestone and Pueblo Indians of the southwestern U.S. used limestone or naturally-occurring soda. Only in the last generation have we understood the importance of lime to the nourishing properties of corn, whose stores of the vitamin niacin it releases. It is also true that limed corn has an earthy "bouquet" that is incomparable.

WHEAT FLOUR TORTILLAS

TORTILLAS DE HARINA

Wheat flour tortillas are very common in Northern Mexico. Making your own is a pleasant experience that will become easier and easier as you acquire the "touch" for it. ~ PATRICIA

3¾ CUPS ALL-PURPOSE FLOUR

1½ TEASPOONS SALT

1 CUP PLUS 1 HEAPING TABLESPOON LARD OR SHORTENING

1¼ TO 1½ CUPS LUKEWARM WATER OR MORE DEPENDING ON THE FLOUR

Sift the flour and salt twice. Place in a bowl and add lard. Work in with two knives until mixture resembles coarse meal. Gradually add water and knead until dough forms a ball and is shiny and elastic. Do not add full amount of water until you can see whether you need it. Kneading is easier if your hands are moist — more moist than they are for the kneading of corn tortillas. Kneading may require 30-45 minutes. Dough should be moist. Cover with a cloth and allow to stand for 30 minutes. (You may use the bread attachment of a food processor for kneading if you prefer.) When dough is elastic enough you will see the "eyes" or stretched places on its surfaces; it should be glossy and warm.

Heat a comal. (Wheat flour tortillas must be cooked on a very hot comal to avoid becoming brittle.) Meanwhile, working on a formica table top or a sheet of plastic, pinch off about 1 inch of dough, form it into a ball, and with a rolling pin, flatten until it is ⅛-¼ inch thick. Turn over while shaping. Then stretch tortilla, pulling slightly to extend. Wipe preheated comal lightly with vegetable oil. Cook the extended tortilla about ½-1 minute on each side, then turn. Do not cook too long. Push tortilla down with a spatula as it is cooking or it will puff up. Keep tortillas warm by wrapping in a cloth. Repeat same procedure for remaining dough. If you plan to store and reheat tortillas, brown them a little more than if you are going to use them immediately.

To serve: Serve directly from a tortilla basket or a cloth. These tortillas are delicious for preparing burritos, machacas, bean or guacamole tacos, and seafood or meat fajitas. **MAKES 18-20 TORTILLAS.**

URES' CAZUELA

CAZUELA DE URES

This is a typical main course served in the northern State of Sonora. It is a stew that is reduced and used as a filling for the famous Sonoran burritos. ~ MARGARITA

FOR THE MEAT AND BROTH

6 QUARTS WATER

2½ POUNDS SKIRT STEAK, CHOPPED INTO PIECES

2 MEDIUM WHITE ONIONS, PEELED AND CHOPPED

1 GARLIC HEAD, CLOVES PEELED

4 BAY LEAVES

SALT TO TASTE

FOR THE VEGETABLES

3 TABLESPOONS CORN OIL

4 CHILES ANCHOS, WASHED, SEEDED AND DEVEINED (SUBSTITUTE OTHER DRIED RED CHILES SUCH AS CALIFORNIA OR MILD NEW MEXICAN)

1½ MEDIUM WHITE ONIONS, PEELED AND QUARTERED

4 GARLIC CLOVES, PEELED

3 LARGE, RIPE TOMATOES (ABOUT 3¾ POUNDS), ROASTED

½ CUP VEGETABLE OIL

1½ TO 2 CUPS COOKED GARBANZOS (CHICKPEAS)

2½ CUPS GREEN BEANS, CHOPPED, COOKED FOR 8 MINUTES IN SALTED WATER, THEN REFRESHED IN ICED WATER

Prepare the meat and broth: Heat the water in a large stockpot. Add meat, onion, garlic, bay leaves and salt to taste. Cook for 1½ hours or until the meat is tender. Remove from heat and allow meat to cool in the broth. Reserve.

Prepare the vegetables: Heat the oil in a large saucepan. Fry the chiles briefly, then soak in meat broth to cover for 10 minutes. Place onion, garlic and tomatoes in a blender or food processor and purée. Strain mixture. Heat remaining oil in saucepan and add strained purée. Cook until the mixture thickens, about 45 minutes. Season to taste and add garbanzos, broth and meat. Simmer for 30 minutes, rectifying seasoning. Add cooked green beans 5 minutes before serving. Serve from a deep bowl.
SERVES 8.

VARIATION

To make Sonoran burritos, cook until the liquid evaporates and use to stuff wheat flour tortillas. Roll up the stuffed tortillas. Heat briefly in a medium oven.

CHICO SALSA

SALSA ESTILO EL CHICO

This sauce comes from the Chico region of Hidalgo. It is perfect with fried eggs and warm corn tortillas. There are as many uses for Mexican salsas as your imagination can create. Try this salsa (or any of the others in this book) with various breakfast dishes, or with meats, poultry, melted cheese dishes, plain tortillas and beans. ~ PATRICIA

3 TO 4 CUPS WATER

15 MEDIUM TOMATILLOS, HUSKED

6 GARLIC CLOVES, PEELED

½ MEDIUM WHITE ONION, PEELED AND QUARTERED

4 CHILES GUAJILLOS, SEEDED, DEVEINED AND FRIED IN A SMALL AMOUNT OF OIL (SUBSTITUTE DRIED RED CHILES CALIFORNIA, NEW MEXICO OR ANAHEIM)

4 CHILES CASCABELES, SEEDED, DEVEINED AND FRIED IN A SMALL AMOUNT OF OIL (SUBSTITUTE DRIED RED CHILES CALIFORNIA, NEW MEXICO OR ANAHEIM)

2 TO 4 RED CHILES CHIPOTLES SEEDED, DEVEINED AND FRIED

4 GARLIC CLOVES, PEELED

½ MEDIUM WHITE ONION, PEELED AND QUARTERED

SALT TO TASTE

Bring the water to a boil in a medium saucepan. Add the tomatillos, garlic, onion and fried chiles and cook for 25 minutes. Allow to cool briefly, then transfer ingredients to a blender or food processor and purée. Gradually add raw garlic cloves, onion and salt to taste. Add a little cooking water to achieve desired consistency. Rectify seasoning, and serve in a molcajete.
SERVES 8.

JICAMA AND OLIVES WITH VINAIGRETTE

JICAMA Y ACEITUNAS CON VINAGRETA AL AJO

Jicama, a root that is eaten raw or cooked, can be found throughout Mexico. Tiny jicamas are stuffed into piñatas around Christmastime, and large ones are eaten raw in round slices. Jicama is even hung from the Day of the Dead altars with bunches of marigolds. This appetizer combines the fresh taste of jicama with salty, pungent olives. ~

FOR THE JICAMA

1   LARGE JICAMA, PEELED AND CUT IN SLICES, THEN CUT INTO THIN STRIPS

WATER TO COVER

FOR THE VINAIGRETTE

½   CUP LIME JUICE

1   CUP PLUS ONE TABLESPOON OLIVE OIL

1   LARGE GARLIC CLOVE, PEELED

1   TEASPOON GARLIC POWDER

1½ TABLESPOONS GARLIC SALT

SALT TO TASTE

CHILE POWDER OR PAPRIKA

FOR THE OLIVES

⅓   CUP OLIVE OIL

2   CUPS PITTED BLACK OLIVES

Prepare the jicama: Soak jicama strips in water, with a little salt, for about 20 minutes in the freezer

Prepare the vinaigrette: Blend the lime juice, olive oil, garlic, garlic powder, garlic salt and salt to taste in a blender or food processor or whisk vigorously. Refrigerate.

Prepare the olives: Heat the olive oil in a medium saucepan. Sauté the olives, then cover the pan with a lid and leave over very low heat for about 15 minutes.

To serve: Drain jicama and sprinkle with a little powdered chile or paprika. Serve olives and vinaigrette on the side. SERVES 8.

SINCRONIZADAS

SINCRONIZADAS

*S*incronizadas *(seen kron ee ZAH dahz) are delicious little hot ham and cheese tortilla "sandwiches," quick and easy to prepare, fit for any hour of the day. They are served in homes and restaurants, to children and adults alike.* ~ MARGARITA

FOR THE SALSA

1½   MEDIUM WHITE ONIONS, PEELED AND FINELY CHOPPED

6   FRESH CHILES SERRANOS, FINELY CHOPPED

4   LARGE RIPE TOMATOES, FINELY CHOPPED

1   CUP CILANTRO, FINELY CHOPPED

1   TABLESPOON OREGANO

THE JUICE OF 3 LIMES

6   TABLESPOONS OLIVE OIL

SALT TO TASTE

FOR THE GUACAMOLE

3   LARGE, RIPE AVOCADOS, PEELED AND FINELY CHOPPED

1½   MEDIUM WHITE ONIONS, PEELED AND FINELY CHOPPED

4   TO 6 CHILES SERRANOS, FINELY CHOPPED

THE JUICE OF 1 LIME

2   TABLESPOONS OLIVE OIL

SALT TO TASTE

FOR THE SINCRONIZADAS

40   THIN CORN TORTILLAS

20   VERY THIN SLICES OF BOILED HAM, FOLDED IN QUARTERS

20   SLICES MILD CHEESE, SLIGHTLY SMALLER THAN THE TORTILLAS, OR STRING CHEESE, SHREDDED

40   TOOTHPICKS

3   CUPS VEGETABLE OIL

2   GARLIC CLOVES, PEELED

FOR THE GARNISH

¾   CUP CILANTRO, FINELY CHOPPED

¾   CUP WHITE ONION, FINELY CHOPPED

Prepare the salsa: In a glass bowl, place the onion, chile, tomato, and cilantro. Stir together, then add the oregano, lime juice, oil and salt. Mix well, then allow to stand for about 40 minutes before serving.

Prepare the guacamole: Stir together the avocado, onion, chile, lime juice, oil and salt. Chop with a knife until ingredients form a thick purée. Place an avocado pit in the guacamole to retard the browning process.

Prepare the sincronizadas: Separate half of the tortillas and place on a table. Place folded ham in center of each tortilla and cover with a slice of cheese. Cover each with another tortilla (making a tortilla sandwich). Secure with toothpicks on the sides. Heat the oil in a frying pan. When it is hot, fry until golden brown, being sure that the tortillas do not get too crisp. Remove from oil and drain on paper towels. Remove toothpicks, and keep warm until serving time.

To serve: Arrange the sincronizadas around bowls containing the Mexican salsa and guacamole. Sprinkle with chopped cilantro and onion, or dot each sincronizada with a spoonful of guacamole and serve immediately. **SERVES 10.**

JICAMA AND OLIVES WITH VINAIGRETTE

JICAMA ≈

The rough brown jicama (HEE KAH MAH) is the tuber of a tropical morning glory vine. Its delicate, crisp white interior tastes something like water chestnuts; peeled and sliced, it is delicious served raw in salads. In Mexican street-corner shops it is offered raw as a refreshing snack, cut into french-fry-shaped slices, arranged in a vertical bundle in a paper cup, and sprinkled with a touch of ground hot chile.

Jicama is delicious sliced extremely thinly and deep-fried to make "chips." Try it raw, slivered, with vinaigrette, chopped onion, sliced jalapeño and crumbled cheese, served over lettuce as a cold salad.

ROYAL MOUNTAIN TURNOVERS

PASTES ESTILO REAL DEL MONTE

TURNOVER VARIATIONS

≈

Royal Mountain Turnovers can be filled with any of the savory stuffings used for Quesadillas (page 72-73).

The Real de Monte area of Hidalgo is an old mining district. When the English arrived there in the 1800s to assist with the mining of precious metals, they brought them memories of the little meat pie or "pasty" that English miners or country folk carried as a portable midday meal. Here is a satisfying Mexican version of the pasty. ~ PATRICIA

FOR THE FILLING

½   CUP BUTTER

⅓   CUP OLIVE OIL

1   MEDIUM WHITE ONION, PEELED AND FINELY CHOPPED

2   LEEKS, CHOPPED OR THINLY SLICED

3   FRESH CHILES SERRANOS OR TO TASTE, FINELY CHOPPED

2   TO 4 TABLESPOONS PARSLEY, FINELY CHOPPED

¾   POUND BEEF FILLET, FINELY CHOPPED

¾   POUND POTATOES, BOILED AND DICED

    SALT TO TASTE

    BLACK PEPPER TO TASTE

1   CUP CHICKEN OR BEEF BROTH

FOR THE DOUGH

1   POUND ALL-PURPOSE FLOUR, SIFTED

1   TEASPOON SALT

¾   CUP PLUS 1 TEASPOON LARD OR BUTTER

1   EGG YOLK

¾   OR 1 CUP VERY COLD PULQUE, BEER, OR SPARKLING WINE (AMOUNT DEPENDS ON THE CONSISTENCY OF THE FLOUR)

3   EGG YOLKS

½   CUP MILK

Prepare the filling: Heat the butter and oil in a medium saucepan. Brown the onion, leek, chile and parsley. Add the chopped meat and diced potatoes and cook for 25 minutes, stirring occasionally, until the meat is browned. Season to taste with salt and pepper and add the broth. Remove from heat and allow to cool.

Prepare the dough: Place the sifted flour in a bowl. Add the salt and work in the lard until the dough takes on a sandy consistency. Then add the egg yolk and gradually add the pulque (or beer or sparkling wine) until the dough is smooth and elastic. Cover with a cloth and set aside in a draft-free place for about 1 hour.

Assemble the turnovers: Roll out the dough on a floured surface until it is ¼ inch thick. Cut into circles about 5 inches in diameter. Place 1½ to 2 tablespoons of filling on one side of the circle and then fold over. Press edges shut, fluting slightly. Mix egg yolks and milk and use it to brush the turnovers. Seal edges by pressing with a fork or decorate with a small braid. Place the turnovers on a buttered baking tray and allow to rest for about 2 hours.

Preheat oven to 350°F. Bake the turnovers for 30 minutes or until golden brown. Serve warm or at room temperature. To transport turnovers as an itacate dish, arrange them in a basket lined with cloth or wrap them individually to avoid breaking.
SERVES 8-12.

VARIATION

You may also fill the turnovers with roasted chile strips, onion and cheese or with Mushrooms in Morita Sauce (page 122).

Minted Chicken Broth with Vegetables

Caldo de Pollo a la Hierbabuena

Spearmint is used frequently in Oaxacan cooking. Its aromatic scent highlights many dishes that date back to the conquest, and the arrival of the Spanish and Arabic customs that have had such a lasting influence on native cuisine. This chicken dish is an outstanding example of the use of spearmint in main courses.

FOR THE BROTH

6	QUARTS WATER
6	CHICKEN LEGS, WITHOUT SKIN, SAUTÉED
4	CHICKEN THIGHS, WITHOUT SKIN
4	CHICKEN WINGS, ROASTED
2	MEDIUM WHITE ONIONS, PEELED AND QUARTERED
1	HEAD GARLIC, CUT IN HALF ACROSS THE GRAIN
2	CARROTS, PEELED
4	RIBS CELERY, WITH LEAVES
	SALT TO TASTE, OR POWDERED BOUILLON

FOR THE VEGETABLES

3	CHAYOTES, PEELED AND CUT IN CHUNKS
2	EARS OF CORN, CHOPPED INTO PIECES
4	ZUCCHINI, SLICED
1	TO 2 BUNCHES MINT

FOR THE GARNISH

½	CUP CHIVES

Prepare the broth: Bring the water to a boil. Add the chicken, onion, garlic, carrots, celery and salt to taste. Reduce heat and allow to simmer for about 1¼ hours, or until chicken is tender. Skim off excess fat and strain broth, reserving the chicken meat for later use if desired. Or you may start with a previously-made good chicken stock.

Prepare the vegetables: Place the broth in a large saucepan. Add the chayotes and corn, and boil for 15-20 minutes or until done. Then add zucchini and cook until they turn bright green.

To serve: Just before serving the soup, season to taste, add the mint and bring the soup to a boil. Allow to cool and bring to a second boil. Garnish with mint and serve piping hot. SERVES 8.

NOTE

The leftover chicken can be used to prepare enchiladas, tacos, or chalupas.

OPTIONAL

You may wish to use baby vegetables, or to add green onions or carrots.

CHICKEN CONSOMMÉ

CONSOME DE POLLO

Curiously enough, chicken consommé is a common breakfast dish in the Mexican markets. This recipe, from my first cookbook, COOKING IS A GAME, *calls for the addition of cilantro and chile to enhance the flavor of the rich broth.* ~
PATRICIA

FOR THE CONSOMME

4	QUARTS WATER
½	CHICKEN
6	CHICKEN FEET, BLANCHED FOR ABOUT 3 MINUTES, THEN SKINNED (CLIP NAILS) OR CHICKEN BONES
4	CHICKEN LEGS (DRUMSTICK AND THIGH)
1	GENEROUS POUND OF BONELESS VEAL
4	CARROTS, PEELED AND DICED
½	LEEK
6	GARLIC CLOVES, PEELED
1	LARGE ONION, PEELED AND QUARTERED
½	STALK CELERY
8	BLACK PEPPERCORNS
2	BAY LEAVES
2	TO 3 TABLESPOONS POWDERED CHICKEN BOUILLON

FOR THE GARNISH

8	GREEN ONIONS, CHOPPED
2	AVOCADOS, CHOPPED
½	CUP CILANTRO, CHOPPED
3	TO 4 FRESH CHILES SERRANOS OR CANNED PICKLED CHIPOTLES, CHOPPED
2	LARGE RIPE TOMATOES, CHOPPED

Prepare the broth: Place the chicken, veal and water in a stockpot or large saucepan. Simmer for about 20 minutes, then skim broth and add carrots, leek, garlic, onion, celery, pepper, bay leaves, and bouillon powder and simmer for about 1 hour and 15 minutes. Strain out chicken and vegetables. Bone and shred chicken. Rectify seasoning. Serve broth steaming hot with chicken, vegetables and garnishes on the side or return chicken and vegetables to broth before serving. Reserve extra chicken for tacos, enchiladas, tostadas, chalupas and other Mexican snacks. SERVES 8-10.

MINTED CHICKEN BROTH WITH VEGETABLES.

CONSOMMÉ VARIATIONS
≈

Consommé is a perfect base for other soups. Try adding shredded chicken and topping with mild cheese. Or add cooked rice, chopped avocado, roasted and chopped chiles chipotle, shredded chicken, chopped onion and shredded mozzarella. It can also be flavored with Mexican Salsa (page 177).

Another variation includes chopped green onions, grated hard-cooked egg, chopped parsley and thinly sliced mushrooms.

To prepare a CALDO TLAPEÑO, *add chopped carrots, celery, potato, corn, garbanzos, cooked rice, shredded chicken, avocado slices and Mexican Salsa.*

MEAT AND VEGETABLE
STEW WITH CHILES,
SAFFRON AND CHORIZO.

MEAT AND VEGETABLE STEW WITH CHILES, SAFFRON AND CHORIZO

CALDO GALLEGO A LA MEXICANA

PUCHERO EN TRES TIEMPOS ≈

PUCHERO EN TRES TIEMPOS, *literally, "broth three times," is a country style of serving stew. First the marrow bone is separated from the meat and cooked alone in boiling water. The remainder of the meat is cooked in a pot filled with water, accompanied by vegetables such as corn and yams, whole chiles, and seasonings. After cooking, the meat and vegetables are strained from the broth. When the family sits down for the meal, they are first served the marrow as an appetizer, with avocado, chopped onion, cilantro and salsas. Next they are served the "puchero," or broth of the meat, from a tureen. Last comes a steaming platter of the meat and vegetables, served separately from the broth.*

My mother often prepared this soup for Sunday meals, in memory of my late grandfather Miguel. He was of Spanish origin and always liked hearty Spanish-style dishes such as this one. He didn't care that mother had adapted it to the Mexican way of cooking. ~ MAGO

1 POUND SMALL WHITE NAVY BEANS OR GARBANZOS (CHICKPEAS), SOAKED OVERNIGHT IF DESIRED

4 BAY LEAVES

1 TEASPOON DRIED THYME

1 TEASPOON DRIED MARJORAM

6 GARLIC CLOVES, PEELED

1 MEDIUM WHITE ONION, PEELED AND QUARTERED

1 TEASPOON LIGHTLY TOASTED SAFFRON

2 CUPS WHITE WINE

4 TO 5 QUARTS WATER

7 OUNCES THICK BACON, DICED

1½ POUNDS BONELESS VEAL, CUT IN CHUNKS

2¼ POUNDS PORK HOCK, CUT IN CHUNKS

1 THICK SMOKED PORK RIB, CUT IN PIECES

10 OUNCES HAM, CUT IN PIECES

4 CHICKEN BREASTS, BONED AND CUT IN PIECES

3 LARGE TOMATOES

3 CHILES DE ÁRBOL OR OTHER SMALL HOT DRIED CHILE, WASHED, SEEDED AND DEVEINED, LIGHTLY TOASTED

3 CHILES GUAJILLOS OR CALIFORNIA, OR DRIED RED NEW MEXICAN CHILES, WASHED, SEEDED AND DEVEINED, LIGHTLY TOASTED

2 MEDIUM WHITE ONIONS, PEELED AND QUARTERED

6 GARLIC CLOVES, PEELED

⅓ CUP OLIVE OIL

3 LARGE CHORIZO SAUSAGES

4 SMOKED PORK RIBS

¾ POUND VIENNESE OR CATALAN CHORIZO SAUSAGE

1½ POUNDS SWISS CHARD, MILD KALE, OR OTHER GREENS, CHOPPED

1 MEDIUM HEAD CABBAGE, CUT IN HALF, CORED AND QUARTERED

1 POUND BABY POTATOES, COOKED

1 CUP CHOPPED PARSLEY

2 TABLESPOONS POWDERED CHICKEN BOUILLON OR SALT TO TASTE

2 TABLESPOONS SUGAR OR TO TASTE

Combine the navy beans, bay leaves, thyme, marjoram, garlic, onion, saffron, wine, water, bacon, veal, pork hock, pork rib, ham and chicken breasts in a large stockpot or saucepan and cook until the meat is tender.

Place the tomatoes, chiles de árbol and guajillos, onions, and garlic in a blender or food processor and blend into a smooth sauce. Heat the oil in a heavy pan and add the sauce. Cook for 45 minutes or until it renders its fat. Then add to the soup.

Fry the chorizo sausage, ribs and sausage until light brown. Drain and add to soup. Add Swiss chard, cabbage, potatoes, and parsley. Rectify seasoning and add bouillon and sugar to taste. Cook 25 minutes. Serve hot from a tureen. **SERVES 12-16.**

GARLIC SOUP TOPPED WITH
TOASTED CUBES OF BOLILLO
AND CHEESE.

GARLIC SOUP

SOPA DE AJO ESTILO TOLUCA

A wide variety of garlic is sold in Mexican markets — tiny to huge, purple, white or yellow, each with its own name.

⅓   CUP OLIVE OIL

⅓   CUP BUTTER

3   HEADS GARLIC, CLOVES PEELED AND FINELY CHOPPED

4   LARGE RIPE TOMATOES, PURÉED AND STRAINED

14   CUPS BEEF BROTH

    SALT TO TASTE

8   SPRIGS CILANTRO OR EPAZOTE

2   EGGS, BEATEN

1   CUP FETA CHEESE, CRUMBLED

3   FRESH CHILES SERRANOS OR 1-2 JALAPEÑOS, FINELY CHOPPED

2   BOLILLOS OR HARD ROLLS, DICED OR SLICED AND FRIED

Heat the oil and butter in a large saucepan. Sauté garlic until light brown. Add the puréed tomatoes and cook until mixture forms a thick sauce. Add beef broth and salt and continue to cook for an additional 20 minutes. Then add cilantro or epazote and bring to a rolling boil.

Add beaten eggs in a thin stream, stirring constantly. Add cheese, chiles and fried rolls (or croutons) just before serving.
SERVES 8.

ALMOND CHICKEN SOUP WITH CILANTRO

SOPA DE POLLO CON ALMENDRA Y CILANTRO

In the state of Veracruz the blending of European and native Mexican cuisine can be seen clearly. This soup is an example of the classical recipes of my grandmother's era, a mixture of two very different cultures, each offering its best. ~ MARGARITA

FOR THE CHICKEN BROTH

4½   QUARTS WATER

4   CHICKEN WINGS

6   CHICKEN THIGHS

6   DRUMSTICKS

6   CHICKEN FEET, CLEANED AND PEELED (OPTIONAL)

1½   MEDIUM WHITE ONIONS, PEELED AND QUARTERED

½   GARLIC HEAD, UNPEELED

½   LEEK, SLICED

2   CARROTS, PEELED, AND CUT IN QUARTERS

20   FRESH MINT LEAVES OR 10 DRIED MINT LEAVES

1½   TABLESPOONS POWDERED BOUILLON

FOR THE SOUP BASE

½   CUP OLIVE OIL

½   HEAD GARLIC, CLOVES PEELED AND FINELY CHOPPED

2   WHOLE CHICKEN BREASTS, BONED AND DICED

6   RIPE TOMATOES, PEELED AND FINELY CHOPPED

2   TABLESPOONS BREAD CRUMBS

1½   CUPS SLICED ALMONDS

1   CUP STUFFED OLIVES, FINELY CHOPPED

½   CUP RAISINS

2   CUPS POTATOES, COOKED, PEELED AND QUARTERED

½   CUP CANNED PICKLED CHILES JALAPEÑOS, FINELY CHOPPED

1   CUP SHERRY

1   CUP CHOPPED CILANTRO

½   CUP PARSLEY, FINELY CHOPPED

½   TABLESPOON FRESHLY GROUND BLACK PEPPER

    SALT TO TASTE

FOR THE GARNISH

1   TABLESPOON FINELY CHOPPED PARSLEY

1   TABLESPOON FINELY CHOPPED CILANTRO

Prepare the broth: Place the water in a large saucepan or stockpot. Add the chicken, chicken feet, onion, garlic, leek, carrots, mint, and bouillon. Simmer ingredients until they foam, then skim off foam and simmer for 1½ hours. Allow to cool. Strain broth and degrease.

Prepare the soup base: Heat the oil in a saucepan. Brown the garlic, then add the diced chicken breasts and sauté. Stir in tomato and cook for about 35 minutes or until the mixture renders its fat. Then add the bread crumbs, almonds, olives, raisins, potatoes, chiles, sherry, cilantro, parsley and black pepper. Cook for about 20 minutes. Stir in hot strained chicken broth and simmer the soup for an additional 15 minutes. If necessary add salt or pepper and thin with additional broth.

To serve: Serve steaming hot from a soup tureen, garnished with parsley and cilantro. SERVES 10.

CILANTRO ≈

Also known as coriander and Chinese parsley, cilantro is part of the essential bouquet of Mexican, Mediterranean, Chinese and Middle Eastern food. It is a uniquely pungent and cooling accompaniment to tomato, chile and onion in salsa and is eaten by the sprig with tacos in Mexico. The seed of the cilantro plant, called coriander, has an entirely different character and is not interchangeable with cilantro. Cilantro loses its spirit when dried, but it is more and more commonly available fresh in North American markets, and can be grown very easily from seed in a small garden space.

GRILLED TROUT WITH
PULQUE SALSA.

GRILLING A CHILE ≈

Chiles poblanos and other large mild chiles or sweet peppers can be roasted, peeled and stuffed with seasoned corn or other vegetable mixtures, then quickly grilled over hot coals as an excellent accompaniment to barbequed meats and seafood.

GRILLED TROUT WITH PULQUE OR BEER SALSA

TRUCHA ASADA A LA MAZAHUA

In the Mazahua Indian region of the state of Mexico are many streams where trout abound. This is a simple way of preparing trout that is delicious. In Mexico the sauce would be prepared with pulque, a native fermented drink made from the juice of the maguey plant. Where pulque is not available, the sauce can be made with beer.

FOR THE TROUT

8	TROUT, BONED AND LIGHTLY SCORED
1	CUP VEGETABLE OIL
6	GARLIC CLOVES, PEELED AND PURÉED
	SALT TO TASTE
	BLACK PEPPER TO TASTE

FOR THE SALSA

4	GARLIC CLOVES, PEELED
½	MEDIUM WHITE ONION, PEELED AND QUARTERED
	SALT TO TASTE
6	MEDIUM TOMATOES, ROASTED
4	FRESH CHILES SERRANOS OR 2 CHILES JALAPEÑOS, ROASTED WHOLE
4	CHILES ANCHOS OR DRIED RED CHILES CALIFORNIA, OR DRIED MILD NEW MEXICAN CHILES, ROASTED, DEVEINED AND SEEDED, WASHED AND SOAKED IN 2 CUPS BEER

FOR THE GARNISH

1	MEDIUM WHITE ONION, CHOPPED
¾	CUP CHOPPED CILANTRO

Prepare the trout: Prepare an open wood fire or a barbecue grill before cooking time.

Arrange the trout in a shallow dish. Brush with oil and sprinkle with garlic. Marinate for one hour. Then drain the fish, reserving the marinade. Sprinkle fish with salt and pepper, then grill for 10-20 minutes on one side. Turn gently with the help of a spatula, brush the exposed side with reserved marinade, sprinkle with salt and pepper, and grill for another 10-20 minutes on the other side. Cooking time will depend on the size of the fish.

Prepare the salsa: Grind the garlic, onion, salt, tomatoes, chiles and beer, preferably in a molcajete, gradually adding each ingredient as you grind. If using a food processor, grind carefully to retain chunky texture. Rectify seasoning. Garnish with chopped onion and cilantro.

To serve: Place the trout on a serving platter. Drizzle lightly with leftover marinade. Serve salsa on the side.

VARIATION

To cook the fish on a conventional stove, follow directions given above, substituting a hot, well-oiled heavy skillet for the barbeque grill. You may also cook the fish directly in the embers of a campfire, if you first wrap it in heavy aluminum foil.

BARBECUED RIBS

AHUJAS

My grandmother Margarita used to take me with her when she went food shopping in Monterrey. There I learned from her about the wide variety of cut meat. AHUJAS *(ah oo hahs) are ribs cut thick in the style of Monterrey.*

FOR THE SAUCE

4   LARGE RIPE TOMATOES (2 GENEROUS POUNDS)

1   TEASPOON FRESH OR DRIED CHILE PEQUIN (TINY, VERY HOT DRIED CHILES)

4   FRESH CHILES SERRANOS OR TO TASTE, STEMMED, WHOLE (SEED FOR A MILDER SAUCE)

8   CUPS WATER

1   MEDIUM WHITE ONION, PEELED AND QUARTERED

4   GARLIC CLOVES, PEELED

   SALT TO TASTE

FOR THE RIBS

   MESQUITE COOKING WOOD

24   RIBS, THICK (MONTERREY CUT) OR THIN

1   CUP VEGETABLE OIL

   SALT TO TASTE

   BLACK PEPPER TO TASTE

Prepare the sauce: Place the tomatoes and chiles in a saucepan. Cover with water and boil until tender, about 15 minutes. Remove from cooking water and transfer to a molcajete, blender or food processor. Add the onion, garlic and salt to taste and purée. Set aside.

Prepare the ribs: Light the firewood or coals before cooking time — about 2 hours for wood and ½ to ¾ hour for charcoal. Brush the meat with oil and sprinkle with salt and pepper. Broil on one side until meat is cooked medium. Turn over and broil on the other side to taste. Be careful not to overcook. Serve immediately, accompanied by Mexican Salsa, flour tortillas and beans. **SERVES 8.**

CHICKEN BREASTS IN ADOBO SAUCE

PECHUGAS DE POLLO EN ADOBO

Adobo, which is often used to baste meats or poultry, is a sauce prepared from vinegar, piloncillo and spices. My great-grandmother used to make adobo sauces frequently. ~ MARGARITA

FOR THE ADOBO

1   POUND CHILE PASILLA OR ANCHO, WASHED, SEEDED AND DEVEINED, LIGHTLY ROASTED ON A COMAL AND SOAKED IN SALTED WATER 30 MINUTES (SUBSTITUTE DRIED RED NEW MEXICAN OR CALIFORNIA CHILES)

1½   LARGE WHITE ONIONS, PEELED AND QUARTERED

6   MEDIUM GARLIC CLOVES, PEELED

2   CUPS CHICKEN BROTH

⅔   CUP VINEGAR

1   TABLESPOON BLACK PEPPERCORNS

1   TEASPOON WHOLE CUMIN SEEDS

3   GARLIC CLOVES, PEELED AND ROASTED

4   BAY LEAVES

2   SPRIGS FRESH THYME OR ½ TEASPOON DRIED

1   CUP OLIVE OIL

½   CUP PILONCILLO OR BROWN SUGAR

      SALT OR POWDERED BOUILLON TO TASTE

FOR THE CHICKEN

16   SPLIT CHICKEN BREASTS, BONED

      SALT TO TASTE

      FRESHLY GROUND BLACK PEPPER TO TASTE

⅓   TO ½ CUP VEGETABLE OR OLIVE OIL

4   GARLIC CLOVES, PEELED AND CHOPPED

2   TABLESPOONS SUGAR

¾   TABLESPOON OREGANO LEAVES, CRUSHED

1   TO 1½ CUPS CHICKEN BROTH

FOR THE GARNISH

½   ROMAINE LETTUCE, WASHED AND CHILLED

6   LITTLE RADISHES, CUT IN THE SHAPE OF A
      FLOWER AND SOAKED IN ICED WATER

16   GREEN ONIONS, CUT IN THE SHAPE OF A
      FLOWER AND SOAKED IN ICED WATER

2   RIPE AVOCADOS, SLICED IN ¾ INCH
      STRIPS

3   RIPE PLANTAINS, PEELED, SLICED IN ¼
      INCH BY 2½ INCH STRIPS, THEN FRIED
      UNTIL GOLDEN BROWN IN 2 CUPS OF OIL
      AND DRAINED ON PAPER TOWELS

¾   TABLESPOON WHOLE OREGANO OR
      MARJORAM LEAVES

Prepare the adobo: Place chiles in a blender or food processor along with the onion, garlic, 1 tablespoon of chicken broth, and soaking water from the chiles. Purée until the mixture forms a heavy paste. Then add remaining chicken broth and vinegar. Transfer to a glass bowl. In a spice mill, grind the black pepper, cumin, roasted garlic, bay leaves and thyme. Stir into the puréed mixture along with olive oil and piloncillo. Season to taste with salt or bouillon.

Prepare the chicken: Place the chicken breasts on a baking tray. Sprinkle with salt and pepper, then drench with adobo sauce and marinate overnight in the refrigerator.

The next day, heat ⅓ cup oil in a large skillet or dutch oven. Sauté the garlic cloves until brown, then sauté the chicken breasts, approximately 6 at a time, over medium heat, for about 6-8 minutes, turning each breast once. Be careful, since the oil may splatter. If necessary, use a lid while cooking. Remove chicken breasts from skillet. Then transfer remaining adobo sauce to the skillet, and cook for about 45 minutes or until the sauce releases its fat. Rectify seasoning, and add sugar and oregano. Stir in enough chicken broth to give the sauce a semi-thick consistency. Add the sautéed chicken breasts to the adobo sauce and cook for 10 minutes.

To serve: Arrange the lettuce leaves on a serving platter. Place chicken breasts over lettuce and drizzle with adobo sauce. Garnish platter with radish and onion flowers, placing avocado slices and plantains in between them. Sprinkle platter with oregano. Accompany with refried beans, white rice, and white or blue tortillas. Serve immediately. **SERVES 16.**

NOTE

Leftover adobo sauce may be used to top fried eggs. It also freezes well.

FOR THE BARBEQUE GRILL ≈

Quail, squab, chicken breasts, turkey breasts and Cornish hens are delicious marinated in adobo and grilled outdoors. Prepare the adobo as specified at left, pour over meat and marinate overnight. Next day, drain the meat and transfer leftover adobo marinade to a saucepan. Cook the meat on a barbeque grill, on a bed of fresh herbs if you have them. Just before serving, bring the leftover marinade to a boil, reduce heat and simmer 5 minutes to cook the meat juices it contains, then serve hot with the grilled meat.

SEAFOOD IN GARLIC AND CHILE DE ÁRBOL SAUCE

ACAMAYAS AL MOJO DE AJO Y CHILE DE ÁRBOL

My mother learned to prepare fresh-water crayfish on the Chapopote Ranch. Typical of northern Huasteca Veracruz cooking, it is very hot. Adjust the recipe to a milder taste by adding fewer chiles. The dish can be made with shrimp or scallops instead of crayfish. ~ MAGO

FOR THE CRAYFISH

¾ CUP BUTTER

1 CUP OLIVE OIL

16 WHOLE GARLIC CLOVES, WITH PEELS

1 TABLESPOON PEELED AND CHOPPED GARLIC

8 FRESH CHILES SERRANOS, SEEDED AND CUT IN STRIPS

8 CHILES DE ÁRBOL OR OTHER SMALL HOT DRIED CHILES, WASHED, CHOPPED

   SALT TO TASTE

   BLACK PEPPER TO TASTE

24 CRAYFISH OR SHRIMP OR SCALLOPS, MEDIUM

FOR THE GARNISH

16 CHILES DE ÁRBOL, FRIED, WHOLE

   BLACK BEANS

   FRESHLY MADE CORN TORTILLAS

Prepare the crayfish: Heat the butter and olive oil in a large saucepan. Add garlic and brown. Stir in the chopped garlic and chiles. Season to taste with salt and pepper and sauté. Add the crayfish and cook over medium heat, stirring occasionally, for about 8-10 minutes or until done. If you are using shrimp or scallops, cooking time will be shorter.

To serve: Arrange the crayfish on a serving platter. Garnish with chiles de árbol. Serve with beans and fresh corn tortillas. **SERVES 8.**

PUMPKIN SEED SAUCE

SIKIL PAK

On a visit to Merida, Yucatan, the Garcia Ponce family taught me how to prepare this pumpkin seed-based sauce. We had it on a picnic at the Uxmal archaeological ruins, to accompany grilled fish. Ground pumpkin seeds have been used to make sauces since pre-Columbian times. They are rich in vegetable oil and very nutritious. ~
PATRICIA

2½ CUPS HULLED PUMPKIN SEEDS, LIGHTLY TOASTED (MAY BE PURCHASED IN HEALTH FOOD STORES AND SOME GROCERY STORES AS *PEPITAS*)

4 MEDIUM TOMATOES, ROASTED

2 GARLIC CLOVES, PEELED AND ROASTED

2 SMALL GARLIC CLOVES, PEELED

   THE JUICE OF ONE LIME

½ TEASPOON BLACK PEPPER

   SALT TO TASTE

   TORTILLA CHIPS

The pumpkin seeds you purchase may already be toasted. If not, toast lightly on a baking sheet at 350°F. Place pumpkin seeds in a blender or food processor and grind well. If possible, transfer to a molcajete (stone mortar) and grind once again. Combine tomatoes, garlic, lime juice, pepper and salt to taste in a bowl. Add ground pumpkin seeds and rectify seasoning. Thin with water, water boiled with epazote, or broth if desired.

Serve with totopos (fried tortilla wedges) or tostadas. **SERVES 8.**

SEAFOOD IN GARLIC AND CHILE DE ÁRBOL SAUCE.

MAYAN CUISINE ≈

The pre-Hispanic cooking of the Mayans used no lard and little oil, as the Spanish had not yet arrived with the domesticated pig. As banana trees grew abundantly in the area inhabited by the Mayans, banana leaves were often used to wrap foods for steaming or for underground pit cooking. Pheasants, deer and fish were part of the cuisine, flavored with sea salt, annatto seeds and chiles, particularly the habanero and the xcatick.

CACTUS PADDLES IN A CACTUS LEAF

NOPALES SUDADOS EN PENCA

NOPAL CACTUS ≈

*Paddles from the nopal cactus (*Opuntia*), called "prickly pear" in the Southwestern U.S., are eaten as a green vegetable throughout Mexico. If you purchase them with thorns, scrape carefully, then peel and dice them. Cook until tender in salted water. To remove the okra-like substance exuded by cactus, rinse the cooked diced paddles thoroughly in cold water. The edible fruit of the nopal cactus is called a* TUNA *.*

*A*s children, we used to collect nopales cactus paddles for my grandmother. We would also bring her the large fleshy cactus leaves in which she steamed the diced, seasoned cactus paddles. This doubling of flavor gives the dish a wonderful aroma, but if cactus leaves are not available, you can use banana leaves or aluminum foil.*

FOR THE FILLING

12 MEDIUM CACTUS PADDLES, FRESH, PEELED AND DICED

1½ MEDIUM WHITE ONIONS, CHOPPED

1 GARLIC HEAD, CUT IN HALF ACROSS THE GRAIN

3 CHILES MANZANOS OR 6 CHILES CASCABEL, LIGHTLY ROASTED, SEEDED, DEVEINED AND CHOPPED

20 SPRIGS CILANTRO

SALT TO TASTE

FOR THE STEAMING

1 LARGE MAGUEY LEAF, WASHED, ROASTED, AND SLIT OPEN AT THE TIP OR 4 LARGE BANANA LEAVES OR ALUMINUM FOIL

FOR THE GARNISH

40 CILANTRO SPRIGS

Prepare the cactus filling: Preheat oven to 350°F. Place the diced cactus paddles in a medium glass bowl. Add the onion, garlic, chile and cilantro. Season to taste with salt and mix ingredients well. Line a baking tray with aluminum foil. Place prepared cactus leaf on tray.

For the steaming: Fill cactus leaf with filling, being sure to place half the garlic head in the middle of the leaf, and the other half at the opening of the leaf. Wrap leaf with aluminum foil and bake for about 1¼ hours or until the juicy liquid of the cactus paddle has evaporated.

To serve: Place the cactus leaf on a serving platter, and slit open at the top with a sharp knife. Garnish with cilantro sprigs. Serve with freshly made corn tortillas and salsa. **SERVES 8.**

TORITOS ≈

Every region of Mexico has its own characteristic alcoholic beverage. The specialty of Mandinga Beach in Veracruz is the Torito, or "little bull." It is prepared with any of a dozen fruit flavors, including guava, coconut, pineapple and mamey.

LITTLE BULLS

TORITOS

8 CUPS WATER

8 LARGE RIPE MANGOS, OR ANY FRESH FRUIT IN SEASON (ABOUT 4 CUPS)

1 CUP SWEETENED, CONDENSED MILK

1 CUP RUM, OR TO TASTE

ICE TO TASTE

Place the water and mangos in a blender or food processor and purée. Add milk and rum and purée again. Pour into wine cups filled with ice and serve immediately. **SERVES 8.**

MOLOTES

MOLOTES

Molotes (mo LO tayz) are a kind of quesadilla shaped into the form of a croquette, typical of Oaxaca and Puebla. I remember the crunchy delight of a hot molote, bought from a corner stand in the main square of Oaxaca, on the night of September 15, as the Independence fireworks exploded. ~ MARGARITA

FOR THE TINGA FILLING

SEE RECIPE ON PAGE 243. YOU MAY PREPARE WITH OR WITHOUT MEAT OR CHORIZO SAUSAGE.

FOR THE POTATO FILLING

8   CUPS WATER

    SALT TO TASTE

4   MEDIUM YELLOW POTATOES, PEELED

⅓   CUP OLIVE OIL

1   MEDIUM WHITE ONION, PEELED AND FINELY CHOPPED

FOR THE CHILE FILLING

⅓   CUP VEGETABLE OIL

12   GREEN ONIONS, THINLY SLICED ON THE DIAGONAL

6   CHILES POBLANOS, ROASTED, SWEATED AND PEELED, SEEDED AND DEVEINED, SOAKED IN SALTED WATER FOR 15 MINUTES, CUT INTO STRIPS

    SALT TO TASTE

    BLACK PEPPER TO TASTE

1½ CUPS OAXACA, MOZZARELLA OR STRING CHEESE, GRATED

FOR THE MOLOTES

3⅓ POUNDS FRESH CORN MASA OR MASA PREPARED FROM MASA HARINA

    WARM WATER

    SALT TO TASTE

½   CUP LARD

6   CUPS VEGETABLE OIL

FOR THE GARNISH

MEXICAN SALSA (PAGE 177)

GREEN SALSA WITH CILANTRO (PAGE 75)

1   RIPE AVOCADO, SLICED

1   BUNCH CILANTRO

1½ CUPS FARMER'S OR FETA CHEESE, CUT IN STRIPS

Prepare the tinga: Follow the recipe, omitting the meat and chorizo sausage if desired. The mixture should be very thick. Allow to cool and place in a cazuela.

Prepare the potato filling: Heat the water in a medium saucepan, with salt to taste. Once it comes to a rolling boil, add the potatoes. Boil 30 minutes or until tender, drain and mash. Heat the olive oil in a frying pan and brown the onion. Add the mashed potatoes and cook for 10 minutes or until potatoes are hot and smooth. Remove from heat and spoon into a cazuela.

Prepare the chile filling: Heat the oil in a frying pan. Sauté the onions and chile. Season to taste with salt and pepper. Remove from heat and spoon into a cazuela. Cover with the cheese.

Prepare the molotes: Place the masa in a large glass bowl. Knead with salt and enough water to form a smooth, firm dough. Cover with a damp cloth and allow to rest for about 20 minutes.

MOLOTES ON A COMAL ATOP A BRAZIER.

MOLOTE VARIATION ≈
Molote dough may be augmented with 2 cups cooked mashed potatoes, 1½ cups grated ricotta cheese, 2 tablespoons flour and a little water.

TOMATILLOS ≈

*The tomatillo (*TOE MAH TEE YO*) looks like a small green tomato in a paper husk, but it is actually a relative of the ground cherry with a distinctive lemony flavor. Standard cooking procedure is to immerse husked tomatillos in boiling water for 10-15 minutes or until they begin to be transparent. They may also be roasted in the husk on a hot skillet or griddle for approximately 10 minutes. Tomatillos are usually used green. When they are ripe they turn yellow. Keep tomatillos under refrigeration for a week or more.*

The husks of tomatillos have a slightly yeasty effect. Water boiled with tomatillo husks is often used to moisten tamales or tortillas, which makes them puffier when baked.

Line a tortilla press with two squares of plastic. Pinch off a little of the masa to form an oblong ball. Place on the tortilla press and flatten with lever to make a small round tortilla about 4-6 inches in diameter. The tortilla should be thin. Carefully peel off the plastic and stretch the tortilla into an oblong shape. Fill with one of the fillings, and fold over. Then shape into a croquette (like the shape of a long egg). Place on a baking tray lined with a damp cloth or cloth. Repeat procedure with remaining masa, using different fillings.

Heat the lard and vegetable oil in a deep frying pan. Fry the molotes until golden brown and drain on paper towels. Serve from a cazuela, with salsas for dipping. Decorate with avocado slices, cilantro and fresh cheese. **SERVES 12.**

PORK LOIN IN CHIPOTLE SAUCE

LOMO DE PUERCO EN TROCITOS AL CHIPOTLE

We *always serve the family's most cherished recipes in September, to celebrate national holidays and to spoil ourselves! This recipe was taught to me by my aunt Elvira Quintana, who was an excellent cook. ~*

3⅓ POUNDS PORK LOIN, CUT IN SMALL CHUNKS

5 GARLIC CLOVES, PEELED

4 CUPS WATER

1 TABLESPOON SALT

4 TABLESPOONS LARD OR VEGETABLE SHORTENING

6 TO 8 CHILES CHIPOTLES MECOS (STRIPED) OR MORITAS

6 GARLIC CLOVES, PEELED

1½ POUNDS TOMATILLO, HUSKED AND COOKED

¼ CUP VEGETABLE OIL OR LARD

1½ TABLESPOONS POWDERED CHICKEN BOULLION

BLACK PEPPER TO TASTE

2 TO 3 CUPS CHICKEN OR BEEF BROTH

Place the chunks of pork loin, garlic and water in a medium saucepan. Season to taste with salt and cook until tender, and the liquid evaporates. Then add lard and brown meat. Remove meat and reserve.

In the same saucepan, sauté the chiles and the 6 garlic cloves. Transfer to a blender or food processor and add tomatillos. Purée. Again in the same saucepan, heat the oil or lard and fry the sauce until it releases its fat, then add the browned meat, bouillon, pepper and broth and cook until the mixture thickens. If it becomes too thick, add more broth. Serve with hot tortillas and frijoles. This dish may also be served in tiny vou-la-vent shells as appetizers. **SERVES 8.**

EL GRITO ≈

AT 11:00 P.M. ON SEPTEMBER 15, THE "GRITO," OR "SHOUT" RINGS OUT IN THE STREETS OF MEXICO CITY, RECALLING PADRE HIDALGO'S CALL-TO-ARMS AGAINST SPAIN IN 1810. FROM THROUGHOUT THE CITY, PEOPLE FLOCK TO THE HISTORIC CITY CENTER, OR ZOCALO, TO SHOUT **VIVA MEXICO!** AGAIN AND AGAIN AS THE CATHEDRAL BELLS RING CONTINUOUSLY IN CELEBRATION OF INDEPENDENCE.

MEXICAN SALSA

SALSA MEXICANA

There are many ways to prepare this ubiquitous hot salsa and every cook seems to have his or her own version. Because the red, white and green of Salsa Mexicana are the colors of the Mexican flag, it is the perfect sauce for the national holidays in September. ~
PATRICIA

1⅓ POUNDS RIPE TOMATOES, DICED

1   LARGE WHITE ONION, PEELED AND FINELY CHOPPED

4   FRESH CHILES SERRANOS OR 3 CHILES DE AGUA, CHOPPED

½   CUP CILANTRO, CHOPPED

1   RIPE AVOCADO, CHOPPED

THE JUICE OF ONE LIME

1   TEASPOON OREGANO, CRUSHED

SALT TO TASTE

Place the tomato, onion, chile, cilantro, avocado, lime juice and oregano in a glass bowl. Mix well and season to taste with salt. Serve from a molcajete (stone mortar), along with freshly made corn tortillas.

This sauce is perfect for accenting tacos, grilled meat or roasted chicken.
SERVES 8.

PORT PICADITAS

PICADITAS DEL PUERTO

We used to visit the port of Veracruz for Independence Day holiday whenever we had the time. I remember the streets lined with open air food stalls offering a wide variety of local snacks. This is a common snack served in the harbor.

FOR THE PICADITAS

1¾ POUNDS FRESH CORN MASA OR MASA MADE WITH MASA HARINA

⅓ TO ½ CUP HOT WATER

SALT TO TASTE

FOR THE FILLING

¾ CUP VEGETABLE OIL OR LARD

1 LARGE WHITE ONION, PEELED AND FINELY CHOPPED

3 CUPS REFRIED BEANS (PAGE 233)

2 CUPS FRESH FETA OR FARMER'S CHEESE, CRUMBLED

FOR THE SAUCE

15 TOMATILLOS, HUSKED

½ MEDIUM WHITE ONION, PEELED AN QUARTERED

2 GARLIC CLOVES, PEELED

4 TO 6 CHILES DE ÁRBOL OR OTHER SMALL HOT DRIED CHILES, FRIED

SALT TO TASTE

½ MEDIUM WHITE ONION, PEELED AND FINELY CHOPPED

2 GARLIC CLOVES, PEELED

FOR THE GARNISH

1 LARGE WHITE ONION, PEELED AND FINELY CHOPPED

Prepare the picaditas: Heat a comal or griddle. Meanwhile, knead the corn masa, adding the hot water and salt, until it forms a smooth dough. Line a tortilla press with two squares of plastic. Pinch off about 1 tablespoon of the masa dough and shape into a ball. Place the ball on the tortilla press and press slightly with the lever to make a small round tortilla, about ¼ inch thick, and 2½ and 3 inches in diameter. Carefully peel off the plastic and place directly on the preheated comal. Cook until slightly brown, then turn over to cook evenly. Pinch the edge all the way around to form a rim, then pinch the center of the tortilla flat, being careful not to perforate it. Repeat this procedure with remaining masa. Keep picaditas warm by wrapping in a cloth or cloth napkin.

Prepare the sauce: Place tomatillos, onion and garlic in a medium saucepan. Cover with water and cook over medium heat for about 20-25 minutes. Remove from heat and drain, allowing to cool. Place the chile in a molcajete, blender or food processor and purée. Add salt, raw onion and raw garlic and purée. Add the cooked tomatillos, onion and garlic and purée once again. If necessary, add more water, and rectify seasoning.

Assemble picaditas: Place picaditas on a hot comal or skillet to reheat. Sprinkle with oil, chopped onion, beans, sauce and cheese. Heat for about 4 minutes. Serve hot.
SERVES 8.

PORT PICADITAS ON A PRE-COLUMBIAN PAINTED VESSEL UNEARTHED IN THE NORTHEASTERN REGION OF VERACRUZ.

PICADITA VARIATIONS
≈

Garnish Picaditas with sautéed shrimp, chile strips, minced onion or chopped cilantro.

Picaditas are also called SOPES *or sopecitos in central Mexico,* PELLISCADAS *in Veracruz, and* MEMELAS *in Oaxaca.*

≈ *The Altar of Sorrows* ≈

Foods
of Lent

LA COMIDA DE CUARESMA

Lent is a season of great intensities: intense gaiety and fierce enjoyment, intense solemnity and abstinence. For Mexican Catholics, the forty days between Ash Wednesday and Easter Sunday commemorate Christ's fasting in the desert and reaffirm the Church's prohibition against eating flesh on Fridays during this period and throughout Holy Week. Between late February and early March, there are carnivals, costume parades, pageants, and fiestas of all kinds all over Mexico, as Mexicans prepare for the fast of Lent with ecstatic feasting.

On Ash Wednesday the palm leaves that have hung in Mexican homes since the previous Palm Sunday, now almost a year past, are brought to the

---

SEAFOOD SOUP WITH CHILES AND TOMATOES.

church and burned, and their ashes emblazoned on the foreheads of the believers in the form of a cross. Throughout the days of Lent, church bells toll loudly and services are sometimes also announced with fireworks.

Holy Week begins the Sunday before Easter with the blessing of the palms, recalling Christ's entry into Jerusalem. From Palm Sunday until Easter the entrances to the churches and the doors of Catholic homes bear the cross of palms to signify the loving protection of a heavenly vault.

On Holy Thursday the sacred images in the church are covered with purple cloths as a sign of mourning and the image of Christ is put away in a dark place in order to preserve its inner light. An aura of overwhelming mysticism pervades the church. On that day, when religious fervor is at its peak, an act of profoundest Christian humility takes place: the washing of feet by the chief priests of the church, who thereby relive the act of love Christ bestowed on the twelve apostles. Subsequently, the faithful make the visit of the Seven Houses, stopping at seven churches, in each of which they receive from the priests a miniature bread in remembrance of the last supper. The faithful, on their part, deposit a coin in each basket containing the bits of bread, in order that it should never be lacking.

On Good Friday morning, the ascent to the cross is reenacted. Afterwards, the inanimate body of the Redeemer is laid at the center of the altar, the light that signifies the presence of Christ is extinguished, and the faithful begin a procession to the feet of the Virgin Mary to pay condolences. The altars are alight with votive candles and white lilies are banked at the feet of the sacred image of the Virgin of Sorrows. A silent procession recalls the events that took place on Holy Thursday and Good Friday through the device of symbols inscribed on banners and standards. On Saturday the populace gives reign to its fierce emotion in the burning of the Judases, cardboard figures created by Mexican artisans to represent the instrument of Christ's betrayal. At 11:00 p.m. in the church atrium, the priest blesses and lights the pascal candle so that the faithful may light theirs from this new flame. A midnight mass initiates Easter Sunday.

From the culinary standpoint the Lenten season is distinguished by the abundance and versatility of its meatless dishes. Mexican tables are loaded with red snapper, mushrooms with garlic, chiles stuffed wih cheese, seafood soup (called "back-to-life"), tamale pie with mole, Judas tamales of corn dough and molasses, turnovers stuffed with dried cod, tuna, young shark and spinach, capirotada, and rice pudding. Perhaps it is typically Mexican that so sober a time as Lent is celebrated through so many ingenuous and prolific dishes derived not from Heaven but from earth.

SEAFOOD SOUP WITH CHILES AND TOMATOES

CALDO LARGO DE ALVARADO

The Port of Alvarado on the Coatzacoalcos River houses a small harbor well known for its delicious food. My grandmother once took me on a trip to Alvarado, where I tasted this famous fish soup for the first time.

FOR THE FISH STOCK

20	CUPS WATER
1½	MEDIUM WHITE ONIONS, PEELED AND QUARTERED
6	GARLIC CLOVES, PEELED
12	WHOLE BLACK PEPPERCORNS
1	TABLESPOON SALT OR TO TASTE
4	FISH HEADS
1⅓	POUNDS RED SNAPPER OR SEA BASS

FOR THE SOUP BASE

½	CUP OLIVE OIL
3	MEDIUM WHITE ONIONS, PEELED AND THINLY SLICED
4	GARLIC CLOVES, PURÉED
2½	GENEROUS POUNDS RIPE TOMATOES, ROASTED, PEELED, SEEDED AND SLICED
¾	TABLESPOON FRESH LEAF OREGANO, OR ½-1 TEASPOON DRIED OREGANO
½	TABLESPOON BLACK PEPPER
	SALT TO TASTE
2	TO 4 FRESH CHILES JALAPEÑO OR SERRANO, OR TO TASTE, STEMMED AND CUT INTO STRIPS, (REMOVE SEEDS FOR A LESS PIQUANT FLAVOR IF DESIRED)
2	GENEROUS POUNDS RED SNAPPER OR SEA BASS, CUT INTO CHUNKS
32	MEDIUM SHRIMP, PEELED AND DEVEINED

FOR THE GARNISH

4	TO 6 FRESH CHILES JALAPEÑOS, STEMMED AND CUT IN STRIPS, (REMOVE SEEDS FOR A LESS PIQUANT FLAVOR IF DESIRED)

Prepare the fish stock: Place the water, onion, garlic, pepper, and salt in a medium stockpot and bring to a boil. Add the fish heads and simmer for 60 minutes, then add fish and continue cooking for 25 minutes. Remove from heat and strain stock.

Prepare the soup base: Heat the oil in a cazuela or heavy saucepan. Brown the onion and garlic. Add the tomato and cook until mixture is thick. Season with oregano, pepper and salt to taste. Gradually add chiles and then add the strained fish stock. This part of the recipe may be prepared a day ahead of serving.

Before serving, heat the soup. Add the fish and shrimp and cook for 8 minutes. Rectify seasoning and serve immediately. Serve chiles jalapeños on the side. **SERVES 8.**

SHRIMP PIE

CAMARONES ESTILO JALAPA EN PASTA FINA

Shrimp, Jalapa style, is a Quintana family recipe passed down to us by an aunt who lived in Jalapa. ~ MAGO

FOR THE DOUGH

2	GENEROUS POUNDS FLOUR
1½	TEASPOONS SALT
3	CUPS CHILLED BUTTER
8	MEDIUM EGGS, BEATEN

TOMATOES

THE WOLF'S PEACH ≈

The tomato, whose name comes from the Nahuatl tongue of the Aztecs, was domesticated in Mexico and brought to Europe after the Spanish Conquest, in 1523. However, for more than 200 years it was eaten only in Italy — other Europeans considering it poisonous. Its Latin name, LYCOPERSICON ESCULENTUM, or "edible wolf's peach," suggests early European ambivalence toward the tomato, the delightful relative of the deadly nightshade.

THE APPLE OF GOLD ≈

Early tomatoes were small and yellow, hence their Italian name, "apple of gold."

THE LOVE APPLE ≈

The French, who thought tomatoes were aphrodisiacs, called them "love apples."

AVOCADOS ≈

Avocados have been cultivated in Mexico and Central America for 7,000 years. The U.S.-grown version comes in two types, one larger and still bright green when ripe, the other smaller and ripening to a rich black, from California. The latter is preferable for Mexican cooking. Called "poor man's butter" in the tropics, the mineral-rich avocado has 20 times the fat content of other fruits. Oddly, the avocado refuses to ripen while still attached to the tree, and so it can be "stored" on the branch for many months. In Mexico there is a seasonal third type of avocado, a very tiny one with thin delicate skin that can be eaten without peeling.

FOR THE FILLING

4 CUPS OLIVE OIL

2 GENEROUS POUNDS ONION, PEELED AND FINELY CHOPPED

8 LARGE, RIPE TOMATOES, DICED

2 CUPS STUFFED OLIVES, FINELY CHOPPED

1 CAN PICKLED CHILE JALAPEÑOS WITH JUICE, APPROXIMATELY 8 OUNCES, FINELY CHOPPED

10 CANS SHRIMP (13 OUNCES EACH), DRAINED, OR 5 POUNDS FRESH BABY SHRIMP, COOKED

1¼ CUP PARSLEY, FINELY CHOPPED

 SALT TO TASTE

 BLACK PEPPER TO TASTE

 EGG YOLK

1 TABLESPOON CREAM

Prepare the dough: Place the flour, salt and butter in a glass bowl. Work the ingredients with the fingertips until the butter is coarsely incorporated into the flour. Add the eggs and continue working with both hands until it forms a smooth dough and is no longer sticky. It may be necessary to add 2-4 tablespoons iced water if mixture is too dry. Shape the dough into a ball and refrigerate for at least 1 hour.

Prepare the filling: Heat the oil in a frying pan. Brown the onions. Add tomatoes, olives and chiles and cook for about 35 minutes. Then add the shrimp and parsley. Season to taste with salt (use salt sparingly since the shrimp is salty) and pepper and cook until the mixture thickens, about 1 hour.

Assemble the pie: Preheat oven to 350°F. Grease two 8-inch oblong serving molds. Divide the dough into 4 equal portions. Roll out 2 portions, cutting 2 rectangles slightly larger than the molds. Use these to line the bottoms of the prepared molds. Spoon shrimp filling into molds, then roll out 2 remaining portions of dough, cutting 2 more rectangles to cover molds. Press edges to seal, brush tops with egg yolk whisked with cream and prick with a fork. Bake for 40 minutes or until the pies are golden brown. Serve immediately, accompanied by a green salad, if desired. **SERVES 24.**

SARDINE-AND-AVOCADO-STUFFED CHILES

CHILES POBLANOS ESTILO LA HACIENDA DE ZAPILA

A roasted and marinated poblano chile could be stuffed with any cold salad you favor — tuna, egg, potato salad, or tabouli. Here the chiles are stuffed with a rich and tasty sardine filling. ~ PATRICIA

FOR THE CHILES

6 CHILES POBLANOS, ROASTED, SWEATED, PEELED, DEVEINED AND SEEDED, SOAKED FOR 20 MINUTES IN HOT WATER WITH 2 TABLESPOONS VINEGAR TO REDUCE PIQUANCY (LEAVE WHOLE EXCEPT FOR SINGLE INCISION TO REMOVE SEEDS)

1 CUP OLIVE OR VEGETABLE OIL (OR MIXED)

½ CUP VINEGAR

2 LARGE WHITE ONIONS, PEELED AND SLICED THIN

 SALT TO TASTE

 BLACK PEPPER TO TASTE

FOR THE STUFFING

1   LARGE CAN BONELESS SARDINES (ABOUT 1 POUND)

1   LARGE WHITE ONION, PEELED AND FINELY CHOPPED

2   POTATOES, BOILED AND DICED

1½ CUPS LETTUCE, SHREDDED

2   CUPS AVOCADO, DICED

⅓   CUP PICKLED CHILES JALAPEÑO WITH 4 TABLESPOONS PICKLING LIQUID

SALT TO TASTE

BLACK PEPPER TO TASTE

OIL AND VINEGAR TO TASTE

FOR THE GARNISH

12 ROMAINE LETTUCE LEAVES

12 RADISHES, SHAPED LIKE A FLOWER

18 SLICES AVOCADO

Prepare the chiles: Place the prepared chiles on a platter and sprinkle with oil, vinegar and sliced onion. Season with salt and pepper and allow to marinate for two hours, turning occasionally.

Meanwhile, prepare stuffing: Place sardines in a glass bowl. Mash with a fork. Fold in onion, potatoes, lettuce, avocado and chiles jalapeño. Season to taste with salt, pepper, oil and vinegar and set aside. When chiles are ready, stuff with sardine filling.

To serve: Arrange stuffed chiles on a serving platter and decorate with lettuce leaves, radishes, avocado slices and the sliced onions marinated with chiles. This dish is delicious with freshly made corn tortillas or tostadas. **SERVES 6.**

VANILLA SHRIMP

CAMARONES A LA XANATH

This *unusual shrimp dish is flavored with vanilla* (XANATH — PRONOUNCED SHAH NAHT — *in Totonaco), which is cultivated abundantly in Mexico. When my son Francisco was born, I prepared this recipe in his honor.* ~ PATRICIA

96 MEDIUM SHRIMP, PEELED AND DEVEINED

3   TABLESPOONS MINCED GARLIC

2   MEDIUM WHITE ONIONS, PEELED AND FINELY CHOPPED

4   TABLESPOONS VANILLA EXTRACT

1   TABLESPOON FRESHLY GROUND BLACK PEPPER

1   TABLESPOON SALT OR TO TASTE

1   CUP BUTTER

¾   CUP OLIVE OIL

2   TO 4 TABLESPOONS VANILLA EXTRACT

SALT TO TASTE

FRESHLY GROUND BLACK PEPPER

1½ CUPS DRY WHITE WINE

3   CUPS CHICKEN BROTH, REDUCED TO 1½ CUPS

Place the shrimp in a large glass bowl. Add garlic, onion, vanilla, pepper, and salt and marinate in refrigerator for 2 hours.

Heat the butter and oil in a paella pan or large skillet. Sauté the shrimp, turning. Season with remaining vanilla extract and salt and pepper to taste. Remove shrimp from the pan. Stir in wine and chicken broth and cook until the sauce thickens. When sauce is ready, return shrimp to the pan.

Vanilla shrimp is excellent with rice. For a change of flavor, add seeded chiles jalapeños, cut in strips, instead of vanilla. **SERVES 8.**

VANILLA ≈

The pod fruit of a climbing vine of the orchid family, vanilla is native to the New World. In its earliest habitat it was pollinated only by one species of bee and one species of hummingbird, making it very difficult to grow elsewhere. The underripe pods are picked and alternately "sweated" in the sun for 10-20 days, then dried for several months. Without this process they have little flavor. XANATH (SHAH NAT), *the Mexican name, comes from the Nahuatl* IXTLILXOCHITL, *for "black flower."*

The great vanilla harvest in Papantla in the Huasteca region of northern Veracruz state occurs in December. In the vanilla-growing region, farmers place vanilla beans among folded clothing for cleanliness and scent. They also braid or wrap the beans into tiny animal figures.

Try a touch of vanilla extract in seafood or in fruits cooked in syrup. You can extend the use of a vanilla bean by keeping it in a tightly-closed jar of sugar, which will become scented and lightly flavored with vanilla.

Shrimp Soup

Caldo de Camaron

*T*his aromatic and spicy shrimp broth
is traditionally served in Mexico in clay
or glass mugs following dinner drinks,
prior to a full-course dinner. It is made
with salt-cured dried shrimp for which
Oaxaca is famous, but it can be made
with fresh shrimp as well. ~ PATRICIA

FOR THE SHRIMP BROTH

2 GENEROUS POUNDS LARGE DRIED SHRIMP,
SHELLED AND SHELLS RESERVED
(SUBSTITUTE FRESH SHRIMP)

1 POUND SMALL DRIED SHRIMP, SHELLED
AND SHELLS RESERVED (SUBSTITUTE FRESH
SHRIMP)

6 QUARTS WATER

2 LARGE FISH HEADS, ANY VARIETY

1 GARLIC HEAD, CLOVES PEELED

2 MEDIUM WHITE ONIONS, PEELED AND CUT
IN HALF

1 LEEK, WHOLE

8 GREEN ONIONS, WHOLE

12 BLACK PEPPERCORNS

2 BAY LEAVES

FOR THE TOMATO BASE

6 LARGE, RIPE TOMATOES

10 GARLIC CLOVES, PEELED

1 LARGE, WHITE ONION, PEELED AND
QUARTERED

¼ CUP OLIVE OIL

2 CUPS PEELED, DICED CARROTS, COOKED

2 CUPS PEAS, COOKED

2 CUPS CHOPPED GREEN BEANS, COOKED

2 CUPS DICED POTATO, UNPEELED, COOKED

¼ CUP VEGETABLE OIL

2 GARLIC CLOVES

12 BLACK PEPPERCORNS

1 GENEROUS POUND LARGE FRESH SHRIMP,
SHELLED, DEVEINED, AND SHREDDED OR
CRABMEAT, SHREDDED

20 SPRIGS PARSLEY

8 EPAZOTE OR CILANTRO SPRIGS

2 TABLESPOONS CHILE PEQUIN (OR OTHER
SMALL HOT RED DRIED CHILE) OR TO
TASTE, WHOLE OR CRUSHED

8 CHILES DE ÁRBOL, WASHED, LIGHTLY
FRIED, CRUMBLED

3 CHILES JALAPEÑOS, CHOPPED

Prepare the broth: Wash the shrimp and
soak shells in water to cover for 30
minutes. Then combine in a large stockpot
the shrimp, shrimp shells, water, fish heads,
garlic, onion, leeks, green onions,
peppercorns and bay leaves, and cook for 1
hour. Transfer half of the leeks, onion and
garlic to a food processor and purée. Strain
the purée. Strain the broth. Reserve broth,
puréed leeks, onion and garlic and cooked
shrimp.

Prepare the tomato base: In a blender or
food processor, purée the tomatoes, garlic
and onion. Heat the oil in a large pot and
add tomato purée. Cook until the mixture
releases its fat. Then add the carrots, peas,
green beans and potatoes. Add puréed
vegetables, shrimp broth, cooked shrimp
and raw, shredded shrimp. Add
peppercorns, parsley, epazote and chiles and
cook soup for 30 minutes. Serve broth
steaming hot. **SERVES 12-16.**

DRIED SHRIMP, WITH
ALMONDS, POTATOES,
ONIONS, GARLIC, CHILES
AND ROMERITOS.

CREPES WITH SQUASH BLOSSOMS, CHILES AND CORN

CREPAS QUERETANAS

As children we oftened traveled to Queretaro during Holy Week to visit my father's sister, Aunt Elena. She served crepes often. This version is filled with squash blossoms, chile poblano and corn, and drenched with cream and cheese sauce.

FOR THE CREPES

24 CREPES (PAGE 45)

1½ TO **2** TABLESPOONS FRESH EPAZOTE OR CILANTRO OR PARSLEY LEAVES, FINELY CHOPPED

FOR THE FILLING

½ CUP OLIVE OIL

⅓ CUP BUTTER

2 MEDIUM WHITE ONIONS, PEELED AND FINELY CHOPPED

4 TO **6** GARLIC CLOVES, PEELED AND FINELY CHOPPED

2¾ POUNDS WHOLE SQUASH BLOSSOMS, CLEANED, LEAVES REMOVED

6 CHILES POBLANOS, ROASTED, SWEATED AND PEELED, SEEDED AND DEVEINED, SOAKED IN WATER AND SALT FOR **15** MINUTES, CHOPPED (SUBSTITUTE **4** CHILES SERRANOS, OR **6** CHILES ANAHEIM)

4 CUPS KERNELS FROM TENDER EARS OF CORN, COOKED IN SALTED WATER **8** MINUTES, THEN DRAINED

SALT TO TASTE

1 TEASPOON FRESHLY GROUND BLACK PEPPER

FOR THE CHILE POBLANO SAUCE

½ CUP BUTTER

1 MEDIUM WHITE ONION, PEELED AND GRATED

4 GARLIC CLOVES, PURÉED

3 TABLESPOONS FLOUR

4 CUPS WARM MILK

1½ CUPS CRÈME FRAÎCHE

½ CUP SOUR CREAM

1 CUP HEAVY CREAM

1 CUP FRESH PARSLEY, CHOPPED

½ CUP FRESH CILANTRO, CHOPPED

½ CUP FRESH EPAZOTE OR CILANTRO, CHOPPED

8 CHILES POBLANOS, RAW, SEEDED AND DEVEINED AND FINELY CHOPPED

½ CUP WATER

½ CUP DRY WHITE WINE

SALT TO TASTE

1 TEASPOON FRESHLY GROUND BLACK PEPPER

FOR THE GARNISH

¾ POUND FONTINA, MANCHEGO, GRUYÈRE, MONTEREY JACK OR OTHER MILD CHEESE, GRATED

Prepare the crepes: Make the crepes according to the recipe. Add the epazote to the batter one hour before cooking. The crepes should be very thin.

Prepare the filling: Heat the oil and butter in a medium saucepan. Sauté the onions and garlic until transparent. Add the squash blossoms, chile and corn. Season to taste with salt and pepper and simmer for about 35 minutes or until the mixture is no longer watery.

Prepare the sauce: Heat the butter in a small saucepan. Sauté the onion and garlic. Add the flour and cook until light brown and bubbly. Remove from heat and whisk in milk. Return to heat and simmer 20 minutes. Then stir in the three creams, parsley, cilantro, epazote, chiles poblano, water, wine and season to taste with salt and pepper. Simmer 40 minutes or until the sauce is semi-thick.

Assemble the crepes: Preheat oven to 350°F. Fill the crepes with the squash blossom filling. Arrange on a baking dish and drench with chile poblano sauce. Bake 40-45 minutes. Cover with grated cheese and return to the oven for another 5 minutes or until the cheese melts. Serve directly from the baking dish. Accompany with a green salad. **SERVES 8-10.**

RICE AND SQUASH BLOSSOM FLOWERS. BEHIND ARE PARTICIPANTS IN THE HOLY WEEK PROCESSIONAL.

≈

"Do men have roots, are they real?/ No one can know completely/ what is Your richness, what are Your flowers,/ oh Inventor of Yourself!/ We leave things unfinished./ For this I weep,/ I lament./ Here with flowers I interweave my friends./ Let us rejoice!/ Our common house is the earth./ In the place of mystery, beyond,/ is it also like this?/ Truly, it is not the same./ On earth: flowers and song./ Let us live here!"

PRE-HISPANIC NAHUATL POEM

SWEETNESS ≈

Pre-Hispanic Mexicans sweetened foods with honey or the sap of the maguey cactus. After the European introduction of sugar cane, the taste for raw, wild sweetness lingered. Mexican sugar is processed less fully than U.S. sugar, and sold in rough brown cones of piloncillo. Substitute dark brown sugar for piloncillo in cooking.

CAPIROTADA

CAPIROTADA

On Good Friday, the altar paying tribute to Our Lady of Sorrows was always lavishly decorated. The Virgin was dressed in black and her hair was carefully groomed and held in place with hair combs, then covered with a black Spanish lace mantilla. White flowers accented the altar, decorated with sprigs of wheat, candles, rosaries and paper cut-outs. We would all gather in front of the image of Mary, praying and mourning. We, too, were shrouded in black. The only thing that lightened the somberness was the delicious food we enjoyed following our prayers and the fast that confirmed our penitence. There were fresh chia, hibiscus and tamarind beverages to quench our thirst, and fritters and capirotada to calm the hunger pains. The capirotada is reminiscent of "French toast," but with a Mexican feeling. ~
MARGARITA

FOR THE BREAD

6 TO 8 EGGS, SEPARATED

½ TEASPOON SALT

2 CUPS VEGETABLE OIL

32 SLICES OF HARD FRENCH ROLLS (PREFERABLY BOLILLO), SLICED 1 INCH THICK AND TOASTED (OR STALE)

FOR THE SYRUP

10 CUPS WATER

6 CONES DARK PILONCILLO OR 4 CUPS DARK BROWN SUGAR, PACKED

4 STICKS CINNAMON, ABOUT 4 INCHES LONG

10 WHOLE CLOVES

1 TABLESPOON ANISE SEED, WRAPPED TIGHTLY IN CHEESECLOTH

2 SHOTS OF RUM OR TO TASTE (OPTIONAL)

FOR THE GARNISH

1 CUP RAISINS

1 CUP PEANUTS, LIGHTLY TOASTED IN THE OVEN

1 CUP ALMONDS, BLANCHED AND LIGHTLY TOASTED IN THE OVEN

1½ CUPS WHITE CHEESE (FARMER'S, DRIED RICOTTA OR FETA), GRATED

Prepare the bread: Beat the egg whites with a pinch of salt until they form soft peaks. Heat oil in a medium saucepan until it is hot. Meanwhile, fold egg yolks into egg whites. Dip slices of bread in egg mixture, then fry on both sides in hot oil until lightly browned. Remove from oil and drain on paper towels. Repeat procedure until all are fried.

Prepare the syrup: Heat water in a large saucepan. Add piloncillo cones, cinnamon sticks, cloves and anise. Stir well and allow to simmer until the mixture thickens, forming a heavy syrup, about 45 minutes. Just before turning off heat, stir in rum to taste. Allow to cool slightly.

To serve: Place a layer of batter-fried toast on a serving platter. Drench with syrup. Sprinkle with half the raisins, peanuts, and almonds. Cover with a second layer of bread and repeat layer of syrup, raisins, peanuts and almonds. Sprinkle with grated cheese and serve immediately. Or serve with syrup only or cheese only. **SERVES 8-12.**

LENTEN TURNOVERS

EMPANADAS DE CORPUS

These turnovers are prepared in Oaxaca starting on Palm Sunday, the first Sunday of Lent. Empanada dough makes an excellent flaky, croissant-like pastry for fish or meat pies. ~
MARGARITA

FOR THE TURNOVER DOUGH

1	POUND PLUS FOUR TABLESPOONS ALL-PURPOSE FLOUR
7	EGG YOLKS
½	CUP BUTTER OR LARD, AT ROOM TEMPERATURE
1	TEASPOON SALT
¾	CUP ICED WATER
1	CUP LARD OR BUTTER, WELL CHILLED

FOR THE FILLING

6	EGG YOLKS
1¾	CUPS SUGAR
⅓	CUP CORNSTARCH
3	CUPS WARM MILK
2	CINNAMON STICKS OR VANILLA BEANS, ABOUT 6 INCHES

FOR THE GARNISH

2	EGG YOLKS, BEATEN
⅓	CUP MILK OR HEAVY CREAM
1	CUP SUGAR

Prepare the turnover dough: Place the flour on a flat surface. Form a hole in the center and place the egg yolks and ½ cup butter in the middle. Knead ingredients together, then work in salt and water. Knead by hand or using the bread attachment of a food processor until the dough is shiny, elastic, and not sticky. Then roll out, sprinkling with flour as necessary, and shape into a rectangle or square approximately ¼ to ½ inch thick. Place remaining cup of butter in the center of the rolled-out dough, and flatten it with the rolling pin. Spread the butter to cover the central one-third of the rolled-out dough. Then fold the top third of the dough downwards. Fold the bottom third upwards, overlapping the previous fold. Fold the left side inwards in the same fashion, then fold the right side inward too. You will now have a compact rectangle of dough that is four layers thick. Roll out the dough slightly, to press the layers together. Wrap in plastic wrap and refrigerate 1½ hours. Remove from refrigerator, roll out, and fold exactly as before. Refrigerate again for 1½ hours, then remove and roll out and fold again. Now roll out the dough on a floured surface and cut into 2½ to 3-inch circles.

Prepare the filling: Combine the egg yolks and sugar in a saucepan, mixing until the dough becomes a pale yellow color. Add the cornstarch, milk and cinnamon and simmer until the mixture thickens, about 20 minutes, stirring constantly. Once the mixture thickens, remove from heat and allow to cool.

Assemble the turnovers: Preheat oven to 350°F. Place a tablespoonful of filling on one side of the circle, and fold over. Pinch edges to seal closed. Brush with beaten egg yolk whisked with cream and sprinkle with sugar. Place on a baking tray. Repeat for remaining turnovers, then refrigerate for 15 minutes before baking. Bake in a preheated oven for 30 minutes or until golden. Serve hot or cold. SERVES 8.

LENTEN TURNOVERS.

TURNOVER VARIATIONS
≈

Add shredded fresh coconut to custard used to fill the turnovers. Turnovers are also delicious filled with blackberry or other homemade preserves.

APRICOT PRESERVES

MERMELADA DE CHABACANO

4	POUNDS FRESH APRICOTS, WASHED, CUT IN HALF, PITS REMOVED
3½	POUNDS SUGAR
6	TO **8** STERILIZED PINT JARS
	PARAFFIN, MELTED (OPTIONAL)

I remember my grandmother preparing a cupboardful of preserves in the springtime. We loved to eat them with crepes, toast or warm biscuits, when the traditional fish dishes of Lent were not filling enough for us hungry children. These are some of the many preserves that she lovingly made for us. To test whether preserves have cooked long enough, place a spoonful on a plate and shake gently. Preserves should not "weep" but should hold together. ~ MARGARITA

Place the fruit and sugar in a large glass bowl and allow to sit at room temperature (or in the refrigerator) overnight. This helps the apricots release their natural pectin. Spoon the fruit and sugar into a large saucepan and simmer for one hour or until the mixture thickens to desired consistency. If you wish, you may add a few drops of lemon juice to reduce foaming. Foam should be gently skimmed as mixture cooks. Remove from heat. Spoon preserves into hot sterilized jars. (To sterilize, place clean jars in water to cover and boil hard for 10-15 minutes, removing with tongs.) Immediately before sealing, you may wish to add a little whiskey or rum, pine nuts, almonds or hazelnuts to each jar. If using water bath method, seal at once with sterilized two-part canning lids and immerse in boiling water for 5 minutes to create a vacuum seal. (Follow the manufacturer's recommendations.) Or you may cool the preserves, spoon them into sterile but cooled jars, then seal with melted paraffin. **MAKES 6-8 PINTS.**

APRICOT AND PLUM PRESERVES

MERMELADA DE CHABACANO Y CIRUELA

6½ POUNDS APRICOTS, CUT IN HALF AND PITTED (RESERVE SEEDS INSIDE PITS)

6½ POUNDS PLUMS, CUT IN HALF AND PITTED

¾ CUP SUGAR FOR EACH CUP OF FRUIT, OR TO TASTE

Measure fruit to calculate correct amount of sugar to use. Place fruit in a glass bowl and cover with sugar. Leave at room temperature for 24 hours. Add the apricot seeds and cook for about 1½ hours or until the mixture thickens. Just before sealing jars, add rum, whiskey, or raisins and almonds, if desired. To seal jars, follow directions for apricot preserves.

MAKES 6-8 PINTS.

APRICOT AND PEAR PRESERVES

MERMELADA DE CHABACANO Y PERA

4½ POUNDS RIPE APRICOTS, CUT IN HALF AND PITTED

4½ POUNDS PEARS, GRATED

¾ CUP SUGAR FOR EACH CUP FRUIT

3 VANILLA BEANS

10 DROPS LIME JUICE

In a blender or food processor purée the apricots. Measure the fruit to calculate correct amount of sugar to use. Place fruit in a glass bowl and cover with sugar. Add vanilla beans and leave at room temperature for 24 hours. Then add lime juice and cook for about 1½ hours or until mixture thickens. Seal as with apricot preserves.

MAKES 6-8 PINTS.

PLUM AND APPLE PRESERVES

MERMELADA DE CIRUELA Y MANZANA

9 POUNDS PLUMS, CUT IN HALF AND PITTED

2 GENEROUS POUNDS APPLES, PEELED AND PURÉED

¾ CUP SUGAR FOR EACH CUP OF FRUIT

2 CINNAMON STICKS, 6 INCHES LONG

Measure fruit to calculate correct amount of sugar to use. Place the fruit in a glass bowl and cover with sugar. Leave at room temperature for 24 hours. Then transfer to a medium stockpot or saucepan and add cinnamon stick. Cook about 1 hour or until the mixture thickens. Remove from heat, then proceed as with apricot preserves.

MAKES 6-8 PINTS.

BLACKBERRY PRESERVES

MERMELADA DE ZARZAMORA

5 POUNDS LARGE BLACKBERRIES, WASHED AND DRAINED

4 POUNDS SUGAR

A FEW DROPS OF LIME JUICE

6 TO 8 STERILIZED PINT JARS

PARAFFIN, MELTED (OPTIONAL)

Place the fruit and sugar in a large glass bowl and allow to sit at room temperature (or in the refrigerator) overnight. Spoon fruit and sugar into a large saucepan and simmer until mixture begins to foam. Skim off foam. Stir in lime juice and continue simmering until the mixture thickens to desired consistency, skimming as required. Remove from heat, then proceed as with apricot preserves. **MAKES 6-8 PINTS.**

PICKLED EGGS

HUEVITOS DE CODORNIZ EN ESCABECHE

Quail eggs can be prepared in a variety of ways. My grandmother Margarita used to pickle them for Lent. I remember eating them for a snack and as an appetizer before a hearty lunch. This recipe may also be made with chicken eggs. Prepare pickled eggs at least a day before you want them. They will keep refrigerated for up to a month. ~
MARGARITA

FOR THE EGGS

40 QUAIL EGGS OR 12 CHICKEN EGGS

FOR THE PICKLING SAUCE

½ CUP OLIVE OIL

8 GARLIC CLOVES, PEELED

4 MEDIUM WHITE ONIONS, PEELED AND SLICED THINLY

5 BAY LEAVES

2 SPRIGS FRESH THYME

2 SPRIGS FRESH MARJORAM

1 TEASPOON BLACK PEPPER

1 TEASPOON GROUND ALLSPICE

9 CARROTS, PEELED, SLICED ON THE DIAGONAL AND COOKED IN WATER WITH 1½ TEASPOON EACH OF SALT AND SUGAR

SALT TO TASTE

4½ CUPS VINEGAR, REDUCED TO 3 CUPS

Prepare the eggs: Boil the eggs in water, about 12 minutes for chicken eggs or 6 minutes for quail eggs. Then refresh in iced water for about 20 minutes. Peel eggs.

Prepare the pickling sauce: Heat the olive oil in a medium saucepan. Brown the garlic cloves. Then remove and purée 4 of the browned garlic cloves in a blender or food processor and return to the saucepan. Add the onion, bay leaves, thyme, marjoram, pepper, allspice, carrots and salt to the saucepan. Stir in reduced vinegar. Simmer ingredients for about 25 minutes. Rectify seasoning. Add the boiled eggs and cook for an additional 10 minutes. Serve the eggs as an appetizer, garnishing with carrots and pickling sauce. **SERVES 8-10.**

PICKLED SHRIMP

CAMARONES EN ESCABECHE BLANCO

Pickled Shrimp is a succulent appetizer or an interesting garnish for a vegetarian main dish during Lent. ~ PATRICIA

1 QUART OLIVE OIL

16 GARLIC CLOVES

10 MEDIUM WHITE ONIONS, PEELED AND THINLY SLICED

8 PURPLE ONIONS, PEELED AND THINLY SLICED

3⅓ CUPS WINE VINEGAR OR SHALLOT VINEGAR

¼ CUP DRIED TARRAGON

2 TEASPOONS POWDERED CHICKEN BOUILLON OR SALT TO TASTE

5 SPRIGS THYME

10 BAY LEAVES

5 SPRIGS MARJORAM

5 WHOLE CLOVES

12 TO 20 BLACK PEPPERCORNS

8 WHOLE CAYENNE PEPPERS

1 TEASPOON SUGAR

2 TEASPOONS COARSELY GROUND BLACK PEPPER

6½ POUNDS MEDIUM OR JUMBO SHRIMP, CLEANED AND DEVEINED

2 CANS PICKLED CHILES GÜEROS LARGOS OR OTHER HOT CHILES, ABOUT 13 OUNCES EACH

3 CUPS LARGE OLIVES, STUFFED WITH PIMIENTOS

Heat the olive oil in a medium saucepan and brown the garlic cloves, pressing a little while frying. Then remove and discard. Add onion and cook on a low heat until it becomes transparent. Then add vinegar, tarragon, bouillon, (or salt), thyme, bay leaves, marjoram, cloves, peppercorns, peppers, sugar and ground pepper. Stir well and cook for about 20 minutes. Then add shrimp and cook 5 minutes. Add chiles and stuffed olives and cook an additional 10 minutes.

Remove from heat, cool and refrigerate overnight. **SERVES 16.**

CORN SOUP WITH CHILES CHIPOTLES

SOPA DE ELOTE AL CHIPOTLE

In our household, this soup was always served during Lent. The tender flavor of the corn blended with the striking, smoky chipotle chile flavor makes for an extraordinary treat. ~ MARGARITA

FOR THE SOUP

6 TO 7 CUPS KERNELS FROM SWEET CORN

½ MEDIUM WHITE ONION, PEELED AND CHOPPED

3 GARLIC CLOVES, PEELED

6 CUPS MILK

SALT TO TASTE

1 TABLESPOON SUGAR

3 CUPS CHICKEN BROTH

4 CUPS WARM MILK

2 CUPS CRÈME FRAÎCHE

2 TO 4 PICKLED CANNED CHILES CHIPOTLES, OR DRIED CHIPOTLES, WASHED AND SOAKED IN HOT WATER 10-15 MINUTES, CHOPPED

2 TABLESPOONS CHIPOTLE CHILE JUICE FROM CAN, OR WATER

⅓ CUP BUTTER, IN CHUNKS

FOR THE GARNISH

½ CUP VEGETABLE OIL

6 MEDIUM TORTILLAS, CUT INTO WEDGES

2 TABLESPOONS PARSLEY OR CILANTRO, FINELY CHOPPED

Prepare the soup: Place the corn, onion, garlic and milk in a blender or food processor. Purée well, then strain the mixture and transfer to a medium saucepan. Add salt and sugar and simmer, stirring occasionally. Gradually add the chicken broth, milk, cream, chiles and chile juice and simmer 15-20 minutes. If the soup is too thick, add milk or chicken broth. Stir in butter before serving.

Prepare the garnish: Heat the vegetable oil in a frying pan and fry the tortilla wedges. Serve the soup from a tureen, garnished with fried tortilla wedges and chopped parsley or cilantro or you may wish to place garnishes in the bottom of individual soup bowls and ladle soup over at the table. **SERVES 8.**

INDIVIDUAL FISH TARTS

PAY DE PESCADO A LA CREMA

As my great-grandmother adapted her cooking to British cuisine to please my great-grandfather, she began to experiment with flavors and ingredients that were foreign to her. This recipe is an outcome of that experimentation. ~
EMILIA

FOODS OF LENT

FOR THE DOUGH

2   CUPS PLUS 3 TABLESPOONS ALL-PURPOSE FLOUR, SIFTED

¼   TEASPOON SALT, OR TO TASTE

1   CUP CHILLED BUTTER

4   TO 5 EGG YOLKS

5   TABLESPOONS ICED WATER

FOR THE FISH

4   CUPS WATER

8   CUPS MILK

1   CUP WHITE WINE

1½   MEDIUM WHITE ONIONS, PEELED AND HALVED

½   LEEK

6   STALKS CELERY, WITH LEAVES

1   TEASPOON BLACK PEPPERCORNS

1   TABLESPOON SALT, OR TO TASTE

1   FISH HEAD

1   FISH TAIL

3   POUNDS FISH, ANY VARIETY, WHOLE

FOR THE SAUCE

6   TABLESPOONS BUTTER

¾   CUP GREEN ONIONS, FINELY CHOPPED

1⅓   CUPS LEEKS (WITHOUT GREEN STEMS), FINELY CHOPPED

½   CUP CELERY, DICED

½   CUP CARROTS, FINELY CHOPPED

1   CUP WHITE WINE OR WHITE VERMOUTH

4   TABLESPOONS FLOUR

1   CUP SLIGHTLY WARMED MILK

½   CUP WHIPPING CREAM, AT ROOM TEMPERATURE

2   TABLESPOONS PARSLEY, FINELY CHOPPED

½   TABLESPOON TARRAGON, FINELY CHOPPED

½   TEASPOON GROUND WHITE PEPPER

    SALT TO TASTE

¾   CUP COOKED PEAS (OPTIONAL)

FOR THE GARNISH

2   EGG YOLKS

3   TABLESPOONS MILK

Prepare the dough: Place the flour and salt in a glass bowl. With two knives, work in butter until the mixture has a sandy consistency. Then stir in the egg yolks, working the dough with the fingers. Add the iced water and continue kneading the dough with the fingers for about half a minute. Then form the dough into a ball and sprinkle with a little flour. Cover and refrigerate for about two hours.

Prepare the fish: Place the water and the milk in a wide saucepan in which the fish will fit easily. Add wine, onion, leek, celery, peppercorns, salt, fish head, and fish tail. Boil for about 30 minutes over medium-to-low heat. Then add fish and poach for 15-20 minutes. The fish should be tender, but cooked. Test with a fork. Once done, remove fish from the stock and reserve. Continue to simmer the stock until it is reduced to 1½-2 cups. Reserve the fish stock. Separate the cooked fish into flakes and set aside.

Prepare the sauce: In a medium saucepan, heat the butter. Sauté the onions and leeks until they are transparent. Stir in celery and carrots and sauté vegetables for an additional 5 minutes. Stir in wine or vermouth and reduce liquid until it has almost totally evaporated. Add the flour and cook until the mixture takes on a light brown color. Remove saucepan from heat and slowly stir in milk, cream and 1¼ cups of reserved fish stock. Return mixture to the heat and simmer until it thickens (if it thickens too much, add milk or fish stock). Incorporate the parsley, tarragon, white pepper and salt to taste. Cook for an

INDIVIDUAL FISH TARTS WITH THE TART MOLDS IN WHICH THEY WERE BAKED. THE PARCHMENT BENEATH THEM IS THE OUTER SKIN OF MAGUEY CACTUS, PEELED, DRIED AND USED TO WRAP MEATS OR FISH FOR ROASTING.

additional 25 minutes on low heat. Stir in cooked peas if desired.

Preheat oven to 350°F. Butter and flour individual 4-5 inch tart molds. Then, working on a floured surface, roll out the pastry dough until it is approximately ½ inch thick. Cut 16 seven-inch circles from the dough, and place them in the prepared tart molds. Spoon flaked fish and cream sauce into individual molds. Leftover filling makes an excellent base for a soup or chowder. Cover with another pastry circle and pinch edges shut. Brush tops with egg yolk and milk, and prick with a fork to allow steam to escape. Bake for about 40 minutes or until the tops are golden brown. This dish is delicious with a green salad. **SERVES 8.**

VEGETABLES AND SHRIMP WITH COLORADITO MOLE

COLORADITO CON VERDURAS Y CAMARÓN DE CUARESMA O DE VIGILIA

My grandmother Margarita used to prepare coloradito — one of the seven famous moles from Oaxaca State — for Lent. ~ MARGARITA

FOR THE COLORADITO

1   CUP VEGETABLE OIL OR LARD

1   RIPE PLANTAIN

6   WHOLE CLOVES

1   TABLESPOON PEPPERCORNS

1½ TABLESPOONS CRUMBLED CINNAMON STICK

4   TABLESPOONS SESAME SEED, TOASTED

2   MEDIUM WHITE ONIONS, PEELED AND ROASTED

12 GARLIC CLOVES, PEELED AND ROASTED

4   MEDIUM TOMATOES, ROASTED

10 TOMATILLOS, HUSKED AND ROASTED

12 CHILES ANCHOS, WASHED, SEEDED AND DEVEINED, ROASTED AND SOAKED FOR ½ HOUR IN SALTED WATER (SUBSTITUTE DRIED RED MILD NEW MEXICAN OR CALIFORNIA CHILES)

10 CHILES CHILCOSLE, GUAJILLOS OR DRIED RED NEW MEXICAN OR CALIFORNIA CHILES, WASHED, SEEDED AND DEVEINED, ROASTED, AND SOAKED FOR ½ HOUR IN SALTED WATER

2   TABLESPOONS CHILE SEEDS, ROASTED

2   SLICES ONION

½   CUP MEXICAN CHOCOLATE (WITH CINNAMON) OR SEMI-SWEET BAKING CHOCOLATE TO TASTE

1   TEASPOON CRUSHED FRESH OREGANO

SALT TO TASTE

FOR THE VEGETABLES

½   CUP VEGETABLE OIL

1½ MEDIUM WHITE ONIONS, PEELED AND CHOPPED

4   LARGE POTATOES, PEELED AND DICED

2   CUPS GREEN BEANS, CHOPPED

2   CUPS PEAS

1½ CUPS CARROTS, DICED

SALT TO TASTE

3   CUPS WATER OR SHRIMP BROTH

FOR THE SHRIMP

1   MEDIUM WHITE ONION, QUARTERED

½   GARLIC HEAD, PEELED OR UNPEELED, CUT ACROSS THE GRAIN

2   GENEROUS POUNDS JUMBO SHRIMP, PEELED AND DEVEINED, SHELLS RESERVED

2   GENEROUS POUNDS LARGE DRIED SHRIMP, PEELED AND WASHED (SUBSTITUTE FRESH SHRIMP)

Prepare the coloradito sauce: Heat ½ cup vegetable oil or lard in a medium saucepan and fry the plantain, cloves, peppercorns, cinnamon and sesame seeds. Place this spice mixture in a processor or blender. Add onion, garlic, tomatoes, tomatillos, chile and chile seeds to the processor and purée. The ingredients should form a heavy paste. Strain through a sieve, adding broth to facilitate process if desired.

Heat remaining oil or lard in a heavy pot. Brown the onion slices. Then remove and discard. Add ½ cup of the strained sauce (it should sizzle). When the sauce begins to bubble, add remaining sauce. Simmer for about 1 hour or until the sauce releases its fat. Stir in chocolate and oregano and season with salt. Simmer for another hour, stirring occasionally.

Prepare the vegetables: Place the vegetable oil in a medium saucepan. Heat oil and then brown the chopped onion. Add potatoes, green beans, peas, carrots and season to taste with salt. Add the water or shrimp broth and simmer for ½ hour, or until the vegetables are tender. Strain vegetables out of stock and set aside, reserving stock.

Prepare the shrimp: Reheat the stock in which vegetables were cooked. Add onion, garlic and shrimp shells and bring to a boil. Then add the fresh and dried shrimp and boil for 8 minutes. Allow to cool and then strain shrimp from broth. Add vegetables and shrimp to the coloradito sauce. Simmer for 40 minutes. If the sauce becomes too thick, add a small quantity of shrimp broth to thin. Serve directly from the clay pot. This sauce is especially tasty with rice seasoned with cilantro or chepil (an herb from Oaxaca) and corn tortillas. You may also wish to reduce the sauce till it is thick and use to spread on a fried tortilla. Top with garnish to make a delicious tostada.

SERVES 8-16.

QUINTONILES OR SPINACH WITH CHILE

QUINTONILES CON RAJAS

Quintoniles *(keen toe NEE lez) are a delicious edible herb. Try this vegetable dish with spinach, chard, arugula or your favorite greens.* ~ EMILIA

5½ POUNDS QUINTONILES OR SPINACH

12 CUPS WATER

2 TABLESPOONS COARSE SALT

WATER AND ICE

⅔ CUP OLIVE OIL

½ CUP BUTTER

2 MEDIUM WHITE ONIONS, PEELED AND SLICED ON THE DIAGONAL

6 CHILES POBLANOS, ROASTED OR FRIED, SWEATED AND PEELED, SEEDED AND DEVEINED AND SOAKED IN SALT AND VINEGAR WATER, THEN SLICED INTO STRIPS

SALT TO TASTE

BLACK PEPPER TO TASTE

1½ CUPS FRESH RICOTTA OR FETA CHEESE, CRUMBLED

Wash the quintoniles or spinach well. Place water in a large saucepan. Add salt and bring to a rolling boil. Add a third of the quintoniles and boil for 6 minutes or until the vegetable is bright green and still somewhat crisp. Remove and rinse in iced water. Repeat procedure until all the greens are cooked. Drain off excess iced water and squeeze dry.

Heat the oil and butter in a medium frying pan. Add the onions and brown. Stir in chile strips and sauté for about 8 minutes. Add the refreshed greens and season to taste with salt and pepper. Sauté, then simmer 10 minutes.

YELLOW JACK MEATBALLS

ALBÓNDIGAS DE JUREL

Meatballs are prepared in Mexico in many ways. This is an example of a meatball not prepared with meat at all, but rather with fish. This recipe comes from Baja California, where fish is more abundant than beef. It can also be made with salt cod. ~ MARGARITA

FOR THE BROTH

½   CUP OLIVE OIL

8   GARLIC CLOVES, PEELED

1½   MEDIUM WHITE ONIONS, PEELED AND QUARTERED

4   MEDIUM, RIPE TOMATOES

1   TEASPOON DRIED OREGANO

1½   TEASPOONS BLACK PEPPER, OR TO TASTE

     SALT TO TASTE

20   CUPS FISH OR SHRIMP BROTH

4   CELERY RIBS

FOR THE MEATBALLS

3⅓   POUNDS YELLOW JACK, SALT COD OR OTHER FIRM, WHITE-FLESHED FISH, GROUND IN A PROCESSOR OR MORTAR

3   CARROTS, PEELED AND CUT IN CHUNKS

1½   MEDIUM WHITE ONIONS, PEELED AND QUARTERED

1   TO 2 TABLESPOONS CHOPPED FRESH CHILE SERRANO, OR ½ TO 1 TABLESPOON JALAPEÑO

½   TEASPOON DRIED OREGANO OR 1 TEASPOON FRESH OREGANO

4   EGGS, BEATEN

2   SLICES BREAD SOAKED IN ½ CUP MILK, CRUMBLED

     SALT TO TASTE

FOR THE GARNISH

FRESH OREGANO

Prepare the broth: Heat the oil in a large saucepan. Brown 4 cloves garlic, then remove and discard. Place the onion, remaining garlic, tomato, oregano, pepper and salt to taste in a blender or food processor and purée. Strain mixture and add to hot oil. Rectify seasoning and simmer until it releases its fat, about 40 minutes. Then stir in fish broth and celery.

Prepare the meatballs: Place the ground fish, carrots, onion, chile, oregano, eggs, bread and salt in a blender or food processor and process. Dampen or oil hands and shape mixture into 2- to 3-inch balls. Drop the meatballs into the boiling broth and cook for 25 minutes.

To serve: Serve meatballs from a soup tureen, or on individual dish plates. Garnish with oregano leaves. **SERVES 8.**

CORN AND GREEN CHILE SOUP

CHILE ATOLE EN VERDE

Atoles are dishes or drinks thickened with corn masa. They may take the form of a beverage or a chile-flavored breakfast porridge, or, as here, a rich soup or stew seasoned with epazote, hierba santa and cilantro. Chile atole is important to Mexican cuisine as a soup. This version is typical of Puebla. ~ MARGARITA

SALT COD, PARSLEY AND TOMATOES.

SALT COD ≈

From the 16th to the 18th centuries, cod made up over half of all fish eaten in Europe. It was exported to colonial Mexico by the Spanish very soon after the Conquest. The cold-water cod cures nicely with salt, which made it very portable for long sea voyages. Most cod eaten in Spain — and Mexico — in colonial times was caught off the coast of Newfoundland and Scandinavia and cured (or dried) with salt exported from Spanish and Portuguese ports. Young cod is called scrod in the U.S. Salt cod is available as whole fillets or in boneless, skinless, thick-cut pieces. Either way, it must be soaked a minimum of 24 hours to remove its saltiness. In Mexico, those who cannot afford dried cod buy the less expensive dried shark instead, trading "gato por liebre," or "cat for hare," as the saying goes.

FOR THE BROTH

6 QUARTS WATER

1 CHICKEN, 2½ POUNDS, CUT IN HALF

2 CHICKEN WINGS

½ GARLIC HEAD, UNPEELED

1 MEDIUM WHITE ONION, PEELED AND CUT IN HALF

4 RIBS CELERY, WITH LEAVES

2 CARROTS, PEELED

10 SPRIGS PARSLEY

½ LEEK

2 TURNIPS, PEELED AND CUT IN HALF

SALT TO TASTE

FOR THE SOUP

⅓ CUP BUTTER

¼ CUP VEGETABLE OIL OR LARD

6 FRESH EARS OF CORN, KERNELS REMOVED

6 MEDIUM WHOLE CHILES POBLANO OR ANAHEIM, ROASTED, SWEATED AND PEELED, SEEDED AND DEVEINED, AND CUT INTO STRIPS OR CHOPPED

1 MEDIUM WHITE ONION, PEELED AND GRATED

4 GARLIC CLOVES, GROUND

SALT TO TASTE

4 CUPS WATER

12 TOMATILLOS, HUSKED

½ MEDIUM WHITE ONION, PEELED

4 FRESH CHILES SERRANOS OR 2 JALAPEÑOS, STEAMED, WHOLE

1 CUP MASA, DISSOLVED IN 4 CUPS CHICKEN BROTH, THEN STRAINED

4 SPRIGS EPAZOTE

10 SPRIGS CILANTRO OR 6 HIERBA SANTA, CHOPPED

SALT TO TASTE

FOR THE GARNISH

VEGETABLE OIL

12 TORTILLAS

2 CUPS QUESO FRESCO OR OTHER MILD FRESH WHITE CHEESE

Prepare the broth: Bring the water to a boil in a stockpot. Add the chicken, chicken wings, garlic, onion, celery, carrots, parsley, leek, and turnips and season to taste with salt. Cook over medium heat for 1¼ hours or until the chicken is tender, skimming as necessary. Remove from heat and allow to cool for about 40 minutes. Skim fat off top of broth. Remove chicken, shred and reserve. Strain broth and degrease.

Prepare the soup: Heat the butter and oil in a medium saucepan. Stir in the corn kernels, chiles, onion, and garlic and salt. Cook until the vegetables are tender. In a separate saucepan, bring the water to a boil. Add the tomatillos, onion and chiles and boil for 30 minutes. Remove with a slotted spoon and grind in a blender or food processor. Strain and add to the corn-chile mixture. Continue cooking until the mixture releases its fat. Then, gradually stir in the dissolved masa in its strained broth, the epazote, cilantro (or hierba santa) and more salt if necessary. The soup should be semi-thick. Just before serving, add one-third of the chicken.

Prepare the garnish: Heat the oil in a deep frying pan. Cut tortillas into small squares and fry in hot oil until crisp. Shred remaining chicken.

To Serve: Place shredded chicken in individual soup bowls. Ladle chile atole over chicken and then garnish with fried tortillas and cheese. **SERVES 8.**

CRAB SOUP

CHILPACHOLE DE JAIBA

My grandmother's friend, Toñita Horta, taught her how to prepare this wonderful seafood soup. ~ MARGARITA

FOR THE CRAB

2½ GENEROUS POUNDS CRAB MEAT, CLEANED

1 CUP WHITE WINE

SALT TO TASTE

BLACK PEPPER TO TASTE

FOR THE FISH BROTH

30 CUPS WATER

2 FISH HEADS (ANY VARIETY)

2 FISH TAILS (ANY VARIETY)

6 CRABS, WHOLE

3 CARROTS, PEELED AND SLICED

4 CELERY RIBS, SLICED

1 MEDIUM WHITE ONION, PEELED AND HALVED

½ HEAD GARLIC

4 WHOLE BAY LEAVES

2 SPRIGS FRESH THYME

2 SPRIGS FRESH MARJORAM

1 TABLESPOON BLACK PEPPER, FRESHLY GROUND

SALT TO TASTE

FOR THE SOUP

3 TO 5 DRIED CHILES ANCHOS, SEEDED AND DEVEINED, LIGHTLY ROASTED AND SOAKED IN WATER FOR 20 MINUTES (SUBSTITUTE DRIED RED CHILES CALIFORNIA)

1 MEDIUM WHITE ONION, PEELED AND QUARTERED

6 MEDIUM GARLIC CLOVES, PEELED

4 RIPE TOMATOES, ROASTED

½ TEASPOON CUMIN SEED

1 TABLESPOON DRIED OREGANO

1 SPRIG FRESH THYME

½ CUP OLIVE OIL

3 GARLIC CLOVES, PEELED

1 SMALL WHITE ONION, PEELED AND SLICED

6 SPRIGS FRESH EPAZOTE OR CILANTRO

1 TO 3 FRESH CHILES SERRANOS OR JALAPEÑOS OR PASILLAS, STEMMED, WHOLE, FRIED LIGHTLY IN A SMALL AMOUNT OF OIL

Prepare the crab: Wash the crab and place it in a large glass bowl. Add the wine and season to taste with salt and pepper. Marinate for about 2 hours in the refrigerator.

Meanwhile, prepare the fish broth: Place the water, fish heads and tails in a large saucepan or stockpot. Add whole crabs, carrots, celery, onion, garlic, bay leaves, thyme, marjoram, pepper and salt to taste. Simmer for about 1-1½ hours. Remove from heat and allow to cool. Strain broth.

Prepare the soup: Place chiles, onion, garlic, tomatoes, cumin seed, oregano and thyme in a blender or food processor. Add 1 cup of the prepared fish broth and purée, then strain. Heat the oil in a medium saucepan and brown the garlic and onion slices. Remove and discard garlic and onion. Then add the strained chile mixture to the pan, and simmer for about 30-40 minutes, or until it releases its fat. Season to taste with salt. Gradually add the remaining fish broth. Then stir in shredded crab and cook for 10 minutes. Add the epazote and chiles and cook soup for an additional 25 minutes. Degrease, then serve hot from a soup tureen. **SERVES 8-12.**

RED SNAPPER WITH PARSLEY

PESCADO CON PEREJIL

My grandmother's friend Toñita Horta, a native of the coastal state of Veracruz, taught her how to prepare several regional dishes, of which this is one. This recipe became a family favorite. ~
MARGARITA

FOR THE FISH

1	6½ POUND FISH (RED SNAPPER, OR BASS), BONED AND CLEANED
	JUICE OF 3 LIMES
	SALT AND PEPPER
1½	WHITE ONIONS, PEELED AND FINELY CHOPPED

1	CUP PARSLEY, FINELY CHOPPED
2	MEDIUM WHITE ONIONS, PEELED AND THINLY SLICED
1½	GENEROUS POUNDS RIPE TOMATOES, THINLY SLICED
3	TABLESPOONS BREAD CRUMBS
	SALT AND PEPPER
1½	CUPS OLIVE OIL

FOR THE VEGETABLES

10	CUPS WATER
10	MEDIUM WHITE OR PINK POTATOES
1½	TABLESPOON SALT, OR TO TASTE
4	OUNCES BUTTER, IN CHUNKS
3	TABLESPOONS PARSLEY, FINELY CHOPPED

For the fish: Preheat oven to 400°F. Brush a baking tray with olive oil. Sprinkle fish with lime juice, salt and pepper. Stuff with half the chopped onion, parsley, sliced onion and tomato. Place on the prepared baking tray and arrange remaining onion, parsley and tomato on top of fish. Sprinkle with bread crumbs, salt and pepper, then pour olive oil over fish. Bake for about 1 hour 15 minutes or until the fish is tender. Test with a fork. When meat flakes easily it is ready. If fish begins to get too crisp while baking, cover it with a piece of aluminum foil.

Prepare the vegetables: Place water in a large saucepan. Add potatoes and salt to water and boil until the potatoes are done. Remove from boiling water and peel. Discard the boiling water and return potatoes to warm saucepan to dry them a little; however do not turn on heat. Press the potatoes through a mesh sieve (do not mash) and arrange pressed potatoes around the fish. Garnish platter with butter, salt and parsley. **SERVES 8-10.**

POTATOES WITH PEPPER AND GARLIC

PAPAS A LA PIMIENTA Y AL AJO

Potatoes *are prepared in many ways in Mexico. They are used as a filling for fried quesadillas or as a side dish, mixed with chiles poblanos, onions, and cheese. They are used to make the traditional omelet —* TORTILLA ESPAÑOLA. *I remember my grandmother saying that the best potatoes in the Republic came from Perote in the State of Veracruz. ~*
MAGO

FOR THE POTATOES

3 TO 5 QUARTS WATER OR TO COVER

1 GARLIC HEAD, CUT IN HALF ACROSS THE GRAIN

16 MEDIUM BOILING POTATOES (WAXY), WHOLE, WITH SKINS

SALT TO TASTE

FOR THE VINAIGRETTE

1½ CUPS WHITE WINE VINEGAR

2 CUPS SEVILLE ORANGE JUICE OR 1 CUP ORANGE JUICE PLUS 1 CUP GRAPEFRUIT JUICE

6 GARLIC CLOVES, PEELED

1 TABLESPOON FRESHLY GROUND BLACK PEPPER

½ TABLESPOON SUGAR

SALT TO TASTE

1½ CUPS OLIVE OIL

FOR THE GARNISH

2 HEADS GARLIC, PEELED AND OPENED TO RESEMBLE A FLOWER

6 TABLESPOONS GREEN ONION, CHOPPED FINELY

Prepare the potatoes: Bring the water to a rolling boil. Add the garlic, potatoes and salt and boil until potatoes are tender. Be careful not to overcook or the potatoes will become mushy. When done, remove from heat and allow the potatoes to cool in water. Peel and refrigerate for about 25 minutes. Then slice.

Prepare the vinaigrette: Place the vinegar, orange juice and garlic in a medium saucepan. Bring to a boil. Add pepper, sugar and salt. Boil until the mixture is slightly reduced. Remove from heat and allow to cool a little. Then gradually add the oil, mixing well with a whisk. Rectify seasoning. Place sliced potatoes on a serving plate. Drench with the vinaigrette sauce. Garnish with garlic heads. Sprinkle with green onions. Refrigerate for one hour before serving. Serve this side dish cold. **SERVES 8.**

GARLIC ≈

Garlic, which originated in the Mediterranean long before the birth of Christ and was brought to the New World by Europeans, is now deeply integral to Mexican cooking. Aromatic and friendly to many other ingredients, the garlic bulbs or heads sold as "fresh" are actually dried. Separate them clove by clove for use, keeping the unused portion of the head in an airy, dark, cool place such as a pierced ceramic crock. Garlic mellows dramatically with long cooking.

Mexican folk wisdom calls for garlic as a cure for insomnia, suggesting that you boil 4 cloves in milk, strain, and drink, to cure sleeplessness. It is also said to be good for circulation and stomach ailments. To peel and mince a clove of garlic with the least trouble, first flatten it with the back of a knife.

BAKED STUFFED RED SNAPPER

XIMBO

Ximbo *(SHEEM bo) is typical of the Hidalgo region, where fresh maguey leaves are used to cook the fish. The fish may also be stuffed with chopped mushrooms (instead of the chiles poblanos) or with cuitlacoche, the fragrant and spicy fungus that is cultivated on ears of corn during the rainy season.*

FOR THE MARINADE

1   CUP OLIVE OIL

1½ MEDIUM WHITE ONIONS, PEELED AND QUARTERED

8   GARLIC CLOVES, PEELED

1½ TO 2 CUPS WHITE WINE

½   TABLESPOON FRESHLY GROUND BLACK PEPPER

    SALT TO TASTE

FOR THE FISH

1   LARGE SEA BASS (7¾ POUNDS) OR RED SNAPPER, BONED

6   SMALL MAGUEY LEAVES OR 8 BANANA LEAVES, ROASTED ON A COMAL (YOU MAY ALSO USE FRESH CORN HUSKS)

FOR THE FILLING

¾   CUP BUTTER

¼   CUP OLIVE OIL

4   MEDIUM WHITE ONIONS, PEELED AND SLICED DIAGONALLY

12 CHILES POBLANOS, ROASTED AND SWEATED, PEELED, SEEDED, DEVEINED, CUT INTO STRIPS

    SALT TO TASTE

1   TEASPOON BLACK PEPPER

Prepare the marinade: Place the oil, onion, garlic, white wine, black pepper and salt in a blender or food processor and purée. Place fish on a baking tray or ovenproof pan. Pour the puréed mixture over fish and set aside for two hours.

Prepare the filling: Heat the butter and oil in a large frying pan. Brown the onion, then add the chiles poblano and cook for about 20 minutes. Season to taste with salt and pepper, and reserve.

Prepare the fish: Preheat oven to 400°F. Place two of the roasted maguey leaves next to one another on a baking tray. Place two more leaves over them, crisscrossing. Place the fish over the leaves and stuff with prepared filling. Cover with remaining leaves and wrap as if in a bag. Then tie together with wire, and wrap with aluminum foil. Bake 1½ to 2 hours, or until the fish is tender (the time depends on the oven and the altitude). Test with a fork. The fish should flake easily when done. Since the maguey leaves will absorb the heat, they may dry out if you are not careful. If you have no maguey leaves, banana leaves or cornhusks, the fish may be baked in an oven baking bag or in aluminum foil.

To serve: Uncover fish and serve on a platter directly from the maguey leaves.
SERVES 16.

≈ *Re-entering the World* ≈

DAY
OF THE
DEAD
EL DIA DE LOS MUERTOS

"El Dia de los Muertos," The Day of the Dead, combines pre-Hispanic Indian beliefs with the Catholic traditions of Medieval Spain. The ancient religions of Mexico saw death as only one state in an endless cycle of being. Even the universe died and was reborn again and again. The line between the living and the dead, so clear to North Americans, was soft and blurred.

When the Spanish arrived in Mexico in the 16th century, they brought with them the heritage of Medieval Europe, which had its own strong, though darker, involvement with the idea of death. During the dangerous and tumultuous early Middle Ages, French poets created the image of the "Danse Macabre," Dancing Death in the form of a cloaked skeleton, coming

A WOMAN GATHERS MARIGOLDS IN A FIELD OF
FLOWERS NEAR THE VILLAGE OF SAN ANTONINO, OAXACA.

to take away everyone in the end, from popes to peasants. The church counseled wise behavior for eternal life, but some were bound for Purgatory, the in-between state of the unredeemed. All Souls Day, in early November, was the day that the faithful prayed for the souls in Purgatory, to shorten their sojourn there.

In the miraculous way that ideas are tranformed through rebirth in another culture, All Souls Day in Spanish-Indian Mexico became The Day of the Dead. Instead of praying for those in Purgatory, Mexicans celebrated with those who had gone before, feasted with them and welcomed them home for a visit.

In the words of the great poet and writer Octavio Paz, fiesta allows us to "throw down our burdens of time and reason." In the fiesta of Muertos (the Dead), time no longer bars one spirit from another by reason of death. Mothers and fathers welcome back the spirits of children by creating altars in their homes. On the morning of October 31, the souls of "los angelitos," the little innocent ones, return. Everything on their altars is new, and there are favorite sweets, toys, flowers and candles. By noon on November 1, the children have left and the souls of the departed adults begin to return, to feast at altars with their favorite foods.

Mexicans believe that the dead wish for the living the things of life, the brilliant colors of flowers, ribbons, costumes, fireworks, candlelight. In all regions, in the great cities and in far-flung villages, fiesta is celebrated. In the cemeteries, entire families devote themselves to washing the tombstones and decorating them with flowers, portraits, refreshing drinks, and garlands of the traditional flower of the celebration, the yellow-orange zempasúchil, or marigold, which floods the markets with a sea of saffron brilliance in the days preceding Muertos. Flowers, so beloved by Mexicans, are everywhere during the fiesta. Cannas, calla lilies, baby's breath, daisies, hollyhocks, and a rainbow of other flowers crowd the markets and are carried by the bale, wrapped in huge straw mats, to the gates of the cemeteries. Burros laden with flowers are led down the dusty roads of the villages, and horse-drawn carts heaped high with flowers rumble behind them.

After a lifetime of feasts celebrated with family and friends of all ages, feasts redolent with strong aromas and vivid with spicy, fresh, colorful foods, it seems appropriate that the spirit would return again yearly to those it knew and loved, to partake once more of the pleasures of earth. The last and forever-recurring feast of Mexico bridges life and death, feeding both body and soul.

THE CEMETERY OF SAN ANTONINO, SOON AFTER DAYBREAK. VILLAGERS ARRIVE TO BEDECK THE GRAVES WITH FLOWERS, CANDLES AND FOOD.

≈

"Must I go like the flowers that perish?/ Will nothing remain of my name?/ Nothing of my fame here on earth?/ At least my flowers, at least my songs!/ Earth is the region of the fleeting moment."

PRE-HISPANIC NAHUATL POEM

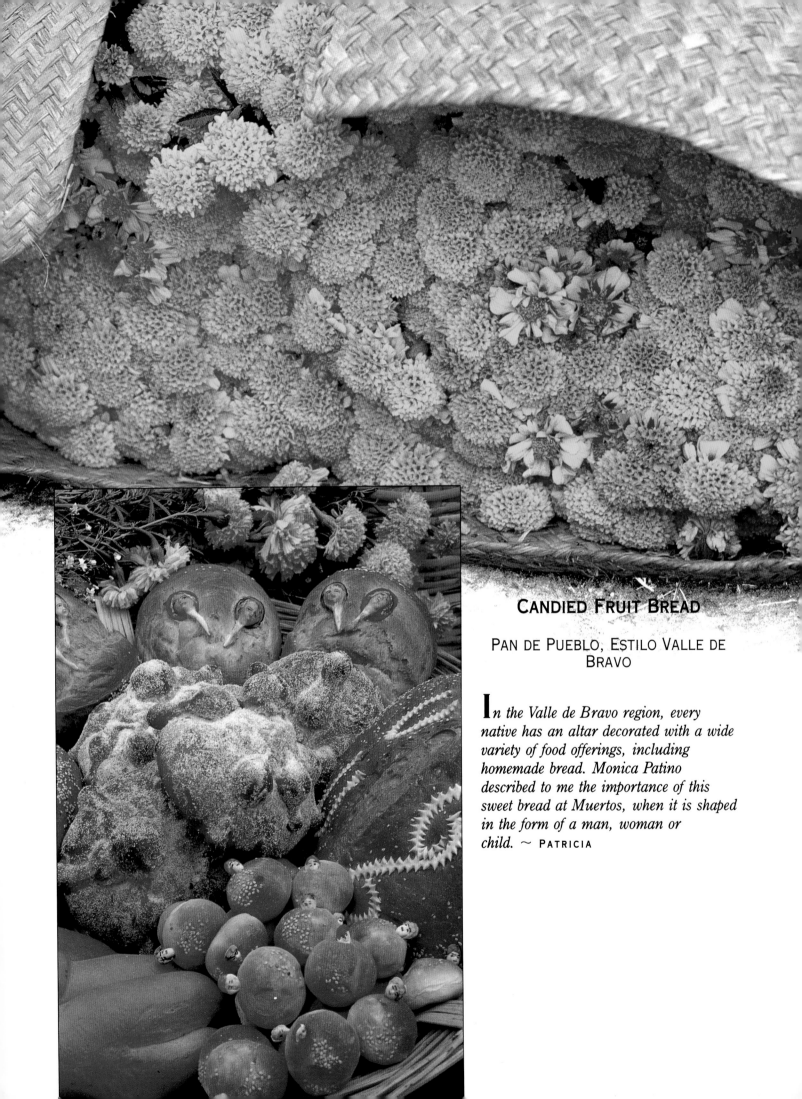

Candied Fruit Bread

Pan de Pueblo, Estilo Valle de Bravo

In the Valle de Bravo region, every native has an altar decorated with a wide variety of food offerings, including homemade bread. Monica Patino described to me the importance of this sweet bread at Muertos, when it is shaped in the form of a man, woman or child. ~ Patricia

½ CUP LUKEWARM WATER

1 OUNCE YEAST (1 HEAPING TABLESPOON)

8 GENEROUS CUPS FLOUR

1 TABLESPOON WHOLE ANISE SEED

1 CUP SUGAR

1 TABLESPOON SALT

10 EGGS

3 CUPS BUTTER

¾ CUP CANDIED FIGS, FINELY CHOPPED

¾ CUP ACITRON, FINELY CHOPPED

¾ CUP CANDIED PINEAPPLE, FINELY CHOPPED

¾ CUP CANDIED PUMPKIN OR SQUASH, FINELY CHOPPED

CONFECTIONERS' SUGAR

Place the water in a medium bowl. Add yeast and stir until well dissolved. Add about 1 cup of the flour, and stir until the mixture can be shaped into a ball. If necessary, add a little more water. Cover with a clean cloth and set aside in a warm, draft-free spot. Place the remaining flour on a flat surface. Form a hole in the center of the flour and fill it with the anise seed, sugar, salt, and eggs. Knead the ingredients together, evenly incorporating them. Knead 25 minutes, or until the dough becomes elastic and is no longer sticky. (You may knead with a food processor if preferred.) Add the yeast mixture and continue kneading until the dough is again silky. If the dough becomes too dry (depending on climate and quality of the flour), add a little milk. Gradually add butter and knead dough until soft. Shape into a single ball and place in a greased bowl. Coat with a little oil and cover with a clean cloth. Place in a warm, draft-free place and allow the ball to double in size. Punch down and refrigerate dough overnight.

The next day, preheat oven to 375°F. Add the candied fruit to the dough, kneading briefly. Shape the dough into the form of a person, or make a braid. Cover with a cloth and allow to rise once again. Then bake for 30-40 minutes or until the bread is golden brown. Remove from oven and allow to cool. Before serving, sprinkle with confectioners' sugar. Serve warm with butter, preserves and a cup of hot chocolate. **SERVES 8-10.**

NAOLINCO BREAD

PAN DE NAOLINCO

We used to prepare Naolinco bread in my great-grandmother Emilia's house to commemorate loved ones on the Day of the Dead. ~ EMILIA

4 CUPS FLOUR

4 CUPS WHOLE WHEAT FLOUR

6 TABLESPOONS LARD OR BUTTER

2 TABLESPOONS SUGAR

1 TABLESPOON SALT

1 TABLESPOON DRIED YEAST

2½ TO 3 CUPS WARM WATER

1 EGG YOLK

In a large glass bowl place the flour, lard (or butter), sugar, salt and yeast. Stir in the water, then knead until the dough is firm and not sticky. Cover with a clean cloth and set aside in a warm, draft-free place for 2 hours, or until doubled in volume.

Preheat oven to 350°F. Knead the dough a few times. Then shape into 2 loaves. Allow the loaves to rest for about 1 to 1½ hours. Brush with egg yolk mixed with a little water. Bake for 45 minutes or until golden brown. Serve with butter or cream, or to accompany a meal. **SERVES 8.**

THE BREADS OF THE DEAD, IN MANY VARIETIES. SOME HAVE PAINTED PORCELAIN HEADS EMBEDDED IN THE DOUGH, OTHERS ARE DECORATED WITH BRAIDS OF DOUGH OR PAINTED WITH FOOD COLORING.

PUMPKIN SEED BUTTER
≈

Grind ½ cup toasted, salted pumpkin seeds in a food processor, then combine with ¾ cup butter at room temperature. Optional additions are minced cilantro, chile purée, cracked black pepper and minced fresh garlic cloves, either raw or roasted. Pumpkin Seed Butter is delicious on flour or corn tortillas and with breads and rolls, especially whole-grain.

EGG BREAD

PAN DE YEMA

The texture of this delicious egg bread makes it perfect for dipping into hot chocolate. ~ EMILIA

3½ TABLESPOONS YEAST

¾ CUP WARM WATER

1 CUP ALL-PURPOSE FLOUR

8 CUPS ALL-PURPOSE FLOUR

1½ CUPS SUGAR

1½ CUPS BUTTER, AT ROOM TEMPERATURE

1 TEASPOON SALT

15 EGG YOLKS

3 EGGS

1 EGG YOLK WHISKED WITH 2 TABLESPOONS MELTED BUTTER OR CREAM

Dissolve the yeast in warm water. Add one cup flour and allow mixture to stand for ½ hour. Then place the yeast mixture, flour, sugar, butter, salt, egg yolks and eggs in a large bowl. Mix thoroughly. Knead the dough until it becomes elastic and not sticky (if necessary, add more flour). You may also use the kneading attachment of a food processor, processing about 20 minutes. Form into a large ball, cover with a cloth, and place in a warm, draft-free place for about an hour or until doubled in volume. Or allow to rise overnight in the warmest part of the refrigerator.

Preheat oven to 350°F. Knead the dough briefly. Shape into 2 or 3 round loaves or into human figures. Place on a greased baking tray and cover. Allow to double in volume. Before placing in the oven, brush tops with egg yolk and butter or cream. Bake 45 minutes or until golden brown.

FLAN ≈

Flan is a regional specialty throughout Mexico, appearing in many characteristic guises. In some areas it is flavored with coconut, in others with cheese or squash.

TO CARAMELIZE SUGAR ≈

Add a desired quantity of sugar to saucepan and heat through till melted, approximately 6-8 minutes. Caramelized sugar can be drizzled over ice cream, used to color sauces or flavor milk dishes such as custard, or poured over nuts or seeds to make praline candy.

CARAMELIZED EGG CUSTARD

FLAN

This classical dessert is found everywhere in Mexico. No Muertos altar is complete without a freshly made flan. ~ MARGARITA

2½ CUPS SUGAR

1⅓ CUPS WATER

10 EGGS PLUS 4 EGG YOLKS

2 CUPS SWEETENED CONDENSED MILK

2 CUPS WHOLE MILK

2½ CUPS EVAPORATED MILK

2 TABLESPOONS VANILLA EXTRACT

Prepare the burnt sugar topping: Place the sugar and water in a heavy saucepan. Stir well, then simmer over low heat until the sugar totally dissolves and the mixture is dark brown color.

Pour the burnt sugar into a 10-inch ungreased ring mold, tipping the mold to evenly line the bottom. Allow to cool.

Preheat the oven to 350°F.

Prepare the custard: Beat the egg and egg yolks. Place the three milks in a separate mixing bowl and stir well. Blend eggs and milk, then stir in the vanilla. Pour custard into the prepared ring mold. Place in a larger mold or pan filled with 1 inch of water. Bake for 1½ hours or until a toothpick inserted into the center comes out clean. Allow to cool, then refrigerate overnight. Unmold before serving. Serve chilled. **SERVES 8-12.**

EGG BREAD (BELOW) IS
BAKED FOR MUERTOS.
BREAD, FLOWERS AND
CHOCOLATE ARE CONSTANTS
ON THE ALTARS CREATED
FOR THE DAY OF THE
DEAD.

PORK AND CHICKEN TAMALES

TAMALES OAXAQUEÑOS

My grandmother Margarita considered Oaxacan-style tamales the most important offering for the altar on the Day of the Dead. These tamales are different from others, since they are steamed in banana leaves rather than corn husks. They are commonly served with Mexican-style coffee or hot atole (page 89). If you cannot get banana leaves, you can use corn husks. ~ PATRICIA

FOR THE FILLING

1 MEDIUM CHICKEN, CUT IN PIECES (APPROXIMATELY 2½ POUNDS)

½ POUND PORK LOIN, CUT IN PIECES

1 MEDIUM WHITE ONION, PEELED AND QUARTERED

6 GARLIC CLOVES, PEELED

SALT TO TASTE

WATER TO COVER

FOR THE DOUGH

2 GENEROUS POUNDS FRESH WHITE MASA (OR MASA PREPARED WITH MASA HARINA)

SALT TO TASTE

1¼ CUPS WATER WITH 1 TEASPOON BAKING SODA

1 POUND LARD, SOFT, BEATEN UNTIL FLUFFY

TO COMPLETE THE TAMALES

1 POUND BLACK MOLE (PAGE 234)

1 LARGE PACKAGE OF BLANCHED BANANA LEAVES (OR STEAM BANANA LEAVES OVER A LOW HEAT UNTIL PLIABLE), CUT INTO 24 RECTANGLES 8 X 12 INCHES

Prepare the filling: Place the chicken, pork, onion, garlic and salt in a stockpot and cover with water. Cook over medium heat for 45 minutes, then check to see if chicken is done. When chicken is tender, remove from pot and set aside. Continue cooking pork another 45 minutes or until it is done. Allow pork to cool in the broth, then remove it from the pot. Shred both chicken and pork.

Prepare the dough: Place the masa in a large glass bowl. Add the salt and the water with baking soda dissolved in it. Beat until the ingredients are well incorporated, and the mixture has the consistency of soft dough. Then add the lard and continue beating. Test masa by dropping a bit into a glass of water. If it floats, it is light enough. If not, continue beating. Season with 3 tablespoons of mole.

Assemble the tamales: Drop one or two tablespoons of dough onto a banana leaf, spreading it with the back of a spoon to form a very thin layer. Place a tablespoon of meat over the dough, then a tablespoon of mole. Fold the bottom part of the leaf upward, and the top part of the leaf downward towards the center. Press the leaf to keep in place. Then fold both the sides inward to form a square. Double-wrap the tamal with a second banana leaf, to be sure that the filling does not escape or become soggy in the steaming process. Tie the tamal with strips cut from banana leaves.

Prepare a steamer: Pour water into a steamer, adding a coin. The coin will rattle if the water evaporates. Line the bottom of the steamer with banana leaves. Arrange the tamales in the steamer and then cover with extra banana leaves. Steam for 1½ hours. Tamales are done when the cooked dough can be peeled easily from the leaf. If

TAMALES WRAPPED IN BANANA LEAVES, OAXACA STYLE, AND IN CORN HUSKS, LYING ON A BED OF BANANA LEAVES.

TAMALE ACCOMPANIMENTS ≈

Serve steaming tamales with cream, cheese and Chile Ancho Salsa (page 113), Green Salsa with Cilantro (page 75), or other salsas. They may be served still wrapped, or unwrapped and garnished with salsas and cheese.

necessary, add more water to the steamer during cooking time. Allow tamales to cool slightly.

To serve: Place the tamales on a large round serving platter, piled high. They can be served for a light dinner, a snack or for breakfast with black coffee or hot chocolate. **Serves 8.**

Fresh Corn Tamales

Tamal de Elote

When a Mexican family makes tamales around the Day of the Dead holiday, they are made for the entire family, including those who are now spirits. Tamales are offered to both the living and the dead. ~ MARGARITA

FOR THE TAMAL BATTER

28 CUPS KERNELS FROM LARGE EARS OF CORN, NOT TOO RIPE (SUBSTITUTE FROZEN WHOLE-KERNEL CORN)

2 CUPS CORN FLOUR, BLUE OR YELLOW CORNMEAL, OR MASA HARINA

1½ CUPS BUTTER, AT ROOM TEMPERATURE

⅔ CUP LARD OR VEGETABLE SHORTENING

1½ CUPS SUGAR OR TO TASTE

2 TEASPOONS BAKING POWDER

4 EGGS

2 TABLESPOONS SALT OR TO TASTE

140 FRESH CORN HUSKS (OR BANANA LEAVES)

FOR THE GARNISH

1½ CUPS HEAVY CREAM OR CRÈME FRAÎCHE

2½ POUNDS FRESH FETA OR FARMER'S CHEESE, CRUMBLED, OR STRING CHEESE, SHREDDED

Prepare the tamales: Husk the ears of corn, reserving the husks to wrap tamales in. Degrain the ears of corn with a sharp knife. Place the corn kernels in a blender or food processor and purée. If the kernels are very dry, add a little milk to facilitate the procedure. Transfer puréed corn and corn flour to a large bowl and beat with a rotary beater or electric beater. Gradually add the butter and lard. When well mixed, add the sugar and beat another 3-4 minutes. Incorporate eggs one by one along with baking powder and salt, and continue beating for about 25 minutes or until the mixture is smooth. Allow mixture to sit for 30 minutes.

Meanwhile prepare a steamer: Fill a steamer with water. Place coin at the bottom (it will rattle if the water has evaporated), then place rack in steamer. Place a thick layer of corn husks in the bottom of the steamer to keep tamales from becoming soggy. Begin to heat water over a medium flame.

Assemble the tamales: Place 1-2 tablespoons of tamale batter in the center of each corn husk and fold shut according to the procedure described on pages 52-53. Arrange tamales in the prepared steamer, overlapping. Cover with fresh cornhusks. Top with a damp cloth and steam for 1 hour or until done. The husks will easily peel from the batter when done. If necessary, add more water to the steamer.

To serve: Arrange corn tamales on an earthenware platter. Serve steaming hot, with cream, cheese and Chile Ancho Salsa (page 113), Green Salsa with Cilantro (page 75) or other salsas on the side. Or unwrap tamales and place on individual dinner plates, garnishing with cream, cheese and salsa. **MAKES 60 TAMALES.**

CHILTOMATE SAUCE

SALSA DE CHILTOMATE

This versatile cooked sauce can accompany tamales, egg dishes or casseroles.

10 LARGE RIPE TOMATOES (ABOUT 4 POUNDS), ROASTED

1 MEDIUM WHITE ONION, PEELED AND ROASTED

6 GARLIC CLOVES, PEELED AND ROASTED

½ MEDIUM WHITE ONION, PEELED AND QUARTERED

3 GARLIC CLOVES, PEELED

½ CUP SAFFLOWER OIL OR LARD

SALT TO TASTE

4 CHILES XCATICK OR GÜERO, ROASTED, SWEATED, PEELED, SEEDED AND DEVEINED, CUT INTO STRIPS (SUBSTITUTE ANAHEIM OR BANANA PEPPERS)

2 SPRIGS FRESH EPAZOTE OR CILANTRO

SALT TO TASTE

Place the roasted tomatoes (still in their skins), roasted onion and garlic, and raw onion and garlic in a blender or food processor and purée, if necessary in batches. Strain the puréed mixture. Heat the oil or lard in a deep skillet and add ½ cup of the strained sauce (it should sizzle). After 1 or 2 minutes, add the rest of the sauce. Season to taste with salt and cook for 25 minutes or until the mixture thickens and its oil is separate and visible on the surface of the sauce. If sauce is too thick, thin with chicken broth. Then add the chiles, epazote and salt to taste.

SERVES 8-12.

LARD

MANTECA

When the Spaniards arrived in Mexico with their pigs, the Indians called this strange animal COCHINO, "the one who sleeps," from the word for sleep, COCHI. Soon the sound of sizzling lard, made from pork fat, joined the music of the Mexican kitchen. Pure, light homemade lard is used in tamales, tacos, moles and many other dishes essential to Mexican cooking. From the Spanish the Mexicans also learned to make chorizo, the spicy, smoked, air-dried pork sausage first made in Toluca. In Mexico, little of the pig is wasted — even its skin is made into a dish called CHICHARRÓN, meaning "to burn or sizzle" after the sound it makes when it is deep-fried into large crunchy, golden sheets. Commercial lard with its stabilizers and preservatives may be used in Mexican cooking, but homemade lard is more wholesome and better tasting.

6½ POUNDS CLEAN PORK FATBACK, CUT INTO PIECES

SALT TO TASTE

WATER TO COVER

Prepare the lard: Place the fatback in a medium saucepan. Sprinkle with salt and cover with water. Bring to a rolling boil, then reduce heat and melt fatback until it resembles pork cracklings, about 45 minutes. Be careful the fat does not burn. Remove from heat and allow to cool, then strain lard. Sediment may be used for preparing beans or gorditas. Can be stored in the refrigerator for up to 2 months.

MAKES 4-6 CUPS.

THE RIPE TOMATO ≈

Out-of-season tomatoes in the U.S. have usually been picked very green and given a vine-ripe color through exposure to ethylene gas. If all you can get are these cottony tomato look-alikes, try substituting your favorite canned tomatoes. If you have half-ripe tomatoes from the vine, do not refrigerate them, but place them in a perforated paper sack in the company of a very ripe apple, whose tiny breath of ethylene gas will gently ripen them. Or place them in a straw basket in strong, indirect light at room temperature.

Tomatoes are very rapidly peeled after being immersed in boiling water for 2-3 minutes. Drain and cool; the skin will easily slip off.

CHICKEN AND VEGETABLES WITH YELLOW MOLE

AMARILLO

In Oaxaca, this mole is called simply AMARILLO — *or "yellow." It is the color of the marigold petals that Oaxacans scatter from their houses to the cemetery to aid the returning souls in finding their way home.* ~ PATRICIA

FOR THE CHILE

½ POUND YELLOW CHILES GUAJILLO OR CHILCOSLE, OR DRIED CHILES CALIFORNIA

¼ CUP VEGETABLE OIL

FOR THE SPICES

1½ CUPS WATER

1 MEDIUM WHITE ONION, PEELED AND QUARTERED

2 GARLIC CLOVES, PEELED

10 TOMATILLOS, HUSKED

1 GARLIC HEAD, CLOVES SEPARATED, PEELED AND ROASTED, OR THE HEAD ROASTED WHOLE, THEN CLOVES PEELED

1 MEDIUM WHITE ONION, PEELED AND ROASTED

1 MEDIUM WHITE ONION, PEELED, RAW

2 MEDIUM RIPE TOMATOES, ROASTED

4 WHOLE CLOVES, LIGHTLY ROASTED

1 CINNAMON STICK, 2½ INCHES LONG, LIGHTLY ROASTED

7 HIERBA SANTA LEAVES OR 15 EPAZOTE LEAVES

¾ TABLESPOON FRESH OREGANO LEAVES OR 1 TEASPOON DRIED OREGANO

⅔ CUP VEGETABLE OIL OR LARD

1 SLICE WHITE ONION

SALT TO TASTE

½ CUP FRESH MASA OR MASA PREPARED WITH MASA HARINA

4 CUPS CHICKEN BROTH

FOR THE CHICKEN

15 CUPS WATER

2 TO 3 WHOLE CHICKENS, EACH 3⅓ POUNDS, CUT IN PIECES

2 MEDIUM WHITE ONIONS, PEELED AND CHOPPED

6 HIERBA SANTA LEAVES OR 20 CILANTRO SPRIGS

3 CARROTS, PEELED

1½ TEASPOONS DRIED OREGANO LEAVES

SALT TO TASTE

FOR THE VEGETABLES

3 CHAYOTES, PEELED AND CUT IN 2-INCH PIECES

½ POUND GREEN BEANS, CUT IN HALF

FOR THE CHOCHOYONES

1½ CUPS FRESH MASA OR MASA PREPARED WITH MASA HARINA

6 TABLESPOONS CHICKEN BROTH

2 TABLESPOONS LARD OR VEGETABLE OIL

½ TEASPOON SALT, OR TO TASTE

FOR THE GARNISH

1½ MEDIUM WHITE ONIONS, FINELY CHOPPED

THE JUICE OF 3 LIMES

Prepare the chiles: Wash, dry, seed and devein the chiles. Heat the oil in a frying pan and fry the chiles, without browning them too much. Then transfer to a bowl and cover with water. Allow to soak for about 45 minutes. Transfer to a blender or food processor and purée with ½ cup soaking water, or use the traditional method of grinding the chiles on a *metate* (a volcanic grinding stone).

Prepare the spices: Heat the water in a medium saucepan. Add the onion and garlic cloves and bring to a boil. Add the tomatillos and cook for 20 minutes. Cool, then transfer to a blender or food processor and purée with roasted garlic, roasted and raw onion, roasted tomatoes, cloves, cinnamon, hierba santa and oregano. Add about 1½ cups chicken broth to facilitate the procedure. It may be necessary to purée in batches.

Heat the oil in a heavy skillet, add the onion slice and brown. Stir in puréed tomatillo mixture and cook for 45 minutes or until the mixture renders its fat. Stir in puréed chiles and cook for 1 to 1½ hours, or until the mole thickens and renders its fat. Season to taste with salt. Combine the masa and chicken broth and add to mole. Thin with more broth if desired. Sauce can be as thick or thin as you prefer. Cook an additional 25 minutes.

Prepare the chicken: Heat the water in a large stockpot. Add the chicken, onion, hierba santa, carrots, oregano and salt to taste. Cook for 35 minutes or until the chicken is semi-cooked. Remove from heat and allow to cool completely in the broth. Then remove chicken from broth, reserving broth.

Prepare the vegetables: Bring the reserved broth to a boil. Add the chayotes and cook for 25 minutes or until tender. Remove and reserve. To the same cooking broth, add the green beans and cook 5-8 minutes or until tender. Remove and reserve.

Prepare the chochoyones (masa dumplings): Mix together the masa, chicken broth, lard and salt and knead for about 5 minutes or until the masa is smooth and no longer sticky. Form into 1½-inch balls and press in the center with the knuckle to make an indention. Reserve.

To serve mole: Reheat the mole, adding cooked chicken and a little broth until you have the desired consistency. Add the chochoyones and cook for 20 minutes. Reheat vegetables separately. Serve a piece of chicken, drenched in mole, on each plate. Arrange the chochoyones and vegetables on the side. Garnish with chopped onion and lime juice. Accompany with hot tortillas. SERVES 10-12.

YELLOW MOLE VARIATIONS ≈

Yellow Mole may be used to fill tamales or turnovers. Thicken mole to the consistency of custard and blend it with shredded chicken for use as a filling.

To intensify the flavor of Yellow Mole, just before serving, add ground garlic cloves, oregano, mint leaves, minced onion and ground cinnamon, ground together in quantities to taste.

CHILE COLOR ≈

All chiles and peppers change color as they ripen, to red, yellow, brown or purple. Most, however, are picked and sold green, in part because they keep better when green.

YELLOW MOLE, WITH YELLOW CHILES GUAJILLO, ALSO CALLED AMARILLO CHILES. INSET IS A STREET PAINTING MADE WITH FLOWER PETALS AND DYED SAND FOR MUERTOS.

OAXACAN BEEF WITH TOMATILLO SAUCE ON TORTILLAS

TASAJO A LA OAXAQUEÑA EN TLAYUDA

When my grandmother arrived in Oaxaca, after having lived on the Veracruz ranch for many years, she was very curious about local Oaxacan cuisine. She used to tell us how she went to the downtown Juarez Market to explore. There she bought strips of flank steak pounded thin and cured with salt and lemon, called FAJITAS or TASAJO. Tasajo is served in the southwestern state of Oaxaca for breakfast. ~ MARGARITA

FOR THE SAUCE

2   QUARTS WATER

3½ POUNDS TOMATILLOS, HUSKED

½   HEAD GARLIC, CLOVES PEELED

1   MEDIUM WHITE ONION, PEELED AND QUARTERED

8 TO 12 OAXACAN CHILES PASILLAS, WASHED, SEEDED AND DEVEINED (SUBSTITUTE DRIED RED CHILES CALIFORNIA) OR CHILES MORITAS OR CHIPOTLES, WASHED, WHOLE

½   MEDIUM WHITE ONION, PEELED AND QUARTERED

4   GARLIC CLOVES, PEELED

SALT TO TASTE

FOR THE MEAT

2½ GENEROUS POUNDS TASAJO (FLANK STEAK OR FAJITAS), THINLY SLICED

FOR THE TLAYUDAS

8   TLAYUDAS OR VERY LARGE TORTILLAS

8   TABLESPOONS LARD OR BUTTER

FOR THE GUACAMOLE

4   RIPE AVOCADOS, FINELY CHOPPED

8   TOMATILLOS, HUSKED AND FINELY CHOPPED

¾   CUP CILANTRO, FINELY CHOPPED

1½ MEDIUM WHITE ONIONS, PEELED AND FINELY CHOPPED

4   FRESH CHILES SERRANOS OR 2 JALAPEÑOS, FINELY CHOPPED

SALT TO TASTE

FOR THE GARNISH

2   MEDIUM WHITE ONIONS, THINLY SLICED

2   CUPS FRESH CHEESE (FETA), CRUMBLED

Prepare the sauce: Place the water, tomatillos, garlic, onion, and chiles in a large saucepan. Bring to a boil and cook for about 25 minutes. Remove from heat and allow to cool. In a molcajete or blender, grind the cooked garlic and onion, adding the raw onion and raw garlic cloves. Season to taste with salt. Add the chiles and tomatillos and grind until the mixture forms a smooth paste. If necessary, grind in batches.

Prepare the tlayudas: Place the large tortillas on a comal or griddle, one at a time. Spread lightly with lard or butter and heat through. Stack on a baking tray, covered with foil, and place in a warm oven (300°F.) for about 10 minutes.

Prepare the guacamole: Mix together the avocado, tomatillo, cilantro, onion, chile and salt to taste. Place an avocado pit in the guacamole sauce to keep it from turning brown.

Prepare the meat: Place a little oil on a comal or skillet and sauté the meat for three

---

SHREDDED BEEF ≈

Mexican butchers often cut meat with the grain (a cut that is coming to be known as "fajita" in the U.S.), which is useful for meat that will be braised or stewed and shredded. The habit may originate with range-fed beef, which is very flavorful but may require the tenderization of long cooking.

For succulent shredded beef, start with meat cut with the grain, such as skirt steak, immerse in simmering water and seasonings, but do not salt until ingredients are well heated through. Salt tends to draw the juices out of the meat and into the water, valuable in soup-making but not when shredded meat will be the star of the dish. You can cook meats to be shredded in an uncovered stockpot, in a pressure cooker, or overnight (or all day) in a crockpot.

minutes. Then turn over and sauté on the other side for about 1½ minutes. You may barbeque the meat on a grill instead, if you prefer.

To serve: Place the tlayudas on individual serving plates. Spread with tomatillo sauce, then cover with cooked meat, garnishing with onion and cheese. Serve the guacamole sauce on the side. This dish is also delicious accompanied with beans. **SERVES 8.**

NOTE

You may also serve the meat wrapped in a tortilla like a soft taco.

CHICKEN WINGS IN PULQUE SAUCE

SOPA DE ALITAS EN PULQUE, ESTILO VALLE

I *love how the natives incorporate local ingredients into their regional cuisine. This recipe was given to me by Monica Patiño, who adapted it from one used by her nanny to prepare a Day of the Dead offering. In Valle de Bravo, it is made with locally-produced* PULQUE — *an ancient liquor fermented from the juice of the maguey plant. Where fresh* PULQUE *is not available, beer can be substituted in this recipe.*

FOR THE CHICKEN

- 32 CHICKEN WINGS (FEWER ARE USED IN MEXICO, SINCE THEY ARE VERY MEATY), WASHED AND CUT IN HALF AT THE WING JOINT
- 8 CHICKEN LEGS, WASHED
- 8 TABLESPOONS LIME JUICE, OR TO TASTE
  SALT

- ½ CUP LARD OR OLIVE OIL
- 8 LARGE GREEN ONIONS OR 20 TINY GREEN ONIONS, CHOPPED FINELY, WITH TOPS
- 6 LARGE GARLIC CLOVES, PEELED AND CHOPPED COARSELY
- 14 CUPS PULQUE OR 3 CUPS BEER ADDED TO 12 CUPS WATER OR BROTH
- 20 FRESH EPAZOTE LEAVES OR 20 SPRIGS CILANTRO
- 2 FRESH CHILES MANZANOS, CARIBES, AMARILLOS OR JALAPEÑOS, OR BANANA PEPPERS, SEEDED AND DEVEINED, CUT IN STRIPS
- 3 CHILES PASILLAS OR DRIED CHILES CALIFORNIA, LIGHTLY FRIED WHOLE

FOR THE GARNISH

- 16 FRESH EPAZOTE OR CILANTRO LEAVES
- 1¼ CUPS WHITE ONION, FINELY CHOPPED
- ¾ CUP CILANTRO, FINELY CHOPPED
- 4 LIMES, CUT IN HALF
- 4 CHILES PASILLAS, CUT IN HALF BUT NOT SEEDED, FRIED LIGHTLY UNTIL THEY PUFF, THEN CRUMBLED
- 4 CUPS COOKED WHITE RICE

Prepare the chicken: Rub the chicken wings and legs with lime juice and sprinkle with salt. Set aside. Heat the lard in a large saucepan. Add the onion and garlic and brown lightly. Then add the chicken and brown until golden. Add pulque or diluted beer. Season to taste with salt and add epazote leaves and chiles. Cover pot and simmer ingredients for about 40 minutes or until the chicken is well done.

To serve: Place 3 chicken wings, one leg and half a chile manzano in each individual dish. Ladle the cooking broth over the chicken and chile. Garnish with epazote or cilantro leaves. Serve the chopped onion, chopped cilantro, limes, chile pasilla and rice on the side and allow diners to serve the garnishes themselves. **SERVES 8.**

PORK LOIN WITH COLORADITO MOLE

COLORADITO

Coloradito, or "little red" mole is another of the seven famous moles from Oaxaca. It is particularly popular around Day of the Dead festivities, when it is prepared as part of the offerings to be placed on the altars. The strong, full aroma of this chile sauce is said to entice the appetites of the deceased, luring them to the festive altars. ~ PATRICIA

"(In the streets we still see those young Indian girls burdened with lilies, in whom Diego Rivera discovered, bridging the centuries, the eternal affinities
of a people who sow the same springtime, again and again.)
Of blood and by flowers the Mexicans live.
Of blood and of flowers live both memory and forgetfulness.
(When I say this thing my heart plunges deep
in my stony bed of limpid, round water.)"

CARLOS PELLICER

DURING MUERTOS, GRAVES ARE DECORATED WITH CANDLES AND FLOWERS. SAND AND FLOWER-PETAL PAINTINGS ARE ALSO MADE IN PUBLIC PARKS, IN CEMETERIES AND ON SIDEWALKS.

FOR THE CHILES

8 CHILES ANCHOS (FOR CHILES ANCHOS AND GUAJILLOS, SUBSTITUTE DRY CHILES CALIFORNIA OR MILD NEW MEXICAN DRIED RED CHILES)

11 TO 12 CHILES GUAJILLOS

1½ TABLESPOONS CHILE SEEDS

¼ TO ¾ CUP LARD

HOT WATER TO COVER CHILES

FOR THE MOLE SAUCE

2 LARGE, RIPE TOMATOES

1 MEDIUM WHITE ONION, PEELED

1½ GARLIC HEADS, CLOVES PEELED

¼ CUP LARD OR SAFFLOWER OIL

1 SMALL PLANTAIN, RIPE, PEELED

⅓ CUP RAISINS

⅓ CUP PEANUTS

⅓ CUP ALMONDS

1 CINNAMON STICK, 1¼ INCHES LONG

⅓ CUP SESAME SEEDS

1½ GARLIC CLOVES, PEELED

½ MEDIUM WHITE ONION, SLICED

3 TO 4 SMALL BAY LEAVES

2 TO 3 SPRIGS THYME

2 TO 3 SPRIGS MARJORAM

5 WHOLE CLOVES

8 BLACK PEPPERCORNS OR WHOLE ALLSPICE

1 TEASPOON CUMIN

1½ GARLIC CLOVES, PEELED

1½ TEASPOONS OREGANO LEAVES

¾ CUP LARD OR VEGETABLE OIL

2 SMALL WHITE ONIONS, SLICED

SALT TO TASTE

4 OUNCES MEXICAN CHOCOLATE OR SEMI-SWEET BAKING CHOCOLATE

1½ TABLESPOONS SUGAR

4 CUPS CHICKEN BROTH

FOR THE MEAT

¼ CUP BUTTER, AT ROOM TEMPERATURE

2 TABLESPOONS OLIVE OIL

3 POUNDS PORK LOIN

5 GARLIC CLOVES, PEELED, SLIGHTLY CRUSHED

1 TEASPOON FRESHLY GROUND BLACK PEPPER

SALT OR POWDERED BOUILLON TO TASTE

FOR THE GARNISH

¼ CUP SESAME SEEDS

Prepare the chiles: Wash, seed and devein chiles. Reserve 1½ tablespoons of chile seed. Heat lard in a saucepan. Fry the chiles lightly, without browning or they will take on a bitter flavor. Transfer to a glass bowl and cover with hot water. Allow to soak for about 1 hour. This procedure will make the chiles easier to purée. Fry chile seeds in a little lard and reserve.

Prepare the mole: On a well preheated comal or skillet, roast the tomatoes, onion and garlic until they are dark brown, turning to expose all sides to the heat. Heat the lard in a saucepan. Fry the plantain until it is golden brown, then remove and drain on paper towels. In the same lard, fry until dark brown the raisins, peanuts, almonds, cinnamon stick, sesame seeds, garlic cloves, onion slices, bay leaves, thyme and marjoram, cloves and peppercorns or allspice. Transfer tomatoes, garlic, plantains and all other fried ingredients to a blender or food processor and purée until a heavy paste forms. If necessary, purée in batches. Add chicken or beef broth to facilitate if necessary. Strain the purée. Separately purée the cumin, garlic and oregano. Then add to the paste.

Heat ¾ cup lard or vegetable oil in a saucepan. Brown onion, then add the prepared paste and cook until the mixture renders its fat, about 1 hour. Stir mixture regularly with a wooden spoon while ·cooking. Place the soaked and reserved chiles in a blender or food processor and purée twice. Stir them into the mole and simmer for 1½ to 2 hours, or until the mixture renders its fat. Season to taste with salt and add chocolate and sugar, stirring to melt. Throughout the cooking procedure, add chicken broth when necessary. At this point, the mole may be cooled and frozen. Or reserve the mole.

Prepare the meat: Preheat oven to 350°F. Butter 2 baking trays. Place the pork loins on the trays and pour oil over. Top with crushed garlic cloves, and sprinkle with black pepper. Bake for 1½ hours or until the meat is tender and golden brown. Remove from oven and cover with aluminum foil. Allow to rest for 10 minutes before cutting. Then cut in thin slices.

To serve: Garnish with sesame seeds and cinnamon stick if desired. Serve with freshly prepared corn tortillas. **SERVES 10-12.**

BEANS

TRADITIONAL COOKERY
≈

Wash dried beans and add 4 cups cold fresh water for every cup of beans, then soak 10-12 hours. Drain, discard water, and proceed to cook beans.

QUICK COOKERY ≈

Place washed beans in a large pot with 4 cups water for each cup of beans, bring to a boil, reduce heat, simmer 2-3 minutes, then remove from heat, cover, and let stand 1-2 hours. Drain and proceed to cook beans.

BEST COOKING
≈

Simmer beans, don't boil them. Stir seldom and with a wooden spoon to avoid breaking beans. Do not salt until beans are almost tender, to avoid toughening them. If water is needed during cooking, add boiling water, so as not to stop the cooking process. To test for doneness, remove a few beans and blow on them. If the skins break, they are done.

SEASONINGS
≈

Epazote, cilantro, green onion (plus stalks), avocado leaves, chiles.

BEANS AND RICE ≈

A common Mexican meal is a simple dish of beans with rice, crumbled cheese, shredded lettuce and pickled chiles.

BLACK BEANS WITH PORK

FRIJOLES CHARROS

Frijoles charros (free HO lez CHAR roz) can be served either as a main course or a side dish. Because of the generous amount of pork, the dish is hearty and filling. ~ PATRICIA

FOR THE BEANS

1⅓	POUNDS BLACK BEANS OR PINTO BEANS, SORTED AND WASHED, SOAKED OVERNIGHT IF DESIRED, DRAINED
2½	QUARTS WATER
1½	POUNDS PORK RIBS
20	GREEN ONIONS, WITH TOPS, CUT IN HALF
1	MEDIUM WHITE ONION, PEELED AND QUARTERED
1	GARLIC HEAD, CUT IN HALF ACROSS THE GRAIN
	SALT TO TASTE
½	CUP LARD OR VEGETABLE OIL
1½	LARGE WHITE ONIONS, PEELED AND FINELY CHOPPED
¾	POUND BACON, DICED
¾	POUND HAM, DICED

FOR THE GARNISH

1	SMALL LETTUCE, WASHED, DRIED AND SHREDDED
1	BUNCH RADISHES, WASHED AND CHOPPED FINELY
½	POUND PORK CRACKLINGS, CHOPPED FINELY
20	CHILES DE ÁRBOL, LIGHTLY FRIED IN ⅓ CUP OIL AND SPRINKLED WITH A LITTLE SALT
2	LARGE AVOCADOS, PEELED AND DICED
6	FRESH CHILES JALAPEÑOS, CUT IN STRIPS (SEEDED IF DESIRED)

20	GREEN ONIONS, FINELY CHOPPED
	THE JUICE OF 2-3 LIMES
	SALT TO TASTE
	OREGANO TO TASTE

Prepare the beans: Heat the water in a pressure cooker or large saucepan. Add the beans, pork ribs, onion, garlic and salt. Cook for about 1 hour or until beans are tender. Presoaked beans will cook faster than unsoaked ones. Allow to cool, then uncover. If using a saucepan, cook longer, until the beans are tender, adding boiling water as needed. Add salt after beans are tender. Set aside. Remove garlic head. Purée 1 cup of beans in a blender or food processor and reserve.

Heat the lard in a large pot or cazuela. Fry the onion until it is light brown. Add the bacon and ham, then gradually add the beans and pork ribs, and the puréed beans. Simmer 30 minutes or until beans thicken.

To serve: Serve directly from a cazuela, with garnishes and hot tortillas on the side. SERVES 10.

BLACK BEANS, SANTIAGO DE TUXTLA STYLE

FRIJOLES NEGROS DE SANTIAGO DE TUXTLA

Beans are served throughout Mexico — black, pinto, CANARIO — and are prepared in many ways. But the beans prepared in Veracruz are famous throughout the country for both the way they are prepared and for the quality of the locally-grown seeds. They are a small black variety that swells as it is cooked, releasing its distinctive flavor.

FOR THE BEANS

1¾ POUNDS SMALL BLACK BEANS, SORTED AND
    WASHED, SOAKED OVERNIGHT AND DRAINED

14 CUPS WATER

2 TABLESPOONS LARD OR VEGETABLE OIL

    SALT TO TASTE

TO REFRY BEANS

⅓ CUP VEGETABLE OIL

6 GARLIC CLOVES, PEELED AND FLATTENED

1½ CUPS WHITE ONION, FINELY CHOPPED

2 MEDIUM WHITE ONIONS, PEELED AND
    QUARTERED

½ CUP LARD OR VEGETABLE OIL

    SALT TO TASTE

FOR THE GARNISH

1½ CUPS WHITE ONION, FINELY CHOPPED

2½ CUPS FRESH CHEESE (FETA OR FARMER'S),
    CRUMBLED

    FRESH CHILES SERRANOS OR JALAPEÑOS,
    OR PICKLED CHILES, TO TASTE

    OLIVE OIL TO TASTE

Prepare the beans: Place the beans in a large pot, along with water and lard. Cook for 1 to 1½ hours or until the beans are tender. If necessary add more water during cooking time. Do not salt until after the beans are almost cooked.

To refry beans: Heat the oil in a large saucepan or skillet. Brown garlic, then remove and discard. Brown the onion. Transfer 2 cups of cooked beans to a blender or food processor and purée. Add puréed beans and cooked beans to saucepan. Add quartered onions, lard and salt to taste. Cook until the mixture thickens. Garnish with chopped onion, cheese and chiles. Sprinkle with olive oil. **SERVES 8-12.**

GARLIC, CHILE AND TOMATO SALSA

SALSA ROJA DE MOLCÁJETE ESTILO CUETZALAN

This salsa, or table sauce, dates back to pre-Hispanic times. In the Cuetzalán region of Puebla, Day of the Dead altars always bear a molcajete filled with SALSA ROJA (sal sah RO hah) along with a basket of fresh, hand-shaped corn tortillas. ~ MAGO

4 GARLIC CLOVES, PEELED

4 TO 6 FRESH CHILES SERRANOS, WASHED,
    WHOLE

3 LARGE RIPE TOMATOES

4 TABLESPOONS WHITE ONION, PEELED AND
    FINELY CHOPPED

    SALT TO TASTE

½ TO ¾ CUP HOT WATER

Roast the garlic cloves, chiles, and tomatoes separately on a hot comal or griddle, then place the garlic and chiles in a molcajete with the onion and salt. In this salsa, as in all others, the salt and onion used as seasoning should be ground into the mixture in the beginning. The flavor will not be the same if they are added at the end. Grind, adding the tomatoes gradually. When the ingredients are semi-thick, add a little water to achieve desired consistency. Salsas can be as thick or as thin as you prefer. (*SALSA ROJA* can be made in a blender or food processor but the flavor will not be exactly the same. Be careful not to overblend. Salsa should have a chunky texture.) Serve directly from the stone mortar. This condiment complements a great variety of dishes. **SERVES 8.**

TO REFRY BEANS ≈
Heat ¾ cup oil in a frying pan. Add 1 medium onion, chopped, and brown. Add the beans and 4 avocado leaves (optional) and cook until the mixture thickens.

BLACK MOLE

MOLE NEGRO DE SANTA ANA CHAUTEMPAN

Mole (MO lay) comes from the Nahuatl MULLI, *meaning "sauce." Moles differ from region to region, from village to village, from cook to cook in the same village. The regional characteristics of moles can be read almost as Mexican history. The moles of Puebla, for example, are sweeter and milder because of the influence of the Spanish nuns. This mole comes from Santa Ana Chautempan in Tlaxcala, where the moles are hotter, slightly thinner, and smoother than elsewhere. When the great Aztec ruler Montezuma was at war with the people of Tlaxcala, he punished them by withholding their ration of salt, which was traded for tribute goods. Perhaps it was then that they began to use honey, fruit and hot chiles in their moles.* ~
EMILIA

"Skeleton was sitting/ in a marsh grove of cane/ eating hard tortillas/ to be fat again./ Skeleton was sitting/ in a sandy place/ eating hard tortillas/ and beans with no salt/ no salt . . ."

SONG SUNG IN A CHILDREN'S GROUP GAME, LE MEDIA MUERTE (SKELETON)

CHICKEN WITH BLACK MOLE, WITH SUGAR SKULLS FROM ABASTOS MARKET IN THE CITY OF OAXACA AND ANCHO CHILES. INSET, SKELETON TOYS APPEAR IN GREAT QUANTITIES IN THE LOCAL MARKETS A FEW DAYS BEFORE THE DAY OF THE DEAD.

FOR THE MOLE

2   CUPS LARD OR OIL
1½   HEADS GARLIC, PEELED
2   MEDIUM WHITE ONIONS, PEELED AND QUARTERED
1½   CUPS SESAME SEEDS, TOASTED
2½   CUPS BLANCHED ALMONDS OR PEANUTS
1½   CUPS PRUNES, PITTED
1   RIPE PLANTAIN, PEELED
2   CHARRED TORTILLAS
10   WHOLE CLOVES
1   CINNAMON STICK, ABOUT 4 INCHES LONG
1   TABLESPOON BLACK PEPPER
1   TEASPOON GROUND ALLSPICE

1   CROISSANT, TORN IN PIECES
UP   TO 4 CUPS CHICKEN OR PORK BROTH
     SALT TO TASTE
2   CUPS VEGETABLE OIL OR LARD
4   WHITE ONION SLICES
2   LARGE, RIPE TOMATOES
14   TOMATILLOS, HUSKED AND BOILED UNTIL TENDER, ABOUT 20 MINUTES
1   GENEROUS POUND CHILE MULATO, WASHED, DRIED, SLIT OPEN ON THE SIDE, SEEDED, DEVEINED AND FRIED
1½   POUNDS CHILE PASILLA, WASHED, DRIED, SLIT OPEN ON THE SIDE, SEEDED, DEVEINED AND FRIED
¼   POUND CHILE ANCHO, WASHED, DRIED, SLIT OPEN ON THE SIDE, SEEDED, DEVEINED AND FRIED
4   CHILES CHIPOTLES, WASHED, SEEDED AND DEVEINED
12   TABLESPOONS CHILE SEEDS, TOASTED UNTIL DARK
½   CUP CHICKEN BROTH
12   OUNCES MEXICAN CHOCOLATE OR SEMI-SWEET BAKING CHOCOLATE
3   TABLESPOONS SUGAR

FOR THE MEAT

20   CUPS WATER
1   MEDIUM WHITE ONION
½   GARLIC HEAD, CUT IN HALF ACROSS THE GRAIN
1   TEASPOON BLACK PEPPER
     SALT TO TASTE
4   GENEROUS POUNDS THICK PORK RIBS
6½   POUNDS PORK LOIN OR LEG, OR TURKEY OR CHICKEN

Prepare the mole: Heat about ½ cup of lard or oil in a large, heavy frying pan. Add the garlic and onion and fry. Transfer to a blender or food processor. Then fry the sesame seeds and almonds until golden brown, and transfer to the processor.

Repeat procedure with prunes, plantain, tortillas, cloves, cinnamon, pepper, allspice and croissant, frying them until golden brown and then transferring them to the blender or processor. Then purée all ingredients together, adding chicken broth as necessary to facilitate. If necessary, blend in batches. Strain the sauce. Add salt to taste.

In a large stockpot, heat the oil or lard. Brown the onion slices, then add the strained mole sauce. Simmer until the ingredients release their fat, about 45 minutes or longer. Rectify seasoning. In a blender or food processor, purée the tomatoes, tomatillos, fried chiles and the chile seed. Add broth and purée again. Then strain the resulting purée and add to the mole. Add chocolate and sugar. Continue to simmer for about 2 hours, stirring occasionally. Rectify seasoning.

Prepare the meat: Bring the water to a boil in a medium saucepan. Add the onion, garlic, pepper, salt and pork and cook for 1½ to 2 hours or until the meat is tender and done. Remove from heat and allow meat to cool in its broth. Remove meat from the bone and add it to the mole. Cook for an additional 30 minutes. If necessary, add more broth to achieve a light consistency.

To serve: Serve mole directly from the cazuela, accompanied by white rice, freshly made corn tortillas and beans. **SERVES UP TO 30.**

CHICKEN BREASTS WITH BLACK MOLE

MOLE NEGRO DE TEOTITLÁN DEL VALLE

Although moles are prepared throughout Mexico, Oaxacan moles are the best known. Among them, black mole is probably the most famous. Once during Muertos I had the opportunity to watch Abigail Mendoza Ruiz prepare this classic dish — toasting the chiles, frying the spices, and grinding in the metate the wide variety of ingredients. The mole was served at the midday meal in a room behind the altar. Before the food was served, water was tossed on the incense burner, raising an aromatic cloud of scent to make the spirits welcome.

FOR THE MOLE

¼ POUND CHILES MULATO OR CHILHUACLE, WASHED, SEEDED AND DEVEINED

¼ POUND CHILES PASILLA OR GUAJILLO, WASHED, SEEDED AND DEVEINED

1½ CUPS CHICKEN BROTH

2½ MEDIUM WHITE ONIONS

3½ LARGE GARLIC HEADS

½ WHOLE NUTMEG

2 OUNCES OF GINGER ROOT

6 MARJORAM SPRIGS

1½ TEASPOONS WHOLE CLOVES

10 WHOLE ALLSPICE

1 CUP SESAME SEEDS

¾ CUP PRUNES, PITTED

1 TORTILLAS

5 TOMATILLOS, HUSKED

5 LARGE TOMATOES

2 TO 3 AVOCADO LEAVES

2 BAY LEAVES

2 CUPS LARD OR VEGETABLE OIL

2 ONION SLICES

SALT TO TASTE

SUGAR TO TASTE

12 OUNCES MEXICAN CHOCOLATE OR SEMI-SWEET BAKING CHOCOLATE

1 CUP BREAD CRUMBS

7 TO 8 CUPS CHICKEN BROTH

½ CUP SUGAR

FOR THE CHICKEN

10 CUPS WATER

2 MEDIUM WHITE ONIONS, PEELED AND QUARTERED

1½ GARLIC HEADS, CUT IN HALF

3 MARJORAM SPRIGS

3 BAY LEAVES

4 BLACK PEPPERCORNS

SALT TO TASTE

20 SPLIT CHICKEN BREASTS, WITH BONES

Prepare the mole: Preheat a comal or griddle and roast the chiles (being careful not to char or they will take on a bitter flavor). Place the chiles and 3 cups chicken broth in a blender or food processor and purée. Reserve puréed chiles.

On a preheated comal or skillet over direct heat, roast the onions and garlic heads until browned or charred. Remove. Brown the nutmeg, ginger, marjoram (lightly or it will become bitter), cloves and allspice on the comal. Remove. Brown the sesame seeds until very dark. Remove. Lightly brown the prunes and remove. Toast the tortillas until charred. Remove. Roast the tomatillos, tomatoes and avocado leaves, then remove. Heat 2 tablespoons lard or vegetable oil in a frying pan and fry the bay leaves. Then place all the ingredients in a metate, blender or food processor and purée. If necessary, add chicken broth sparingly to facilitate the procedure. Reserve puréed fruits and spices.

Heat the lard in a large saucepan and add onion. Brown until a dark rich color. Remove from lard and discard. Add puréed fruit and spice mixture and cook over low heat for 45 minutes or until it begins to render its fat. Stir in the puréed chiles and cook slowly for 1½ hours. Season to taste with salt, chocolate and sugar. Add bread crumbs and continue cooking until the mixture renders its fat. Rectify seasoning. At this point part or all of the mole may be frozen if so desired. If not, add chicken broth until the mole is semi-thick in consistency. This mole should be thicker than other moles. Strain the mole to make it very smooth.

Prepare the chicken breasts: Heat the water in a large stockpot or saucepan. Add the onion, garlic, marjoram, bay leaves, peppercorns and salt to taste. Bring to a boil and add the chicken breasts. Cook over a medium heat for about 20 minutes or until the chicken is tender. Remove chicken from broth and add to the prepared mole. Cook 20-25 minutes. Serve in soup bowls. Accompany with blanditas (large white tortillas) and white rice. **SERVES 20.**

VARIATION

Bone and cut the chicken breasts into strips before adding to the mole. Or you may oven-roast the chicken breasts (dot with butter, sprinkle with olive oil, salt and pepper and bake at 350°F. for 40 minutes), then slice very thinly and serve with mole on the side.

This mole is delicious for preparing tamales, enchiladas, fried or poached eggs or chilaquiles.

GROUND CHOCOLATE, COCOA BEANS, CHOCOLATE TABLETS, CINNAMON STICK, A CONE OF PILONCILLO, AND WOODEN CHOCOLATE BEATERS (MOLINILLOS).

CANDIED PUMPKIN WITH SYRUP.

CANDIED PUMPKIN

CALABAZA EN TACHA

Candied pumpkin is a typical sweet served around the Day of the Dead holiday. This tradition dates back to pre-Hispanic times when it was originally sweetened with honey or the sap extracted from the maguey plant. Today it is placed on altars as an offering to the dead. ~ PATRICIA

FOR THE SYRUP

10 CUPS WATER

14 PILONCILLO CONES OR 14 CUPS DARK BROWN SUGAR

4 CUPS SUGAR

8 CINNAMON STICKS, EACH 2½ INCHES LONG

1 TABLESPOON ANISE SEED

1 TEASPOON WHOLE CLOVES

FOR THE PUMPKIN

2   SMALL PUMPKINS OR WINTER SQUASH
     WATER TO COVER

4   TABLESPOONS UNSLAKED POWDERED LIME
     (LIMESTONE), AVAILABLE WHERE ROCK AND
     BUILDING MATERIALS ARE SOLD.

Prepare the syrup: Heat the water in a very large stockpot or canning kettle. Add piloncillo, sugar and cinnamon sticks. Wrap the anise and cloves in cheesecloth, forming a little bag, and add to water. Cook for 3 hours or until the consistency of molasses.

Prepare the pumpkin: Perforate the pumpkins or squashes with holes that pierce through the shells. Then place them whole in a large stockpot or other container and cover with water. Add lime and allow to soak for 3 hours. Drain and wash well. Add the syrup and cook for 2 hours or until done, basting occasionally. Allow to cool for 15 minutes before removing from syrup. **SERVES 16.**

SPICED LENTIL STEW WITH PLANTAINS AND PINEAPPLE

LENTEJAS ESTILO ANTEQUERA

This hearty Oaxacan recipe, a favorite of my great-grandmother's, combines sweet and salty flavors, giving an otherwise simple lentil dish an exotic taste. The name given by Cortes to Oaxaca was Antequera. ~ MARGARITA

8   CUPS WATER

1   POUND LENTILS

1   MEDIUM WHITE ONION, PEELED AND
     QUARTERED

1   HEAD GARLIC, CLOVES PEELED

4   WHOLE CLOVES

8   BLACK PEPPERCORNS
     SALT TO TASTE

½   CUP OLIVE OIL

5   GARLIC CLOVES, MEDIUM, PEELED AND
     MINCED

1½   MEDIUM WHITE ONIONS, PEELED AND
     FINELY CHOPPED

2   PLANTAINS, PEELED AND CHOPPED

3   SLICES FRESH PINEAPPLE, PEELED AND
     FINELY CHOPPED

2   RIPE TOMATOES, FINELY CHOPPED

4   WHOLE CLOVES, GROUND

10   ALLSPICE, GROUND
     SALT TO TASTE

½   CUP CHOPPED PARSLEY

Prepare the lentils: Wash the lentils in a colander under running water. Place water, lentils, onion, garlic, cloves, peppercorns and salt in a heavy saucepan. Bring to a boil, then reduce to a simmer. Simmer approximately 20-30 minutes, until lentils are tender but still retain their shape. (Cooking time for lentils varies widely.) While lentils are cooking, heat the oil in a medium saucepan. Brown the garlic, then add the onion and brown. Stir in plantains and pineapple and fry until light brown. Add the tomatoes and cook until the mixture releases its oil. Season with cloves, allspice and salt. Add cooked lentils and a little of their broth. Continue cooking until the mixture thickens (if it becomes too thick, add more lentil broth). Garnish with chopped parsley. Serve hot. **SERVES 8.**

VARIATION

Serve with slices of fried plantains.

NEW WORLD NATIVES ≈
Many foodstuffs imported to Europe in the 15th and 16th centuries originated in Mexico and the regions to her south. Among them are: Potatoes, sweet potatoes, corn, pumpkins, squashes, tomatoes, kidney beans, black beans, fava beans, lima beans, sweet peppers, chiles, avocados, pineapples, allspice, vanilla, and chocolate.

CANDIED SWEET POTATOES WITH CINNAMON AND CLOVES, WITH DECORATIVELY CUT TISSUE PAPER THAT IS FESTOONED IN HOMES AND PUBLIC PLACES DURING FIESTAS.

RABBIT IN SPICY CHILE SAUCE

CONEJO ADOBADO ESTILO AMECAMECA

Adobo is a thick sauce or paste in which chiles and spices are blended with a touch of vinegar. It is used as a marinade for meats, seafood or chicken. Rabbit in adobo is often placed on altars to revere deceased relatives on the Day of the Dead. This recipe may also be prepared with chicken or pork. ~
PATRICIA

FOR THE ADOBO SAUCE

8	CUPS WATER
2	TABLESPOONS VINEGAR
15	CHILES GUAJILLOS
8	CHILES GUAJILLOS PUYA (SUBSTITUTE DRIED CHILES CALIFORNIA OR DRIED NEW MEXICAN CHILES FOR GUAJILLOS AND GUAJILLOS PUYA)
1	MEDIUM WHITE ONION, PEELED AND QUARTERED
8	GARLIC CLOVES, PEELED
1	TEASPOON CUMIN SEEDS
1	TEASPOON CORIANDER SEEDS
3	SPRIGS FRESH OREGANO OR ½ TABLESPOON DRIED OREGANO LEAVES
1½	TEASPOON WHOLE ALLSPICE
1½	TEASPOON BLACK PEPPER
	SALT TO TASTE
½	CUP VINEGAR
½	CUP OLIVE OIL

FOR THE RABBIT

4	MEDIUM RABBITS, 1½ POUNDS EACH, SKINNED AND WASHED, OR 3 POUNDS CHICKEN PIECES
½	CUP VEGETABLE OIL

FOR THE GARNISH

8	RADISHES, SCULPTED INTO FLOWERS
8	GREEN ONIONS, SCULPTED INTO FLOWERS

Prepare the adobo sauce: Wash, seed and devein the chiles, then roast on a hot skillet and soak in hot water plus 2 tablespoons vinegar for about 20 minutes to remove piquancy. Then place the chiles, onion, garlic, cumin, coriander, oregano, allspice, black pepper and salt in a blender or food processor and purée well, if necessary in batches. Add vinegar and olive oil. The mixture should form a stiff paste that will cling when it is rubbed over the surface of the meat. Rub the adobo over the rabbits and allow them to marinate in the refrigerator for one day. Roast the rabbits, preferably on a barbecue grill. If a grill is not available, bake in an oven at 350°F. Baste the rabbits and turn them every 4-5 minutes if cooking on a barbecue grill. Baste and turn every 10 minutes if cooking in the oven. Cook until the meat is tender and juicy.

To serve: Cut the rabbit into pieces and serve immediately, garnishing with sculpted radishes and green onion flowers. Accompany with freshly made corn tortillas.
SERVES 8.

CANDIED SWEET POTATOES WITH CINNAMON AND CLOVES

LOS CAMOTES

*M*exico *produces several varieties of sweet potatoes, yellow, white and purple, as well as true yams (*DIOSCOREA BULBIFERA*), the tubers of a tropical climbing vine. True yams are sweeter than North American sweet potatoes and are less rich in vitamins A and C. Either can be used in Mexican sweet potato or yam recipes.* ~ EMILIA

FOR THE SYRUP

6	CUPS WATER
4	CUPS SUGAR
6	PILONCILLO CONES, 6 OUNCES EACH OR 4½ CUPS DARK BROWN SUGAR
2	CINNAMON STICKS, EACH 3 INCHES LONG
6	WHOLE CLOVES

FOR THE POTATOES

4	LARGE YELLOW SWEET POTATOES, EACH 1 POUND, PEELED
½	CUP BUTTER, MELTED

Prepare the syrup: Place the water in a medium saucepan. Add sugar, piloncillo, cinnamon and cloves and cook for 2½ hours or until the syrup is thick.

Prepare the sweet potatoes: Preheat oven to 350°F. Arrange the sweet potatoes in a large baking dish with a lid. Brush potatoes with melted butter and cover. Bake for 2 hours or until done, basting the sweet potatoes every 20 minutes. Test with a toothpick or fork to be sure they are tender. SERVES 6-8.

TINGA ≈

The classic spiced meat mixture called TINGA *has many uses. Serve spooned around a mound of steaming rice, decorated with slices of avocado, onion and chipotle chiles, with hot tortillas. It makes a wonderful filling for tacos, a toasted-flour-tortilla "pizza" topping, a hot sandwich with bolillos, a filling for turnovers or to fill a flaky meat pie pastry. It is excellent served simply with shredded lettuce and fresh salsa.*

To make a delicious marinated Salpiçon, or Skirt Steak Salad, prepare meat as for Tinga, then combine with a vinaigrette made of ½ cup orange juice, ½ cup grapefruit juice, juice of 3 limes, ¾ cup vinegar, cracked black pepper, 1½ sliced white onions, 1 cup vegetable oil, thyme, marjoram, bay leaves, oregano, allspice, salt and chicken bouillon to taste.

Garnish with onion, avocado, tomato, shredded lettuce, pickled chile and grated fresh cheese. Serve at room temperature.

TINGA

TINGA

Tinga *is a delicious and versatile filling believed to have been invented in the Santa Rosa Convent in Puebla. The nuns were the first to experiment with blending European flavors with Mexican ingredients.*

FOR THE MEAT

12 CUPS WATER

2 GENEROUS POUNDS FLANK STEAK

1 MEDIUM WHITE ONION, SPIKED WITH 4 WHOLE CLOVES

½ GARLIC HEAD, CUT IN HALF ACROSS THE GRAIN

2 BAY LEAVES

1 SPRIG THYME

1 SPRIG MARJORAM

SALT TO TASTE

FOR THE SAUCE

¾ CUP OLIVE OIL OR LARD

6 GARLIC CLOVES, PEELED AND MINCED

2 MEDIUM WHITE ONIONS, CUT ON THE DIAGONAL

1½ CUPS CHORIZO SAUSAGE, FRIED

6 LARGE TOMATOES (ABOUT 2¾ POUNDS), ROASTED AND SKINNED

4 GARLIC CLOVES, PEELED

2 TO 4 CANNED CHILES CHIPOTLES, IN ADOBO SAUCE, CUT IN STRIPS

3 DRIED CHILES CHIPOTLES, WASHED, FRIED AND SOAKED FOR 10 MINUTES, CUT IN STRIPS

4 BAY LEAVES

2 WHOLE CLOVES, GROUND

½ CINNAMON STICK, 4 INCHES LONG, GROUND

1 TEASPOON GROUND BLACK PEPPER

SALT TO TASTE

⅓ CUP VINEGAR

3 TABLESPOONS BROWN SUGAR

FOR THE GARNISH

WHITE RICE OR RICE WITH SQUASH BLOSSOMS AND CORN

2 RIPE AVOCADOS, SLICED

1 MEDIUM WHITE ONION, PEELED AND SLICED THINLY

4 CANNED CHILES CHIPOTLES, IN ADOBO SAUCE

Prepare the meat: Bring the water to a boil in a pressure cooker or medium saucepan. Add the meat, onion, garlic, bay leaves, thyme, marjoram and salt to taste. Cook for 1¼ hours if using a pressure cooker, and 2½ hours if using a regular saucepan, or until the meat is tender. Add water if necessary. Allow the meat to cool in the broth. Remove from broth and shred finely. Reserve about 1 cup of strained cooking broth.

Prepare the sauce: Heat the oil in a medium saucepan. Sauté the garlic and onion. Stir in fried chorizo, tomato, garlic, chiles chipotles with adobo sauce and fried chipotles. Sauté. Add bay leaves, cloves, cinnamon, pepper, salt, vinegar and brown sugar. Cook until the mixture thickens, about 45 minutes. Stir occasionally, seasoning to taste. Then add the shredded meat along with a cup of cooking broth, and cook another 25 minutes.

If the sauce is too thin, add about 2 tablespoons of masa dissolved in ½ cup water. Stir into the sauce, and cook until the mixture takes on desired consistency. (Or you may add 1 tablespoon cornstarch dissolved in cold water.) **SERVES 8-12.**

BEEF STEW WITH CHILES AND VEGETABLES

MOLE DE OLLA

This mole is not a heavy chile sauce, but rather a rich meat and vegetable stew, enhanced with the pungent flavor of pasilla, guajillo *and* ancho *chiles. It also contains little corn-masa dumplings called* CHOCHOYONES. *Its aroma is one of the earthly sensations that is intended to lure the souls of the dead back to the hearthside at Muertos.* ~ MARGARITA

FOR THE MEAT

5   QUARTS WATER

3½   POUNDS BEEF CHUCK, CUT INTO 2½ X 2½-INCH CUBES

2   MEDIUM WHITE ONIONS, PEELED AND QUARTERED

1   HEAD GARLIC, UNPEELED, CUT IN HALF ACROSS THE GRAIN

4   EARS OF CORN, EACH CUT INTO THREE PIECES

  SALT TO TASTE

FOR THE STEW

¾   CUP VEGETABLE OIL

6   CHILES ANCHOS

4   CHILES PASILLAS

4   CHILES GUAJILLOS (SUBSTITUTE DRIED RED CHILES CALIFORNIA OR NEW MEXICAN DRIED CHILES FOR ANCHOS, PASILLAS, AND GUAJILLOS IF NECESSARY)

3   TO 4 CUPS RESERVED BEEF BROTH

2   MEDIUM WHITE ONIONS, PEELED AND QUARTERED

20   TOMATILLOS, HUSKED

8   GARLIC CLOVES, PEELED

⅔   CUP VEGETABLE OIL OR SHORTENING

2   SLICES ONION

2   SPRIGS FRESH EPAZOTE OR CILANTRO, OR TO TASTE

FOR THE VEGETABLES

  REMAINING RESERVED BEEF BROTH

8   VERY SMALL ZUCCHINI, SLICED LENGTHWISE

1   GENEROUS POUND GREEN BEANS, CUT IN HALF

3   CHAYOTES, PEELED AND CUT INTO QUARTERS

  CHOCHOYONES

FOR THE CHOCHOYONES

1½   CUPS FRESH MASA (OR MASA MADE WITH MASA HARINA)

¼   CUP WATER

1   TABLESPOON VEGETABLE OIL OR LARD

  SALT TO TASTE

TO COMPLETE THE STEW

  ADDITIONAL EPAZOTE OR CILANTRO TO TASTE

Prepare the meat: Bring the water to a boil, preferably in a clay pot. Add the meat, onions, garlic and corn. Simmer for about 2½ hours or until the meat is tender. Remove from heat, season to taste with salt, and allow to cool. Once cool, skim off fat. Remove and reserve meat and corn. Strain and reserve beef broth separately.

Prepare the stew: Heat the oil in a frying pan. Wash, seed and devein chiles, then lightly fry them. Soak chiles in 3 cups of reserved beef broth for about 30 minutes. Transfer the chiles and broth to a medium saucepan. Add the tomatillos and cook over

CHAYOTES ≈

*Chayotes (*CHAI OH TAYS*), also called mirlitons, water pears, or vegetable pears, are members of the squash family grown on a vine native to Mexico. The prodigious vine of the chayote may grow to 100 feet and may carry up to 200 chayote squashes at once. The delicious chayote was relished by the Aztecs in pre-*

has a cool green furrowed skin and a single seed which is edible after being cooked. The flesh retains its shape after cooking more readily than that of other squashes. Cook chayotes (whole, halved or quartered, depending on size) in boiling water for 20-25 minutes. Peel after cooking.

Try cooked, chilled, peeled and cubed chayotes in salads, simmer them in a stew, or add them to bread-crumb stuffings for poultry. Cut a cooked chayote in half, scoop out the seed and stuff the hollow with cheese, press the two halves back together, dip it in egg batter, and deep-fry. Serve with tomato-chile sauce. The small white chayotes, which are firmer, can be stuffed and baked like zucchini.

medium heat for 25 minutes. Place chiles, broth, tomatillos, onion and garlic in a blender or food processor and purée. Strain chile purée. Heat oil in a separate pot. Brown the two onion slices in the oil. Add the strained chile purée and simmer until the mixture thickens and the sauce releases its oil. Add 4-6 cups reserved beef broth (depending on the consistency of the sauce and the desired consistency of the stew) and cook for an additional 20 minutes. Add the epazote sprigs and the reserved meat and corn. Continue to simmer until mixture is hot and its flavors have mingled.

Prepare the vegetables: Heat the remaining reserved beef broth in a medium saucepan. Add the zucchini and cook for 6 minutes. Remove and reserve. Add the green beans and cook 8-10 minutes. Remove and reserve. Add the chayotes and cook about 25 minutes or until tender. Remove and reserve.

Prepare the chochoyones (masa dumplings): Place the masa in a glass bowl. Add the water, oil and salt. Knead for about 5 minutes. Then pinch off a small piece of dough and form into a 1-inch ball. Press the center of the ball with your knuckle to form a slight indention. Repeat procedure until all the dough is made into balls.

To complete the stew: Place the mole stew in a large clay cazuela or pot. Stir in the cooked zucchini, green beans, chayotes and masa balls. Rectify seasoning, adding additional epazote or cilantro if desired, and cook for another 30 minutes. The consistency can be that of soup or of thick stew, depending on your preference.

To serve: Ladle into deep soup dishes. Accompany with freshly made corn tortillas.
SERVES 8-10.

"I am come too,/ here I am standing;/ now I am going to forge songs,/ make a stem flowering with songs,/ oh my friend!/ God has sent me as a mesenger./ I am transformed into a poem."

PRE-HISPANIC NAHUATL POEM

INDEX